SHOWDOWN

JFK and the Integration of the Washington Redskins

Thomas G. Smith

Beacon Press
Boston

BEACON PRESS
25 Beacon Street
Boston, Massachusetts 02108-2892
www.beacon.org

Beacon Press books
are published under the auspices of
the Unitarian Universalist Association of Congregations.

Printed in the United States of America

14 13 12 11 8 7 6 5 4 3 2 1

This book is printed on acid-free paper that meets the uncoated paper
ANSI/NISO specifications for permanence as revised in 1992.

Text design by Yvonne Tsang at Wilsted & Taylor Publishing Services

Library of Congress Cataloging-in-Publication Data

Smith, Thomas G. (Thomas Gary).
Showdown: JFK and the integration of the Washington Redskins / Thomas G. Smith
p. cm.
Includes bibliographical references and index.
ISBN 978-0-8070-0074-8 (hardcover : alk. paper)
1. Washington Redskins (Football team)—History—20th century.
2. African American football players—Civil rights—Washington (D.C.)
3. Racism in sports—Washington (D.C.) 4. Discrimination in sports—Washington (D.C.) 5. Kennedy, John F. (John Fitzgerald), 1917–1963—Relations with African Americans. 6. Washington (D.C.)—History—20th century.
7. Washington (D.C.)—Race relations. I. Title.
GV953.W3S65 2011
796.332'64097530904—dc22 2011012345

For Sandra

CONTENTS

PROLOGUE

"Redskins Told: Integrate or Else"

In 1961—as America hummed with racial tension—the Washington Redskins stood alone as the only team in professional football without a black player on its roster. In fact, in the entire twenty-five year history of the franchise, no African American had *ever* played for George Preston Marshall, the Redskins' cantankerous principal owner. But that was about to change.

On March 24, 1961, Secretary of the Interior Stewart L. Udall warned Marshall to hire a black player or face federal retribution. A crew-cutted, youthful, athletic Arizonan, Udall in many ways embodied the image of a vigorous, can-do New Frontiersman. As a three-term Democratic congressman in the 1950s, he had won respect as a hard-working legislator who supported liberal causes, including the preservation of the environment and civil rights. When named Interior secretary by John F. Kennedy, he seized the opportunity to promote racial equality by pressuring the Washington "Paleskins," as he called them, because he "considered it outrageous that the Redskins were the last team in the NFL to have a lily-white policy."

If Marshall did not integrate his team, threatened Udall, then the government would withhold the use of the Redskins' home playing field, D.C. Stadium—a publicly financed and newly built 56,000-seat arena located on public terrain at Anacostia Flats. Marshall had recently signed a thirty-year lease to play all home games at D.C.

Stadium, and as the "landlord" of the parks system, the Interior Department could deny use of the stadium to any entity practicing discriminatory hiring policies.

Realizing that racial justice and gridiron success had the potential to dovetail or take an ugly turn, civil rights advocates and sports fans alike anxiously turned their eyes toward the nation's capital. There was always the possibility that Marshall—one of the NFL's most influential and dominating pioneers—might defy such demands from the Kennedy administration to desegregate his all-white team. With slicked-down white hair and angular facial features, the nattily attired, sixty-four-year-old owner presented a formidable visage in 1961. He had a well-deserved reputation for flamboyance, showmanship, and mercurial behavior. And, like other Southern segregationists, Marshall stood firm against race mixing. "We'll start signing Negroes," he once boasted, "when the Harlem Globetrotters start signing whites."

With its abysmal record of 1 win, 12 losses, and 1 tie the previous season, the Redskins had a real opportunity to improve themselves by making a competent selection. The player draft rules for the fledging American Football League (AFL) and the older National Football League (NFL) were the same: teams would "draft" or select players in inverse order of their won-lost records. In other words, teams with poor winning percentages, like the Redskins, would be given an opportunity to select talented college players before teams with higher winning percentages. The AFL's Oakland Raiders had first pick in 1961, with the NFL's Redskins to follow two days later.

As the two stubborn and strong-willed titans, Udall and Marshall, clashed over federal desegregation efforts, Americans waited in great anticipation for the start of the December 1961 draft. Washington could draft Ernie Davis, a powerful Syracuse University running back who had become the first African American to win the Heisman Trophy. Drafting Davis might mean later losing him to the rival AFL for more money. The team could select Davis and trade him for two or three less-talented white or black players; or it could bypass Davis entirely to select a white player. It seemed unlikely that Marshall would defy the government and renege on his agreement to hire black players, but he was difficult to intimidate and unpredictable to boot. No one, including a well-intentioned presidential cabinet member, he said, could tell him who to hire for his private business. With the possibility of noncompliance in mind, on December 1, Udall issued a final warning to Marshall to honor his pledge to desegregate the team. The draft, he said, "is the showdown on this."

CHAPTER 1

Boston Beginnings

The Redskins professional football team was founded in New England by a bigoted Southerner. Lean and loquacious, brash and uninhibited, George Preston Marshall wore his black hair slicked back and parted down the middle. Dressed in a Bond Street suit and tie, with a gold-headed walking stick, he cut an imposing figure and was often identified in the press as "Marshall the Magnificent," "George the Gorgeous," or "the well-dressed man." "The sports writers have had a lot of fun with Showman Marshall," he once wrote. "I've enjoyed every word of it." As a "leading sportsman," he could be seen in choice seats at the ballpark, racetrack, or boxing arena.

Marshall was born in 1896 in Grafton, a West Virginia railroad and coal-mining town of 5,200 people (160 of whom were black) where his father, T. Hill Marshall, published a newspaper, the *Grafton Leader*. George grew up in the racially segregated South and likely had no black acquaintances. While he never learned racial tolerance, he did learn about the power of marketing. At age nine, when he had trouble selling a female rabbit for 25 cents, he advertised it in his father's newspaper as a rare Jacksonville hare. "Both the buyer and a couple of would-be buyers attracted by my ad," he later wrote, "inspected all points of my rabbit and learnedly agreed that she was a very fine specimen of Jacksonville hare indeed." He sold the "rare" hare for $1.25. That promotion led to others. "I'm guilty of having ideas and being a showman," he once said. "My defense is that promotional ideas and showmanship have never done anybody any harm."

As a youth, he also displayed an interest in athletics, playing baseball and serving as a batboy during the 1909 season for the Grafton team in the Pennsylvania–West Virginia Class-D minor league. The following year, at age fourteen, he organized a football team to compete against teams from adjoining towns, and donations from fans watching those contests sometimes totaled more than $20 (the equivalent of more than $400 today). He attended schools in Virginia and, later, in Washington, D.C., where his father had opened a laundry business.

George attended the tenth grade at Central High, a segregated public school in Washington, and the eleventh grade at the privately run Friends' Select School. Established in 1883 by Thomas Sidwell, the nonsectarian school was located four blocks from the White House. Emphasizing "Christian values," the school began with 28 pupils and grew to more than 200 when Marshall attended from 1913–14. The school accepted girls from its beginnings, but it did not enroll its first African American student until 1956, two years after the U.S. Supreme Court mandated the desegregation of public schools in the *Brown* decision. Eventually, the private school morphed into a college preparatory school (now the Sidwell Friends' School) emphasizing academic excellence, community service, earth stewardship, and racial, religious, and economic diversity. Bobby Mitchell, the first black player for the Redskins, enrolled his two children in the school in the late 1970s, and in 2009, President and First Lady Obama sent their children there.

At the Friends' Select School, Marshall played baseball and also developed a passion for dramatic acting. His love for the stage prompted him to quit school at age eighteen to join an acting company. The closest he came to expressing misgivings about this failing came in a letter recalling the nurturing influence of the Sidwells. "The only real regret I have ever had in my life," he wrote in 1934, "was I did not spend more time with Mrs. Sidwell and yourself in my youth."

As an actor, he performed with his company in cities across

America and in Canada. After three years on the stage, Marshall entered the military, serving in the 63d U.S. Machine Gun Corps without ever leaving the country. Discharged from the army in December 1918, he returned to Washington, D.C., his adopted home, to run the Palace Laundry, which he had inherited from his father.

Marshall had a flair for business and self-promotion. He once ran an advertisement in Washington's daily newspapers consisting of a single blank page except for a few words in small print at the bottom reading: "This space was cleaned by the Palace Laundry." He had the store and the laundry's delivery trucks painted in blue and gold, provided blue-and-gold uniforms for the employees, put fresh flowers in the window, and advertised with the slogan "Long Live Linen." Within a few years, Marshall transformed the small family business into a chain of more than fifty stores. Having amassed a fortune, he searched for additional investment opportunities, including real estate, theater companies, and, in 1925, a professional basketball team, the Washington Palace Five, in the newly formed American Basketball League (ABL). Marshall's team, nicknamed the Laundrymen, was unsuccessful financially and folded in 1928, four years before the collapse of the whole league. During that time, though, Marshall became acquainted with Joe Carr, president of the ABL and the future head of the National Football League (NFL), and with George Halas, a sponsor of the Chicago Bruins basketball team and one of the founders of the NFL. Carr and Halas proposed the idea of investing in a professional football franchise.

Meanwhile, Marshall actively participated in Washington social activities and continued to be a shameless self-promoter, opinionated and domineering. "Whether having a shampoo in the Statler-Hilton barber shop, dining at Duke Zeibert's, or holding court at the Shoreham [hotel] terrace, Marshall considered it a lost opportunity were he not the center of attention," wrote Jack Walsh of the *Washington Post.* He would be the only one at a funeral, as someone once said about Theodore Roosevelt, who would be envious of the corpse. "Marshall is not always offensive," stated one sportswriter, "but he is *never* inoffensive. He dominates any group of people he finds himself in. He does not hold conferences, he holds court."

A young, dapper, rather severe-looking George Preston Marshall. (Associated Press)

Nor was he shy about being a laundry tycoon and social climber. He once sent out Christmas cards featuring himself with a laundry sack slung over his shoulder climbing a ladder labeled "SOCIETY." On another occasion, a Newport, Rhode Island, socialite, peering through her lorgnette, asked: "Who, exactly, are you?" He replied: "I'm in laundry, Ma'am, and I'd like your business." He knew he had arrived socially in Washington, he once joked to friends, when his store obtained the laundry business of Borden Harriman, of one of the city's leading society families. Having reached celebrity status, he was named publisher of the *Washington Times,* a Hearst newspaper, but he was meddlesome and lasted only a year in the post.

Marshall was a social climber in New York as well as Washington. He attended Broadway plays, dined at the Colony Restaurant, the Stork Club, and 21, and frequented nightclubs, often with his friend, Mayor Jimmy Walker. Marshall was financially hurt, but not devastated, by the 1929 stock market crash that triggered the Great Depression. During those hard times, he traveled to Europe, vacationed in Virginia, California, and Florida, and lived lavishly with a butler-valet. His luxurious apartment in Washington featured black marble floors and a mirrored bedroom ceiling. He also maintained a suite in New York's swank St. Regis Hotel. He feared flying and never learned to drive a car, so he traveled by railroad and by a chauffeur-driven Cadillac with a back seat that could be converted into a bar and bed. When he traveled by rail during the Prohibition years, he took along a cowhide satchel full of premium liquor.

So, Marshall had enough money to invest in a professional football franchise, and in July 1932, he approached the NFL with three investment partners: Vincent Bendix, an Indiana auto parts supplier; Larry Doyle, a Wall Street stockbroker; and Jay O'Brien, an international polo star who married into the Fleischmann yeast fortune. It was the Depression's darkest year. The Depression, said former secretary of state Frank Kellogg, was merely a hangover caused by the "financial drunk" of the Roaring Twenties. But nationwide, nearly 32,000 businesses failed in 1932, including 1,500 banks. The unemployment rate topped 20 percent, and the gross national product tumbled from $104 billion in 1929 to $41 billion in 1933. Without significant federal or state assistance, charities tried unsuccessfully to help the needy. The NFL, which had downsized from ten to eight teams, engendered considerable goodwill by hosting a charity game, attended by more than 50,000 fans, in December between the New York Giants and former Notre Dame players coached by Knute Rockne.

Throughout America, millions of people lived in squalor. In urban areas, they huddled together in Hoovervilles, shantytowns named after Herbert Hoover, the president who seemed insensitive to their suffering. In Washington, D.C., the U.S. Army under Gen. Douglas MacArthur used tear gas, bayonets, and tanks to disperse a shabby settlement of World War I veterans who demanded immediate payment of their wartime monetary bonuses.

Lingering hard times and the rousting of the "Bonus Army" was a public-relations nightmare for President Hoover's reelection bid. Representing Washington, D.C., at the Democratic National Convention in Chicago, Marshall endorsed the presidential nomination of New York governor Franklin D. Roosevelt, although he would have preferred a states' rights candidate like Maryland governor Albert Richie. He eventually turned against Roosevelt because he believed that the administration's New Deal relief, recovery, and reform programs intruded too much on the rights of the states. "I am a strong believer in local autonomy or states' rights," he once intoned. "Every effort to centralize has been a failure in government."

A week after the Democratic convention, the Marshall group was awarded an NFL franchise in Boston, at the time a predominantly Irish-American city of 770,000 people. Marshall later boasted to *New York Mirror* sportswriter Harold Weissman that he "got the NFL franchise absolutely free of charge." All he had to do was pay the expenses of operating the team. (In 2010, *Forbes* estimated the financial value of the Redskins at $1.55 billion, slightly trailing only the Manchester United soccer team, the Dallas Cowboys football team, and the New York Yankees baseball team.)

Birthplace of the American Revolution, and home to the Red Sox and Braves baseball teams, Boston in 1932 was regarded as a choice sports town. Its colorful but corrupt mayor, James Michael Curley, was in the midst of his third term. In all, Curley would serve four terms as mayor, one term as governor, two terms in the U.S. House of Representatives, and two terms in prison.

Amid parades and great fanfare, Curley had directed Boston's three-hundredth anniversary in 1930. But merrymaking, historical remembrance, and jaunty talk did little to alleviate the city's jobless rate of nearly 30 percent. He persuaded Boston College and Holy Cross to play a football game at Harvard Stadium, with the profits going to the needy. And at a harborside ceremony in December 1931, he brought a symbolic end to hard times by placing "General D. Pression" in a coffin and burying him at sea. Bostonians (or at least those with the means) could also drown "General D. Pression" at one of the city's four thousand illegal speakeasies—four on the same block as the main police station. Only occasionally did police interfere with illegal liquor activities. Generally, dodging Prohibition was easier than getting around economic hard times. Harvard University had fired twenty cleaning women rather than raise their pay from thirty-five to thirty-seven cents. College athletes and students were required to provide some of the labor for the construction of the new stadium at Boston College. Neighboring towns threatened to fire teachers whose husbands were gainfully employed. Curley terminated 18,000 city workers and, fearing insurrection, denied permits to Communists and other so-called radicals who sought to protest their grievances on Boston Common. Ravaged by unemployment, shuttered businesses, foreclosed homes, and flagging spirits, Bostonians should have welcomed the startup of a new professional sports team. But they proved a hard sell, even to a crack salesman like George Marshall.

Marshall did some early "missionary" work by sponsoring a party in the spring of 1932 for Boston's sports leaders and writers. Held at a swank downtown hotel and hosted by Emil Fuchs, president of the Boston Braves baseball team, the soiree featured plenty of illegal booze and heaps of food on a table about the length of the Queen Mary, recalled one invitee. But instead of listening to speeches by the Marshall syndicate about bringing winning professional football to Boston, the inattentive guests clustered in small groups to talk baseball and drink liquor. The missionary effort largely failed, recalled a *Boston Post* writer, foreshadowing the difficulty that Marshall would have marketing his team in Boston.

From the start, Marshall took control of the football operation. He contracted with the Boston Braves baseball team to use their stadium (now Boston University's Nickerson Field). He also took advantage of the popularity of Major League Baseball by adopting the Braves name. The Chicago Cardinals, Chicago Bears, Staten Island Stapletons, Green Bay Packers, Brooklyn Dodgers, New York Giants, and Portsmouth Spartans made up the remaining teams in the league in 1932. Marshall also set team rules of decorum, some of which he did not heed himself. In public, the team was to dress in suits and ties and, above all, refrain from rowdy, boisterous, and "ungentlemanly" behavior. Nightclubs, bars, and gambling establishments were also off-limits.

To avoid going against the Braves and Red Sox baseball teams, Marshall did not schedule games until October. But then he had to compete against popular college football squads like Harvard, Boston College, Tufts, and Holy Cross. In 1932, there was little doubt that professional football players were superior to college athletes in terms of talent, but college games were more popular with fans. While college games were played on Saturdays rather than Sundays, most Depression-era fans did not have the time or money to attend games on both days.

Marshall expected to lure fans by building a competitive team and promoting it in the same way that he had done his laundry business. Originally, the team sported the same colors as the Palace Laundry: blue and gold. He named as head coach J. R. Ludlow "Lud" Wray, a University of Pennsylvania center who had played in the NFL in the early 1920s. Marshall raised eyebrows by paying the lavish sum of $1,500 to Albert Glen "Turk" Edwards to sign with the Braves. A future Hall of Famer, Edwards was an All-American tackle who played for Washington State University and was sought by several NFL teams. Rather than pay separate transportation fees for western and midwestern players, Marshall told Edwards to rent a bus and drive cross-country to Boston, picking up his teammates along the way. Marshall also recruited running backs Erny Pinkert and Jim Musick from the University of Southern California, and the little-acclaimed Cliff Battles from West Virginia Wesleyan College. Marshall was so taken with the latter player that he instructed the scout to "sign Battles for the Redskins, or just keep going South."

Like Edwards, Battles would be elected to the Pro Football Hall of Fame.

At training camp in Lynn, Massachusetts, forty players competed for twenty roster spots. Athletes in those days played both offense and defense for about $100 per game. The Braves played exhibition games in towns near Boston, hoping to build fan support. They defeated semipro teams from Quincy and Beverly but lost to the Providence Steam Roller, a one-time NFL team that fielded several players cut by the Braves.

Marshall hyped the team by advertising in Boston's five daily newspapers. He promised quality football at bargain prices: 55 cents for bleacher seats, $1.10 for grandstand seats, and $1.65 for box seats. At the inaugural game in Boston on October 2, Mayor Curley delivered a short speech, a local band played at halftime, and 5,000 fans watched as the Braves lost to the Brooklyn Dodgers, 14–0. The following week, however, the Braves defeated the New York Giants, 14–6, before 8,000 customers. All in all, the first season proved disappointing. The team finished with a record of four wins, four losses, and two ties. Fan support was tepid, and the team lost $46,000. Unable to tolerate the financial losses, Marshall's partners pulled out, leaving him in full control of the team.

Marshall was determined to succeed. He promised fans that he would make the team more entertaining and competitive. And he had talent to build on. Turk Edwards was a superior lineman, and Cliff Battles led the league in rushing, amassing 576 yards on 148 carries. Other NFL owners also wanted the NFL games to be more entertaining. There were too many ties and too little scoring. New York Giants owner Tim Mara recommended doing away with the extra point after a touchdown and settling ties with a ten-minute overtime period.

That proposal was rejected as too drastic, but at Marshall's insistence, league owners approved several changes prior to the 1933 season. One moved the goalposts from the end line to the goal line to facilitate extra points and field goals. Another permitted passing from anywhere behind the line of scrimmage, not just five yards beyond it as in previous seasons. Yet another established a ten-team league by dropping the Staten Island Stapletons and adding the Philadelphia Eagles, Pittsburgh Pirates (later the Steelers), and Cincinnati Reds. The league was divided into East and West divisions, with the winners playing a championship game.

Marshall initiated changes for his team as well as the league. He signed a contract to play home games at Fenway Park, and, with an eye towards fashion, he attired his players in gold and burgundy uniforms. When Lud Wray left to lead the newly formed Philadelphia Eagles, Marshall renamed his team the Redskins, an apparent tribute to his new coach, William "Lone Star" Dietz, an American Indian. He also continued to win over local sportswriters. On one occasion, he invited Austen Lake of the *Boston American* to his posh ninth-floor suite at the Ritz-Carlton, overlooking the Public Garden. At his host's invitation, Lake helped himself to some booze, inspected the new satin uniforms, and then listened to Marshall' s "colloquy" about the upcoming season. As Marshall hyped the new uniforms, players, and Indian coach who "put Purdue football on the map," Lake wrote, street-level fruit and vegetable vendors were simultaneously hawking their merchandise. As he departed Marshall's suite, Lake considered it fitting that one vendor was trying to peddle horseradishes.

Marshall's new coach had a colorful but checkered past. Raised in northern Wisconsin, Dietz claimed to be an American Indian. Yet doubt arose concerning his ancestry. A talented athlete and artist, he attended the Carlisle Indian School in Pennsylvania in 1907, where he played football and served as an art instructor. While there, he married an older Winnebago woman who was a trained, professional artist. In 1912, he served as an assistant to the acclaimed Carlisle football coach Glen "Pop" Warner. Their most celebrated player was Olympic gold medalist Jim Thorpe, who would go on to play professional football and baseball.

Upon Warner's recommendation, Dietz was appointed head football coach at Washington State College (now Washington State University) in 1915. At college functions, including football games, Dietz sometimes appeared in Sioux regalia, including headdress, moccasins, and leggings. The student body developed a chant: "Lone Star! Lone Star! Yip, Yip, You! How we love you! Oh, you Sioux!"

Successful in his first season, Dietz took his team to the Tournament of Roses game in Pasadena, California, on New Year's Day. Coaching in top hat and tails instead of Indian costume, Dietz guided Washington State to a 14–0 victory over Brown University in the Rose Bowl. He also had winning seasons in 1916 and 1917, but no bowl bids. Successful on the gridiron and popular with students, the college newspaper *Evergreen* wrote that he "is not only one of the finest football coaches; he is a true sportsman, and above all, a gentleman. He is always genial and courteous. . . . We are glad to have him and that we have manly fellows under him. Such a combination is almost sure to win. But win, or lose—we would have no other."

Unfortunately for Dietz, the president of the college, Ernest Holland, did not share the opinion of the student newspaper. Hired a year after Dietz, Holland seemed jealous of Dietz's success and was, according to his private secretary, a segregationist. "He felt deeply about this—much more deeply than was known outside the office. He felt there was something unmoral, if not actually immoral about having an Indian here," he wrote in a letter decades later. To avoid a potential "social disaster," Holland did not renew Dietz's contract.

Dietz did not remain jobless for long. In 1918, he appeared as an Indian in an unsuccessful Hollywood movie called *Fool's Gold,* and he coached the U.S. Marines football team at Mare Island in Vallejo, California. Once again, he coached his team to the Rose Bowl, but he lost to a Great Lakes Naval Training Station team boasting George Halas.

For Dietz, the year 1919 was a nightmare. His wife, whom he had divorced for desertion a few months before, died in February from the influenza epidemic that ravaged the land. A few months later, in late June, Dietz was nearly disgraced in a messy trial. A Spokane grand jury indicted him for dodging the draft during World War I. Dietz had registered as a non-citizen Indian who was not subject to the draft (Native Americans did not become citizens until 1924). The federal government challenged not only his bravery and patriotism, but also his Indian ancestry. The government claimed that Dietz's parents were both Caucasians whose son was dark-haired and dark-skinned. Dietz testified that as a youngster, his father told him that his biological mother was Sioux. Given the racial attitudes of the day, he said, he would not have attended Indian schools in Oklahoma and Pennsylvania if he believed he was white. Pop Warner and other character witnesses defended Dietz's patriotism by asserting that he served his country by coaching the Marines football team at Mare Island. At the trial, his mother testified that when her baby was stillborn, her husband went away and, about a week later, he brought her a newborn baby that he had obtained from the Sioux, and Dietz's maternal grandmother and two cousins verified that story. The trial ended in a hung jury, but the government retried him.

During the second trial, the prosecution did not make an issue of Dietz's ancestry, arguing that even if he was Indian, he had to live on a reservation or hold an Indian land allotment to be exempt from the draft. Dietz could not afford the expense of bringing back witnesses, so he pleaded no contest and served a month in jail, leaving the issue of his ancestry unresolved. It is possible that Dietz was a white scam artist with a dark complexion. It could be that his mother, grandmother, and other relatives lied under oath to keep him out of prison, but it is likely that at least one of his biological parents was an Indian. Tom Benjey, Dietz's able biographer, argues that Dietz believed himself to be an Indian and embraced his ancestry. But since he had no siblings or children of his own, there is no way to prove his ancestry short of doing a DNA test.

Marshall promptly played on Dietz's Indian ancestry to entertain fans. Not only did he hire a Native American coach and recruit four Indian players from the Haskell Institute, he required Dietz and the players to wear Indian feathers and war paint before home games. "In the thirties," Cliff Battles remembered, "we would, at the urging of George, put on war paint before a game and do a little Indian dance to entertain the paying customers. None of us liked that very much." Battles also complained that the paint and makeup drained them physically for the games because it "clogged their pores." The showmanship, he declared, "was so overdone it was embarrassing."

Although Dietz decried movies and print advertisements portraying Indians as "vagabonds," and "bloodthirsty savages," he helped promote the stereotype of Indians as noble savages. A gifted artist, Dietz probably designed the original team logo and letterhead, which featured an Indian as mascot. Insisting that the team nickname and logo were demeaning, seven Indian activists in the early 1990s sought redress in court.

It is perhaps not surprising that a team that banned black players for nearly thirty years did not consider the term "Redskins" racially insensitive. Team representatives argued that their trademark and nickname were meant to honor Native Americans, not offend them. In a 1986 letter to the *Washington Post,* Marshall's granddaughter, Jordan Harrison Price, maintained that, contrary to the story told by a club spokesperson, Marshall himself had no Indian blood. "Fact is," she continued, "he chose the name because he had always been an admirer of the American Indian and because one of the coaches, 'Lone Star' Dietz, was himself an American Indian." Bob Addie shared that viewpoint in his book *Sportswriter.* "Whatever other ethnic faults Marshall may have had," he wrote, "he was not an Indian-hater. Marshall had a cigar-store Indian in front of his office along with paintings and portraits of famous Indian chiefs, Indian blankets, and other artifacts of Indian lore." In 1999, the U.S. Patent Office adjudged the Redskins trademark disparaging and cancelled it, but that decision was overturned on appeal in 2003 and again in 2009, mainly on the grounds that too much time—at least twenty-five years—had elapsed to challenge the 1967 registration of the trademark.

While Dietz had a well-deserved reputation as a college coach, he proved to have more style than substance at the professional level. In addition to the four Indian players he had coached at the Haskell Institute, he also recruited Jack Riley, a highly regarded lineman from Northwestern University. "Dietz was a man of keen intelligence and fantastic ability and understanding," Riley recalled. "I could have played for George Halas but wanted so much to play for Lone Star." But to the chagrin of some of his players, Dietz was fond of using trick plays. In one, a player would fake a fumble; in another, he would pretend to tie his shoelace. Both were intended to dupe the defense into believing that the play was dead. While the defense was off guard, the Redskins player then would throw a pass or run with the ball. The Redskins players didn't like the plays because they seldom worked, and the defense would retaliate with punishing hits. But Dietz would continue to try them. "Lone Star used to take our quarterbacks aside and bribe them," Battles remembered. "He'd give them money out of his own pocket if they would call those trick plays."

The opening game of the 1933 season against the Packers in Green Bay ended in a tie. To save money, Marshall had the team stay in the Midwest, where they played an exhibition game against a semipro team, the Fort Atkinson Blackhawks, followed in subsequent weeks by a regular season 7–6 loss to the Chicago Bears and a 21–6 win over Pittsburgh. Boston won two of its next three games at home before 50,000 fans. After an October 22 shutout against the Chicago Cardinals, Marshall "was chortling with glee all over the Fenway offices boasting about 50,000 paid attendance in three games," according to the *Boston Globe*. He would soon have an opportunity to put those attendance figures in perspective when the Harvard-Yale game alone matched his three-game total.

The Redskins completed the season with a respectable record of 5 wins, 5 losses, and 2 ties. The team featured a potent running attack, and their backs, Jim "Sweet" Musick and Cliff Battles, led the league in rushing, gaining 809 and 737 yards, respectively. Overall, Marshall was satisfied with the support of the fans, the team's performance, and Coach Dietz, whom he called "a genius, an innovative, brilliant strategist."

The 1934 season, however, was less satisfying. A home game against the Giants on October 8 set the tone for the season and illuminated Marshall's growing tendency to meddle. At the start of that game, Marshall instructed Dietz to kick off if the Redskins won the coin toss. While he made his way to his box seat to watch the game and communicate with the sideline by telephone, he heard "Redskins win toss." But when he reached his seat, he saw the Giants preparing to kick off. He promptly telephoned Dietz and thundered: "Dammit, Dietz, I thought I told you to kick off, not receive." Dietz replied: "Where have you been, George? We did kick off, and they ran it back for a touchdown." Harry Newman scored all the points in the Giants' 16–0 victory by running back the opening kickoff, converting the extra point, and booting three field goals.

That incident, however, did not dissuade Marshall from interfering. He often sat on the bench, recommended plays and strategy, and berated players and officials. *New York Times* columnist John Kieran asserted that, in Boston, "Marshall law has been established on the gridiron." Until his players threatened to strike, he would "sit on the Boston bench and give more orders than a commanding general in a world war." "Resplendent in a Piccadilly hat, a Bond Street suit, and a Rue de la Paix scarfpin," he was the "Beau Brummel[l] of the sidelines." On one occasion in 1933, "George Preston Knute Rockne Walter Camp Marshall" tried to tell Jim Musick how to run through a hole in the line. Musick replied: "What year were you an All-American?" Marshall retaliated with a low salary offer, and Musick decided to sit out the 1934 season.

The 1934 season was also a disappointment for Marshall. Attendance dwindled, and the team ended with a 6–6 record, good for second place behind the Giants, who would go on to win the NFL championship against the Bears. The team's mediocre record cost Dietz his job.

While Boston players resented Marshall's meddlesome hand, the league benefited from some of his suggestions. In a late November game against Boston, Giants owner Tim Mara obtained a quarterback from Pittsburgh to replace his starter, Harry Newman, who went down with a season-ending neck injury. Marshall objected because the late-season trade would benefit the Giants at Boston's expense. Mara said that the trade was agreed upon between consenting owners and that if the situation were reversed, he would not object. Marshall appealed to NFL president Joe Carr, who submitted the issue to a vote of the owners, and they agreed with Marshall. The Giants still won the game 3–0, but after the season, owners instituted the so-called waiver rule that forbade player transactions after the sixth game of the season unless all the clubs waived their objections. At that same December meeting, Marshall and the other owners agreed to use a tapered ball in 1935 to promote passing.

Marshall hired former Harvard coach Eddie Casey to coach the Redskins for the 1935 season. If Marshall thought that hiring a Harvard coach would boost attendance, he was mistaken. When the Redskins played a preseason evening exhibition game in Beverly against a semipro team, they drew only five thousand fans. Desperate to save money, Marshall asked fans to return any footballs kicked into the stands.

Losing money in football, Marshall became involved in other sports activities that potentially promised financial success. In February 1935, he became a principal investor and president of Roosevelt Raceway, a European-style, 4.5-mile oval auto racetrack on Long Island. And in early August 1935, he finally received major coverage in the Boston dailies when he and some unnamed partners made a bid to take over the Boston Braves baseball team. "Marshall Group Near Control," blared the *Boston Globe*. As always, the thirty-nine-year old sportsman had big plans. "I'm a nut on accommodations for spectators," he said. "We can't do any worse than the Braves have been doing, and if we don't improve, we can at least let the fans see us lose in comfort." He promised cushy seats, flashy uniforms, night baseball, and beer. "We're going to pep up baseball." He would also bring quality ballplayers, not has-beens like Babe Ruth, and he assured Bostonians that his baseball operation would not "interfere in any way" with the Redskins football program.

After two meetings, C. F. Adams, the Braves major officer and stockholder, called Marshall a "man of big ideas" who had made an attractive offer. "I have studied Marshall carefully," he told the press. "I firmly believe that he is a hustler who can do things, that he has sound business judgment and good sporting, promotional instincts. I am making all haste in attempting to complete the deal." Unfortunately for Marshall (and perhaps the Braves), the bank holding the mortgage killed the deal.

Marshall not only lost out on baseball, but he had to endure an abysmal football season, suffering losses on the field and at the gate.

He also had to endure criticism from a heretofore indifferent Boston press. One report stated that fans were becoming irritated because Marshall's band music drowned out public address announcements. "Just when the announcer starts to give the crowd some interesting sidelights on the visiting team, up starts the band," complained a *Globe* writer. "Every week, it has been the same."

Frustrated by his team's poor performance, Marshall sometimes went berserk. Right after a mid-October loss to the Detroit Lions, he "hopped onto the gridiron and laced into the gold pants brigade." Nearly homicidal, he followed the players into the locker room, where he continued to berate them. His rants did little to improve fan attendance or team performance. At one point, the team lost eight consecutive games, and it ended the season with a record of 2 wins, 8 losses, and 1 tie. At the final home game of the season, the team again attracted only five thousand fans. And once again, Marshall fired the coach.

Marshall then hired Ray Flaherty to coach the hapless Redskins. Flaherty had played for a decade with the New York Giants, winners of the NFL championship in 1934. Marshall expected Flaherty's success with the Giants to carry over to the Redskins and draw more spectators. At the same time, he sought to offset financial losses by raising prices, with the cheapest ticket jumping from 55 cents to $1.10. Marshall had difficulty selling tickets before the price hike, when he had the only professional football team in town. But in 1936, the Redskins had to compete for spectators with the Boston Shamrocks, a team in the newly established American Football League (AFL).

The Redskins had an excellent opportunity to improve their record because they had the second overall pick in the NFL draft. Established by owners the year before for the 1936 season, the selection of amateur players would occur based on a team's overall record, in inverse order. The Bears traded for the first pick and chose University of Chicago Heisman Trophy winner Jay Berwanger, who decided not to play professional football. With the second pick, the Redskins took Riley Smith, a running back from the University of Alabama. In a subsequent round, they selected Wayne Millner, an end from

Notre Dame who would eventually be elected to the Pro Football Hall of Fame.

Smith had never been out of Alabama before playing with the College All-Stars against the Bears in Chicago. From there, he took his first plane ride to Boston and played all sixty minutes in his first exhibition game two days later. He played quarterback on offense and cornerback on defense. "I went from there to New York, where I played another all-star game, 60 minutes," he related in 1981 to *Boston Globe* writer Leigh Montville. "I had to catch a boat back to Boston in time to catch a train to Pittsburgh, where I played another exhibition with the Redskins. I played four games, 60 minutes, in 10 days. That was the start of the season." Smith retired after three seasons because "there just wasn't any money in it." Playing sixty minutes every week for $250 per game "just wasn't good arithmetic. Just didn't add up."

Unlike some players, however, Smith got along with Marshall. "I'll tell you this about George Preston Marshall," he said to Montville. "If you acted scared of him, he'd eat you alive. But if you stood up to him, he was all right. I stood up to him. He came into the shower room, right there at Fenway Park, screaming after a game about something he thought I'd done. Walked right through the shower heads, wearing a $150 suit and $50 shoes, yelling at me. Well, I told him, 'Damn it, if you don't like the way I do things, then you go and get yourself another quarterback.' I was going for him, too, but he hurried out of the shower room. We got along fine after that. Matter of fact, when I was out of football and got married, he threw me a big party."

While new head coach Flaherty was building a team, Marshall was pursuing a romance with Corinne Griffith, a former silent-film star. Both had been married before, he to a Ziegfeld entertainer, Elizabeth Mortensen, who bore him two children, and she to a Hollywood producer. Marshall first proposed to her during dessert after their first date. But she put him off. "George spends half his life in nightclubs, Corinne remembered saying to a friend. "We've been to 29 different nightclubs for 29 different nights now. . . . If there's one thing I don't care about, it's spending half my life in nightclubs."

As a change of pace, Marshall recommended a weekend summer trip to a farm in the Blue Ridge Mountains at Mt. Airy, Virginia. In a scene reminiscent of *Gone With the Wind,* published that very year, he wooed her amidst fragrant honeysuckle while a group of hired African American performers sang "Carry Me Back to Ole Virginny" and other Southern ballads. "Then Mint Juleps, in frosted silver cups, were brought out by two, overly costumed, pretty Negro maids," Griffith later recalled. "They wore long, full skirts with tiny aprons. Around their heads bandanas were tied." It was a better act of salesmanship, she wrote, than MGM Studios had shown her. Upon their return to Washington, she accepted Marshall's proposal, and he presented her with an engagement gift: a Confederate flag that had been a family heirloom since the Civil War. The couple formally celebrated their engagement in New York at 21, toasting each other with burgundy in gold-rimmed glasses—trademark Redskins colors.

In July, they were married at a small ceremony in Armonk, New York. As they were about to enter a limo after attending a small reception, a scene unfolded that foreshadowed difficulty in their relationship. Marshall said to the chauffeur: "Well, Welles, I got married!" "Yes, sir," he smiled. "I suspected as much, sir." "Yes," interjected Corinne, "we both got married." It was the first time that Marshall would regard Corinne as an afterthought—but it wouldn't be the last.

Marshall could "sell" Corinne, but he had more difficulty "selling" his team to Boston spectators. Corinne and George complained that Boston sportswriters never warmed up to the team, but they overstated the case. The *Boston Post,* the leading city newspaper of the day, provided regular favorable coverage of the Redskins. Claiming that professional football was gaining on baseball in popularity, it carried a Bill Coyne illustration, "Bursting into Space," showing a helmeted football player smashing through a sports page dominated by baseball headlines. Jack Barnwell recapped Redskins games and delivered short, newsy items about the team in a weekly feature called "Scalpings," and *Post* columnist Bill Cunningham wrote upbeat articles on Marshall, the Redskins, and football in general.

Newly returned from Berlin, where he had covered the Olympic Games and reported on a new broadcast technology called television, he reminded readers that, though they faced a depressed economy, they did not have to endure civil war and political oppression. They also had sports as a distraction. "If they had a little more baseball over on the other side, they might have a little less bombing. If they had more racing, there might be less revolution. Football might dilute Fascism some."

Post writers were also optimistic about the Redskins prospects on the field and at the gate. Cunningham contributed a column called "Pro Football Is Booming on Its Fifth Birthday," commemorating the anniversary of the professional game in Boston. Admittedly, he wrote, Bostonians showed little initial zeal for the team. But after four years of "drilling," Marshall was about to "strike oil." "The game has arrived in this town and figures, this year, perhaps, to be sensational." Fellow *Post* writer Jack Barnwell expressed similar sentiments.

Marshall, too, expressed optimism at the beginning of the 1936 season. Making a pledge in late August that would come back to bite him, he said that if the Redskins won the division, they would play the title game "right in Fenway Park, if we have to play it in three feet of snow. Boston deserves that playoff game, and Boston is going to get it before I quit."

The season opened in the "City of Soot" with a 10–0 loss to the Steelers. The Redskins then won the next two road games against the Eagles and Dodgers before opening at home against the Giants on October 4. The owner was in attendance, and "I don't mind telling you," wrote Arthur Duffey of the *Post,* "that high pressure George expects a clean cut victory." Despite increased ticket prices, 15,000 fans watched the Redskins lose 7–0 in a lackluster effort. The team, if not the fan base, rebounded from that loss. Led by the league's best defense and the crafty running of Cliff Battles, the Redskins vied with the Steelers and Giants for the Eastern division title. Boston could prevail with victories over those teams in its last two games.

On November 29, the Redskins trounced the Steelers 30–0 before a meager crowd of 4,800 at Fenway Park. Marshall was outraged over the lack of fan support. After all, in a preseason game in Chicago against college All-Stars, the Detroit Lions had drawn 70,000 fans; and in Massachusetts, nearly 50,000 customers went to Narragansett Park to bet on animal races. Yet the Redskins, competing for the division title, could not attract 5,000 spectators. Privately, Marshall decided that if the Redskins won the division, he would ask league officials for permission to move the championship game to a more receptive venue, and he would also seek league approval to move the franchise out of Boston.

Boston sportswriters tried to build enthusiasm for the team, not initially realizing that a victory over the Giants in New York would not result in the championship game being played at Fenway Park. Newspapers across America at the time carried headlines reading "King May Abdicate" and "King to Leave Throne." Those headlines, of course, referred to King Edward VIII of Britain, who planned to surrender his crown to marry Wallis Simpson, the divorced American woman he loved. But similar Boston headlines in early December were written about Marshall's decision to desert the city. The *Boston Post* referred to early December as "abdication week," as both King Edward and Marshall were going to leave their posts. Both men were leaving "just as they were about to be crowned," wrote Bill Cunningham. "The King goes into exile with Wally; Marshall with his Redskins." "Redskins May Quit This City for Good," declared the *Globe,* and "Boston Fumbles Chance to See Play-Off Game," proclaimed the *Evening Transcript.*

Already agitated over the possibility of losing the championship game and the franchise, Bostonians were further aggrieved when Marshall decided that the town was not even good enough for his players to practice. "Pro Football Goes Sissy," announced the *Boston Evening American* when Marshall moved his players to the Westchester Country Club in Rye, New York. It was bad enough, wrote Murray Kramer of the *Evening American,* for the team to practice on a polo field at an effete country club, but they would also travel there in luxury. "It wasn't so many years ago that professional gridmen were college misfits who couldn't get a job and who traveled by bus," he sneered. "Contrast this to the present Redskin squad . . . who left for New York by train this morning."

While most of the team traveled by train, Cliff Battles and John "Pug" Rentner drove by automobile and were stopped in Webster, Massachusetts, where they were fined $10 for speeding. Their "final salute to Massachusetts," declared one writer, was symbolically appropriate because George Marshall had hastily closed the team office and ordered workers to tear down the portable wooden bleachers at Fenway Park. Although no announcement had been made, it was growing increasingly clear that even if the Redskins defeated the Giants, neither the championship nor any future games would be played in Boston. The only way the Redskins would ever return to Boston, wrote Paul Craigue of the *Globe,* would be to get their luggage.

On a chilly, drizzly, murky day the Redskins captured the division title by defeating the Giants 14–0 before 17,000 fans at the Polo Grounds in New York City. Soon after that game, Marshall confirmed reports that the championship game against the Green Bay Packers would be played at the Polo Grounds, not Fenway Park. Though hardly a surprise, one offended Boston scribe said the move would be like the Boston Red Sox playing World Series games at Yankee Stadium.

Marshall explained that he was hosting the game in New York mainly to benefit the players, who would get 60 percent of the net proceeds. Not only would the gate be larger, but New York City had tamer weather than Boston, and the Polo Grounds had lights if needed, unlike Fenway Park. Besides, "we certainly don't owe Boston much after the shabby treatment we've received. . . . Imagine losing $20,000 with a championship team."

Marshall substantiated rumors that the Boston franchise would be transferred to another city in 1937. Writers guessed that the team might be moved to Buffalo, Chicago, Newark, or Washington, D.C., or it might be merged with the Philadelphia Eagles. Marshall refused to name the new home of the Redskins because he wanted to concentrate on the championship game. Moreover, he needed time to "clean my fingers of some of the red ink I picked up in Massachusetts." In five years, he continued, the Boston franchise had lost slightly more than $85,000. The laundry tycoon, cracked one Boston writer, had been "taken to the cleaners." Marshall could not fathom why fewer than five thousand paying fans showed up at Fenway Park in ideal weather for the pivotal game against the Steelers. He had counted more people than that, he joked, "in the waiting room at South Station." He could transfer the team to a defunct NFL franchise like Stapleton, he said, and draw more spectators than Boston. In New York, by contrast, 17,000 spectators attended the Redskins-Giants game on a day when it "was raining cows and horses and you couldn't see your hand in front of your face," as Marshall described it.

"I'm licked as far as Boston is concerned," he told a writer. "Boston is a great town. I like everything about it and everybody in it," he said disingenuously. Actually, he didn't like the town, many of the writers, or the indifferent spectators. He thanked the small group of loyal fans who supported the team. "But fans in paying quantities don't seem to want us. Maybe they don't want me." He would remain in the sport, he said, "but it will be somewhere else."

Years later, Marshall heaped blame for his lack of success in Boston on the local sportswriters, who he claimed gave more coverage to high school sports than the Redskins and who "agreed that our existence should be kept a close secret." Neither claim was true. While many writers did not like Marshall personally, they did provide regular coverage of his team, including action photos. Moreover, he had developed a close friendship with Bill Cunningham, the city's top sportswriter.

In postmortems, New York and Boston writers speculated on the reasons why the Redskins were not successful in Boston. Stanley Woodward of the *New York Herald Tribune* noted that no group of faithful fans accompanied the team to New York for the title-deciding game, the *Boston Post* was the only local paper to send a writer to that game, and the West Roxbury band that played at halftime had to pay its own way. Bostonians, he concluded, were more interested in dog and horse racing than professional football. Boston was once the most rabid sports town in the nation, he said, but its "sporting heritage apparently had been passed through the pari-mutuel window."

Boston observers conceded that racetrack betting captured dollars that might have gone to professional football otherwise, but there were other factors that contributed to the demise of the franchise. A *Globe* editorial believed that professional football simply could not match the excitement and traditional rivalries of the college game. Other newspapers blamed the slow economy, the rise in ticket prices, and the team's ho-hum performance against the Giants in the home opener. And then there was the issue of Marshall's strong personality. He was arrogant, tactless, egotistical, and an absentee owner who too often made himself, not the team, the center of attention. "He thought he was responsible," John Kieran of the *New York Times* once wrote, "for thirty-five inches of every yard the team gained." Boston writers referred to him derisively as "Long-Live Linen," "Pooh-Bah," and the "Wet Wash King."

Even his defenders, like Bill Cunningham of the *Post,* conceded that "there was undoubtedly a little of the city-slicker about him. He gave the impression, unfortunately for him, that he felt he was doing Boston a favor. His personality was a little too hot for some of the locals to handle." Another problem, Cunningham continued, was that Marshall's antics during games often took attention away from the team. "It was impossible to keep him back in the stands while the battle was on, and he often gave a better show going crazy on the bench than his mercenaries did on the field." Since there was no public outcry over the Redskins leaving, he concluded, fans should just forget about them.

Cunningham was one of the few Boston sportswriters who had accepted Marshall. "I just happen to like the fellow, and the feeling is mutual," he wrote. "I can easily grant that he's stubborn, headstrong, explosive, and opinionated," but he was also honest, forthright, entertaining, and generous. On numerous occasions, Cunningham continued, Marshall picked up checks that totaled more than the weekly wages of the individuals seated at his table. He was also passionate about the game. Indeed, for Marshall, football was "an insanity." And there was little reason to feel sorry for Marshall. He had built a solid team and might thrive in a new city.

Corinne also claimed to have influenced the move to Washington. At the New York club 21, with her husband and the popular writer Damon Runyon, she set forth her displaced citizen theory. "You see," she theorized, "there are so many displaced citizens in Washington from places such as Muleshoe, Texas; Ekalaka, Montana; and even Beverly Hills, California. I know. As a matter of fact, the D.C. after Washington means: Displaced Citizen. Most of these D.C.'s are alone in Washington with nothing to do on Sunday afternoon other than sit in parks and feed the squirrels and pigeons. . . . I have a definite feeling that Washington's D.C.'s would welcome a little more action on Sunday afternoon." Runyon and Marshall, she recalled, agreed.

For Boston fans, the championship game was anticlimactic. Green Bay featured the best offense in the league, especially its passing combination of quarterback Arnold Huber to end Don Hutson, and it had lost only one game all year. The Redskins had the best defense in the league and a darting runner in Cliff Battles, but the team had lost five games, including two to the Packers. The championship game, played on December 13, attracted thirty thousand spectators to the Polo Grounds. Adorned in what one writer called "atrocious looking mustard-brown and green uniforms," Green Bay struck quickly in the first quarter with a 52-yard touchdown pass from Huber to Hutson. Early in that same quarter, Boston's Cliff Battles injured his knee and sat out the remainder of the game. Another Boston starter was ejected for fighting. All in all, Green Bay dominated with a convincing 21–6 win, picking up its fourth championship.

A few days after that disappointing defeat, Marshall announced that the league had approved his request to transfer the Redskins to Washington, D.C., home of the Senators baseball club. *Boston Post* writer Bill Cunningham could not resist a parting shot. He noted that the defunct Boston Shamrocks won their final game in Washington, D.C., before fewer than a thousand customers. Moving a sports franchise to Washington, he cautioned, was a risky move because "the national capital is pretty much a country town where sports are concerned." Marshall would find football and financial success in that "country town," but he would also initiate a team and league-wide ban against black players that would embarrass the sport forever.

CHAPTER 2

Out of Bounds

Reflecting late in life about racism during the NFL's infancy, two icons, one black and one white, held contrasting views. Fritz Pollard, who pioneered in the NFL as a black quarterback and coach, accused league owners of blatant racism. Chicago Bears owner George Halas, he bluntly charged, "was prejudiced as hell."

"He's a liar," Halas retorted. "At no time did the color of skin matter. All I cared about was the color of blood. If you had red blood, I was for you."

During the 1920s and early 1930s, the formative years of the NFL, a few blacks graced the gridiron and doubtless shed some blood. It was a time of NFL franchise fluidity, a time of jazz, Prohibition, speakeasies, and flappers. It was also a time of emotionally crippling Jim Crow segregation laws, lynchings, and open Ku Klux Klan activity. Although there were no Southern NFL franchises, blacks on Northern teams endured many indignities. They were denied accommodations and dining access in many hotels. In Canton, Ohio, Jay "Inky" Williams was permitted to join some whites at a hotel dining table, but only if a portable screen shielded them from other guests. In a few cases, according to Pollard, opposing teams like the Bears insisted that black players be benched or else no game would be played.

Robert "Rube" Marshall and Fritz Pollard were the first black players in what was to become the NFL, playing for the Rock Island

Independents and Akron Pros, respectively, in 1920. Fred "Duke" Slater, a premier tackle, starred for the Independents, and later the Chicago Cardinals, from 1926 to 1931. In 1933, Ray Kemp and Joe Lillard were the lone African American representatives in the NFL. A graduate of Duquesne University, where he played three years of football, Kemp first signed with Art Rooney's newly created Pittsburgh Pirates in 1933. After playing two games at tackle, he was released by Pirates coach Forrest Douds. Recalled to the team in December, Kemp played the final game of the season against the New York Giants. When he attempted to join his teammates at the hotel in New York following the game, he was informed that no rooms were available, and he reluctantly agreed to stay at a YMCA in Harlem. Released in 1933 after one season, he began a long career as a college football coach. In a December 1983 interview with the football publication *Coffin Corner,* he cited racism as the reason for his release. "It was my understanding," he noted, "that there was a gentlemen's agreement in the league that there would be no more blacks."

Joe Lillard's career, though more spectacular, was also cut short. Nicknamed the "Midnight Express," he was a gifted athlete who excelled at baseball, basketball, and football, and played for the Chicago Cardinals in 1932 and 1933. His career as a star running back at the University of Oregon ended when a rival coach discovered that the "Midnight Express" had played baseball and basketball for semipro black teams. Signed by the Cardinals, Lillard was the only African American in the NFL in 1932. In a mid-October scoreless contest against the cross-town Bears, he gave a strong performance as a punt returner, kicker, and running back. The following week, he helped the Cardinals defeat George Marshall's Boston Braves. An ebullient Boston columnist wrote: "Lillard is not only the ace of the Cardinal backfield but he is one of the greatest all-around players that has ever displayed his wares on any gridiron in this section of the country." This was high praise indeed, coming from someone who had seen the running prowess of Cliff Battles and Jim "Sweet" Musick. But a month later Lillard was suspended by the Cardinals and out of football.

Apparently, Lillard lost favor with teammates and management. Like the fullback Jim Brown, who would come later, Lillard had an abundance of surliness and pride, possessing a volatile temper that could be baited easily. Coach Jack Chivigny explained that Lillard disrupted practice by being tardy or absent, missed blocking assignments in games, and disobeyed team rules. The team's public relations officer, Rocky Wolfe, claimed that teammates resented his selfishness and swaggering style. "Football players, like anyone else, will always be jealous," remarked Wolfe. "But a fellow can always clear up such a situation by living, walking, and breathing in a manner that does not bespeak supremacy—a thing Lillard hasn't learned." Worried that his cocky demeanor might deny opportunities to other minority candidates, Al Monroe, a writer for the black weekly *Chicago Defender,* urged Lillard to kiss up to whites because he was "the lone link in a place we are holding on to by a very weak string."

The following year, Paul Schissler, the new coach of the Cardinals, gave Lillard another opportunity. He showed no signs of being more accommodating, but he played well when he was not sitting out games with injuries (he missed four of eleven games). On October 7 he threw three passes for seventy-five yards, but he missed a point after a touchdown in a 7–6 loss to the Portsmouth Spartans in Ohio. The next week he drop-kicked a field goal to defeat Cincinnati, 3–0. And the following week, in a 12–9 loss to the Bears, he kicked a field goal and returned a punt fifty-three yards for a touchdown. On that day, he outperformed Chicago's Red Grange, then the game's best player. The *Chicago Defender* described Lillard as "easily the best halfback in football," but his contract was not renewed for the 1934 season.

The black press claimed that Lillard had been "Too Good For His Own Good," or so the headline ran, and that the "color of his skin had driven him out of the National Football League." In 1935 Coach Schissler conceded that an unwritten rule barred blacks from the game for their own protection. A hundred years earlier, President Andrew Jackson had relocated thousands of southeastern Native Americans to the Trans-Mississippi West supposedly for the same reason—to protect them against violence. Lillard, like American Indians, was a victim of racism. "He was a fine fellow, not as rugged as most in the pro game, but very clever," Schissler explained. "But he was a marked man, and I don't mean that just the Southern boys took it out on him either; after a while, whole teams, Northern and Southern alike, would give Joe the works, and I'd have to take him out." Lillard's presence, the coach continued, made the Cardinals a "marked team . . . and now the rest of the league took it out on us! We had to let him go, for our own sake, and for his too!"

Likely led by George Marshall, professional football owners at their annual meeting in 1933, privately and diabolically, agreed to ban the use of African American players in the NFL. Professional football owners, like their Major League Baseball counterparts, publicly denied the existence of a racial ban. "For myself and for most of the owners," Art Rooney of the Pittsburgh Steelers explained to me decades later, "I can say there never was any racial bias." George Halas of the Chicago Bears declared to sportswriter Myron Cope in 1970 that there had been no unwritten exclusionary agreement, "in no way, shape, or form." Tex Schramm of the Los Angeles Rams did not recall a gentleman's agreement: "You just didn't do it—it wasn't the thing that was done." Tim Mara of the Giants also denied that minorities had been blackballed. Despite the disclaimers, however, blacks had disappeared from the game altogether. After Ray Kemp and Joe Lillard were released in 1933, no African American played major-league football until 1946.

The racial climate of the 1930s no doubt contributed to the policy of discrimination. True, blacks made important strides toward racial justice during the Roosevelt years. Above all, Roosevelt's New Deal offered hope. Encouraged by the promise of "no forgotten men and no forgotten races," blacks deserted their traditional allegiance to the Republican Party. In 1936, Roosevelt attracted about 75 percent of the black vote, and New Deal relief programs, especially the Works Progress Administration (WPA), helped blacks cope with hard times. In all, about 40 percent of the African American population received some federal assistance during the Great Depression.

Despite modest gains and heightened expectations, African

Americans continued to experience injustice. Only the American Communist Party consistently and openly championed full equality for blacks. In agriculture, tenant farmers and sharecroppers suffered from plunging prices. In industry, the jobless rate soared as blacks were the "last hired and first fired." Some New Deal assistance programs discriminated against minorities. More than 60 percent of black workers were ineligible for Social Security benefits, because the plan did not cover farmworkers and domestics.

In the South, where more than two-thirds of the black population resided, a vicious system of segregation existed. Blacks were terrorized and lynched. They were denied access to hospitals, colleges, hotels, restaurants, churches, polling places, playgrounds, and parks. Transportation facilities, movie theaters, public schools, and cemeteries were segregated too.

Discrimination extended beyond regional boundaries. Northern employers, unions, schools, and colleges denied opportunities to African Americans. Movies and radio shows portrayed them in stereotypical roles like Uncle Tom, Sambo, and Aunt Jemima. It is little wonder that some minorities found the 1937 celebration of the 150th anniversary of the U.S. Constitution hypocritical. Some drew parallels with the discriminatory treatment of Jews in Nazi Germany. Until Jim Crow ends, commented the *Pittsburgh Courier,* "only hypocrites will condemn the German Nazis for doing all of a sudden what America has been doing for generations."

Once war erupted in Europe in September 1939, black leaders urged neutrality. The *Pittsburgh Courier* cautioned that "before any of our people get unduly excited about SAVING DEMOCRACY in Europe, it should be called to their attention that we have NOT YET ACHIEVED DEMOCRACY HERE." The *Boston Guardian* noted in an editorial that there was not much difference between the aims of Hitler and Jim Crow. "In each case, the result is to defeat the aims of humanity." Expecting American involvement in the war, the *Guardian* said that blacks would fight out of patriotism, but they would also fight to integrate the military service. In only five states, it observed, could African Americans join the Reserves.

It is not surprising that discrimination and segregation extended to the field of sports. While some African Americans, like Joe Louis and Jesse Owens, were distinguishing themselves in boxing and track, others were being denied opportunities in professional baseball and football. Even most "major" colleges excluded blacks from their teams. In response, blacks organized their own professional football teams and leagues, although these never reached the stability or stature of the Negro Leagues in baseball. In football, the most successful team was the New York Brown Bombers, coached by Fritz Pollard. Joe Lillard played for the Bombers, and later the Union City Rams in the American Association. Asked to compare the quality of play between major- and minor-league football, Lillard conceded that there was more talent in the NFL, but the black professionals were just as tough.

Many reasons were offered to explain the absence of African Americans from the professional game. Some blacks charged that NFL owners used Joe Lillard's volatile personality as an excuse to ban other minority athletes. Proud and hot-tempered, Lillard rarely overlooked a racial slur or dirty play against him. When he felt wronged, he always retaliated, which earned him a reputation for being a "bad actor." In a game against the Pirates in 1933, he was ejected for fighting. Lillard was an angry man, Ray Kemp recalled, "and the players on the other teams knew what would set him off."

During the 1920s, Fritz Pollard has observed, fledgling NFL teams may have signed All-Americans who were African American to gain recognition and fan support. But after gaining popularity and relative stability in the 1930s, the league was no longer willing to sign high-quality black players. And during the Depression decade, it was bad public relations to hire blacks when so many whites were without jobs.

George Marshall never admitted to the existence of a racial ban, nor did he ever admit to being racially prejudiced. But as Ed Linn of *Sport* wrote in 1957: "In ordinary conversation, Marshall refers to the Negroes in a manner which leaves little doubt that his objection to them [as players] is based along purely racial lines." Marshall informed African American sportswriter Ric Roberts in 1942 that paternalism, not prejudice, explained the absence of blacks in the NFL. If blacks played in the league, he said, white players, especially those from the South, would go to extremes to physically disable them. By not signing blacks, he lamely declared, NFL owners were preventing on-field mayhem and keeping them out of harm's way.

Besides protecting blacks from physical abuse, some owners, according to Harry March, author of the 1934 book *Pro Football: Its Ups and Downs,* maintained that hiring blacks created too many hassles, such as separate arrangements for lodging, dining, and traveling. Bears owner George Halas attributed the absence of blacks in the NFL to the poor quality of the college talent pool. Still others, like Art Rooney, claimed that financial constraints prohibited NFL teams from developing adequate scouting systems. "In those days," he told me, "the great thrill was not only winning the game on Sunday but also meeting the payroll on Monday." In addition, Rooney continued, black schools did not do a very good job of publicizing their athletes. Once NFL teams had the money to establish sound scouting systems after World War II, they could tap into the "wealth of untapped talent" at small colleges. "In brief, I believe it was the lack of scouting funds and the lack of publicity at the smaller schools that helped cause this problem."

Financial realities no doubt did discourage owners from scouting black colleges, but there were standout African American athletes on major college teams in the 1930s. White players were scouted and signed, so it seems reasonable to expect black athletes who played in the same conferences to have been discovered as well, but none were.

Blacks who sought to play for desegregated college teams faced enormous challenges. They had to have extraordinary ability and a serene temperament. They also created logistical problems. Coaches had to deal with discrimination in travel, lodging, and restaurants. Should they insist upon equal treatment for all team members or ask minority players to endure humiliating Jim Crow laws? Was the principle of equal treatment worth the battle? There were also scheduling problems. Southern colleges usually refused to play against desegregated teams. Consequently, the black players were benched, or games were cancelled outright. University of Iowa coach Ossie Solem benched his black players against George Washington University, he said, "for the good of the sport." The U.S. Naval Academy refused to play against Bill Bell of Ohio State, but it had no objections to NYU's Manuel Riviero because he was a light-skinned Cuban. And despite heated protests from University of Michigan students, Willis Ward was not in uniform against Georgia Tech. Finally, race prejudice prevented African Americans from winning the recognition they deserved. Those who excelled often did not win team captaincies, conference honors, or All-America recognition. They were rarely chosen to play in an annual game between college stars and the NFL championship team.

Despite obstacles, some blacks did play big-time college football, especially in the Big 10 (later Big 12) Conference. Ozzie Simmons, a 185-pound running back at the University of Iowa, was perhaps the most talented and celebrated player in the conference in the 1930s. A four-sport high school star from Fort Worth, Texas, Simmons played on the team with his brother, Don, and two other blacks, Sandy Wallace and Homer Harris. In his first varsity game against Northwestern in 1934, he ran back a kickoff for a touchdown, returned seven punts for 124 yards, and rushed for 166 yards on twenty-four carries. An elusive, speedy running back, he was nicknamed the "Wizard of Oze." The Northwestern coach, Dick Hanley, who had seen Fritz Pollard and Red Grange, called Simmons "absolutely the best I've ever seen." The junior continued to impress the following year, scoring five touchdowns on runs of over fifty yards. "Simmons is All-America, sure fire," wrote white scribe Harold Parrott of the *Brooklyn Eagle.* But Simmons made only the Associated Press's second team.

Acrimony, more than accolades, surrounded Simmons during his varsity year. Rumors that had begun in 1934 persisted about how his teammates resented the attention he was getting and refused to block for him. Simmons was the logical choice for team captain in 1936, but his teammates voted to do away with that honorary position for that year. At the end of the season, they selected Homer Harris, a black end, as the team's most valuable player and captain for 1937. Harris became the first black player to captain a Big 10 football team.

Simmons also had a falling-out with his coach, Ossie Solem. In mid-November, after a 52–0 loss to Minnesota, he left the team after being berated by Coach Solem for lack of effort. Reinstated for the final game against Temple, Simmons romped for a 72-yard touchdown. On the whole, however, it was a disappointing season. Despite considerable talent, he was bypassed for both the team's most valuable player award and for All-America honors. Shunned by the NFL, Simmons signed with a black semipro team, the Patterson Panthers, in 1937.

Skilled black athletes also appeared on Eastern college gridirons. Two of the best players were Wilmeth Sidat-Singh of Syracuse University and Jerome "Brud" Holland of Cornell. The adopted son of a Hindu physician, Sidat-Singh attended DeWitt Clinton High School in New York. A basketball standout, he made the Syracuse varsity team as a sophomore but bypassed the football tryouts. A coach who noticed him playing intramural football urged him to try out for the varsity squad. In 1937, he made the starting backfield as a junior. He was coached by Ossie Solem, who had moved over from Iowa. Sidat-Singh developed into one of the finest passers in the nation. Sportswriters compared his skills to professionals like Sammy Baugh, Sid Luckman, and Benny Friedman. "Singh's Slings Sink Cornell," ran one alliterative headline. "It Don't Mean a Thing If It Ain't Got That Singh," ran another. In 1937, Singh helped Syracuse beat Penn State and Cornell, two tough rivals. Against the University of Maryland, another strong opponent, Sidat-Singh was benched when the Southern college objected to playing against an African American. Syracuse lost, 14–0. The following year at Syracuse, Sidat-Singh played against Maryland and led the Orangemen to a 51–0 victory tagged "Sweet Revenge" by Randy Dixon in the *Pittsburgh Courier.*

Sidat-Singh's most celebrated performance came against Cornell in October 1938. Heavily favored, Cornell led 10–0 with nine minutes to go in the fourth quarter. Sidat-Singh threw three passes covering fifty yards to narrow the score to 10–6 (after a missed try for the extra point). Cornell then ran back the kickoff for a touchdown to take a commanding 17–6 lead. Obtaining the ball on the 31-yard line, Sidat-Singh tossed two passes covering 69 yards for a quick touchdown that cut the score to 17–12 (after another missed extra point kick). When Syracuse recovered a fumble on the 30-yard line of Cornell, Sidat-Singh promptly completed a touchdown pass to win the game, 19–17. In the final nine minutes of play, he had thrown six passes for 150 yards and three touchdowns. Famed sportswriter Grantland Rice called the performance "one of the most amazing exhibitions of machine-gun fire I've ever seen, where the odds were all the other way." And Sam Butler, a respected NBC radio broadcaster, proclaimed it "the outstanding one-man show of the gridiron season of 1938."

Cornell, the team that had been victimized by Sidat-Singh, itself boasted one of the premier football players in the nation. Jerome "Brud" Holland from Auburn, New York, played end on the varsity squad from 1936 to 1938. Strong and agile, he was famous for the end-around play and excelled at his position on offense and defense. In his first season, he was voted to the All-Eastern college football team.

In 1937, Holland led Cornell to a record of 5 wins, 2 losses, and 1 tie. In the team's biggest game of the year against favored Colgate, he scored three touchdowns in a 40–7 victory. During the season, his superb offensive and defensive play won plaudits from both black and white sportswriters. The Yale coach, Clint Frank, called him the best end in the nation. The black press touted Holland for All-America honors. The odds seemed "virtually insurmountable" because he was black and only a junior; nevertheless, he was named to five different All-America teams, and he was the first minority athlete to win the honor since Paul Robeson in 1918. When he was again honored in 1938, he became the first African American since Robeson to be recognized in consecutive years.

Despite the acclaim, Holland failed to receive an offer from an NFL team. Sidat-Singh also was snubbed. Both athletes were chosen by writers to play for the college All-Stars in a game against the New York Giants, the first time blacks had been invited. "Neither Holland nor Sidat-Singh will play in the national Professional Football League this season," lamented one black weekly, "but it's not because they haven't got what it takes."

To NFL owners like Marshall, those players were invisible. From 1937 to 1945, the Redskins were one of the NFL's two dominant teams (the Bears were the other), the Redskins alone winning five division and two national titles. Successful on the field and at the gate, the Redskins and Bears were not desperate enough to tap into the pool of black talent. Less successful teams that should have leaped at the chance for improvement were also headed by bigoted owners who dared not challenge the code of invisibility.

Like those in the East and Midwest, Western colleges had long produced talented gridiron athletes. Marshall had his eye on the West, but not as a source of black talent. He saw the West as a land where he could advance the interests of the NFL, spread the Redskins brand, and maybe, someday, relocate the franchise. He was the first NFL owner, he once boasted, to bring major-league football to the West Coast, opening a training facility in Cheney, Washington, in August 1939 and then relocating it to San Diego two years later. He also began to play an annual game for charity in Los Angeles in 1946. He was too consumed by football not to have known about three elite athletes who played in this part of the country: Jackie Robinson, Woodrow Wilson Strode, and Kenny Washington. But those players did not fit his team's all-white profile.

In the late 1930s, the University of California at Los Angeles (UCLA) had three minority athletes with NFL potential: Robinson, Strode, and Washington. A transfer student from Pasadena City College, Jackie Robinson was a year behind Strode and Washington, class of 1940. NFL owners had a chance to sign the "cyclone-gaited hellion" long before he broke baseball's color barrier in 1947. At UCLA, he was the only athlete ever to letter in four sports: baseball, football, basketball, and track. He was the national champion in the long jump, the leading basketball scorer in the Pacific Coast Conference and still holds the school football record for highest average per carry in a season (12.2 yards, in 1939). The assistant coach at Stanford University referred to him as "just about the best sprinter on the coast, and he's a great ball carrier. He's rugged and can play just as hard and long as anyone. We are scared to death of him." Robinson appeared in the college All-Star game in Chicago in 1941, but the NFL passed him by. "In those days, no major football or basketball clubs hired black players. The only job offered me was with the Honolulu Bears," Robinson recalled. The football Bears, his first professional team, "were not major league, but they were integrated." Robinson's football career ended with the bombing of Pearl Harbor in December 1941.

Woody Strode and Kenny Washington played together on the UCLA Bruins for three seasons (1937–39). Strode was a 220-pound end with speed and sure hands. He also excelled defensively. He was not considered as talented as Brud Holland, but he did win selection to the Pacific Coast All-Star team in 1939. Overlooked by the NFL, he played with minor-league professional teams on the West Coast until 1946.

Kenny Washington, a 195-pound halfback, was one of the best players in college football in the late 1930s. Jackie Robinson described him as "the greatest football player I have ever seen. He had everything needed for greatness—size, speed, and tremendous strength. Kenny was probably the greatest long passer ever." He was impressive in a game played in Los Angeles against SMU, and the SMU coach, Madison Bell, regarded him as "one of the best players I have ever seen." Washington and Strode even drew praise from the white Texas press. Horace McCoy of the *Dallas Times Herald* wrote that the "two black boys were everywhere; they were the entire team; they were playing with inspiration and courage, and they cracked and banged the Mustangs all over the field." At the conclusion of the game, which SMU won 26–13, the Mustang supporters joined UCLA fans in giving Washington an ovation. "In that moment, you forgot he was black; he was no color at all; he was simply a great athlete." The following year, his running and passing prowess earned him a spot on the Pacific Coast All-America team.

In 1939, UCLA enjoyed an unbeaten season and Washington performed spectacularly. "King Kenny" led all college players in total yardage with 1,370. The University of Montana coach, Doug Fessenden, said that he was "greater than Red Grange." West Coast sportswriter Dick Hyland described him as the "best all-around football player seen here this year." A victory over the University of Southern California (USC) in the final game of the year would have sent UCLA to the Rose Bowl. Unfortunately for the Bruins, the game ended in a scoreless tie, and USC received the invitation. Washington won praise for his spirited play. Syndicated columnist Ed Sullivan reported that when Washington left the field, he was given a standing ovation from 103,000 spectators. "I have never been so moved emotionally, and rarely so proud of my country," he remarked.

Sportswriters, both black and white, touted Washington for All-America honors. Wendell Smith wrote that his ability surpassed that of other All-America candidates that year, such as Nile Kinnick of Iowa, Tom Harmon of Michigan, and Paul Christman of Missouri. "You can look this country over from coast to coast and back again, but you'll find nary a pigskin toter the likes of Kenny Washington!" Another writer declared that if Washington "is kept off this year's All-America, then the West coast has a right to secede from the football union." NBC sportscaster Bill Stern, writing for *Life* magazine, named Washington a first-team All-American. But with the exception of *Life,* Washington earned only second-team All-America recognition. Relegating the UCLA back to second-team honors infuriated the black press. Randy Dixon of the *Pittsburgh Courier* called the slight "unadulterated hokum" and the "biggest joke of the year."

Washington was ignored in the NFL draft, too, despite setting UCLA records in career rushing and passing. NBC broadcaster Sam Balter blasted the NFL's black ban. In an "open letter" over the airwaves, he asked NFL owners why "nobody chose the leading collegiate ground gainer of the 1939 season." Those who had seen him play agreed that he was "not only the best football player on the Pacific Coast this season, but the best of the last ten years and perhaps the best in all that slope's glorious football history—a player who has reduced to absurdity all the All-American teams selected this year because they did not include him—and all know why." NFL scouts, he continued, all ranked Washington the best player in the nation, but "none of you chose him." Balter expressed bitter disappointment "on behalf of the millions of American sports fans who believe in fair play and equal opportunity." He concluded by offering airtime to owners to explain why neither Washington nor Brud Holland was "good enough to play ball on your teams." The offer was not accepted.

Jimmy Powers, a columnist for the *New York Daily News*, also scolded NFL owners. After watching Washington play for the college All-Stars against the Green Bay Packers in 1940, he urged Tim Mara and Dan Topping, owners of the New York Giants and Brooklyn Dodgers, respectively, to sign the UCLA star. "He played on the same field with boys who are going to be scattered through the league. And he played against the champion Packers. There wasn't a bit of trouble anywhere." The black ban, however, was not lifted.

Black football players were frustrated by the lack of opportunity at the professional level. Kenny Washington, Jackie Robinson later observed, "had a deep hurt over the fact that he never became a national figure in professional sports. Many blacks who were great athletes years ago grow old with this hurt." In boxing, Joe Louis could punch his way to the heavyweight championship. In the entertainment industry, Duke Ellington, Louis Armstrong, and Paul Robeson could earn a comfortable living showcasing their talent. In baseball, blacks were banned from the major leagues, but they could eke out a living and display their skills in the Negro Leagues and in postseason games against white barnstorming teams. All-black professional football teams, however, had little fan support and little opportunity to measure their players against white stars.

George Halas of the Chicago Bears did agree to play a black All-Star team in a charity game at Soldiers Field in 1938. Many African Americans saw this charity game as an opportunity to show that minority athletes could compete in the NFL. In fact, some black sportswriters predicted that the "sons of Ham" would win easily. Coached by Duke Slater and Ray Kemp, and selected by popular vote, the All-Stars were made up of players who had already graduated. Many represented black colleges. The backfield consisted of Big Bertha Edwards of Kentucky State, Tank Conrad of Morgan State, Ozzie Simmons, and Joe Lillard. But unlike the backfield, the line was light, inexperienced, and no match for the Bears. Coach Ray Kemp, who had not played the game since 1933, toiled at tackle for nearly the entire game. Moreover, the team had less than two weeks of practice.

The game turned out to be a rout, with the powerful Bears winning 51–0. The All-Stars made only four first downs and lost 51 yards rushing. The Bears, forced to punt only once, amassed 605 total yards. "We've just finished witnessing the most disappointing sports spectacle of the decade . . . a 'promotion' which will set Negro college football back years," lamented William G. Nunn of the *Pittsburgh Courier*. Actually, most black fans took the game in stride. "Grin and Bear it," joked one sportswriter. Coach Ray Kemp pointed out that the Bears were a great football team. (Indeed, they would defeat the Redskins in a 1940 championship game, 73–0). Still, he regretted the fact that they didn't have more time to practice. The game was a disappointing loss, but it seemed to make blacks more eager than ever to achieve desegregation in both professional and college football. Increasingly, they were unwilling to swallow what the *Boston Guardian* referred to as the "sport's bitter pill."

CHAPTER 3

The Redskins March

George Washington made a questionable call when he selected a steamy, sweltering swamp along the Potomac River for the nation's capital. For George Marshall, however, the choice of Washington, D.C., for the relocation of his football franchise was a shrewd move. *Washington Post* sports columnist Shirley Povich wrote in mid-December 1936 that the Redskins "are a team that Washington could take to its collective heart. . . . Personally, I'm thinking that Washington fans would go mildly nuts over the Redskins." His hunch proved accurate. Washingtonians, perhaps intent to prove that their home was not a sports backwater, embraced the transplanted team and over the years elevated it to a status rivaling politics'.

Prompted by the growth of government during the Great Depression, Washington was a bustling city whose population swelled from 486,000 in 1930 to 663,000 by the end of the decade. Seventy percent of its population was white, 30 percent black, a ratio that would be reversed by the turn of the century. Franklin Roosevelt's New Deal offered hope and opportunity to whites and blacks, who poured into the District looking for jobs in government or public works. Some New Deal relief programs attracted more than 50,000 blacks to the District, most of them indigents from Southern states. The number of federal employees soared from 63,000 in March 1933 to 166,000 in 1940. While Roosevelt appointed scores of blacks, the overwhelming majority of black federal employees worked in domestic, custodial, or clerical positions.

Washingtonians paid taxes but were not represented in the U.S. Congress (and still are not today, except by a nonvoting delegate), and they could not vote for president and vice president until the Twenty-third Amendment was adopted in 1961. They had no elected municipal government until 1977. Nearly a century earlier, Congress enacted legislation authorizing three commissioners, appointed by the president, to administer the District. They would be in charge of public safety, education, and the many other responsibilities associated with governance. Congress would help Washingtonians share the cost of governance and established two standing committees, one in the House and another in the Senate, to oversee District affairs and recommend appropriations. Unfortunately, these District Committees were not very prestigious and were often staffed by incompetent and indifferent legislators, like Senator Theodore Bilbo of Mississippi, who chaired the Senate Committee on the District of Columbia from 1943 through 1946. A nasty white supremacist, Bilbo shared Adolf Hitler's belief "that the conservation of racial values is the hope for future generations." Bilbo advocated the deportation of all African Americans to Africa, with Eleanor Roosevelt accompanying them to serve as their "queen."

While the white community generally looked down on people of color, Washington was not as rigidly segregated as cities in the Deep South. Tradition, not law, separated the races in Washington in the 1930s. Public recreation areas—playgrounds, golf courses, swimming pools, and picnic grounds—were segregated, but not professional baseball and football games at Griffith Stadium. Blacks were denied access to hotels, restaurants, taverns, theaters, and movie houses, except those specifically reserved for them. And in Washington, the color line often defied logic. An editorial in the *Pittsburgh Courier* observed, "If a Washingtonian is a colored person, he is permitted on the stage of the National Theatre, but not in the audience; permitted in the audience at Constitution Hall, but not on the stage; permitted to attend prizefights at Uline Arena, but no other spectacles; and barred from the audience at the Lisner Auditorium of George Washington University."

Whites attended Central High School, where George Marshall had spent the ninth and tenth grades, or McKinley Tech, if they were interested in business or the trades. Blacks attended Dunbar and Cardozo high schools or the Armstrong Vocational School. College-bound white Washingtonians who wanted to remain close to home could attend Georgetown, American, Catholic, or George Washington universities. Blacks had Howard University. Five daily newspapers competed for mainly white readers, while the *Washington Afro-American* catered to the black community. While major-league baseball and football leagues banned African American players, blacks still attended their games, so much so that the Washington Elite Giants, and later the Black Senators, could not make it financially in the Negro Leagues. In the depressed economy, Griffith Stadium was commended by the *New York Amsterdam News* for employing blacks to maintain restrooms, serve food, and maintain the grounds. "This is in direct contrast to parks in New York, for instance, where few Negroes are employed."

Although a black man who won a District-wide Abraham Lincoln look-alike competition could not attend the theater showing the premiere of *Abe Lincoln in Illinois,* he could travel on (but not operate) integrated District buses, taxicabs, and trolleys; visit the public library and museums; attend professional baseball and football games at Griffith Stadium; and take his dirty clothes to George Marshall's Palace Laundry.

On Easter Sunday, April 9, 1939, the gifted contralto Marian Anderson gave a free, open-air concert on the steps of the Lincoln Memorial that attracted 75,000 rapt listeners. Howard University had booked her to sing, but it did not have an auditorium large enough to accommodate the four thousand or so patrons that were expected to attend. The District did not have a municipal auditorium, so Howard University officials sought to use Constitution Hall, which was owned by a whites-only patriotic group, the Daughters of the American Revolution. The DAR rejected the request because it allowed only white artists to perform at its facility. Outraged by the decision, First Lady Eleanor Roosevelt resigned her membership in the DAR. When no other suitable arena could be found, sponsors decided to hold the concert outdoors at the Lincoln Memorial.

More than 130 prominent individuals sponsored the event, including Eleanor Roosevelt and interior secretary Harold Ickes. An ardent supporter of racial equality, Ickes delivered a moving introduction, paying tribute to Anderson's musical genius and Lincoln's basic humanity. Gathered along the Reflecting Pool, the hushed audience choked with emotion when Anderson began with "My country, 'tis of thee," the first line of "America," and ended with the spiritual "Nobody Knows the Trouble I've Seen." The "Concert That Awakened America," according to the able historian Raymond Arsenault, was one of the singular moments in the history of twentieth-century American race relations because it dramatized the paradox between the ideal of democracy and the reality of racism. That same paradox was evident, at least to some people, on professional and collegiate playing fields throughout the United States. If George Marshall saw such a paradox, he was apparently untroubled by it.

Marshall had business, not democratic ideals, on his mind in the summer of 1937. Not only did he have to market his football team, but he had signed a $100,000 contract with a group of Dallas business executives to promote the Greater Texas and Pan American Exposition. With the assistance of his wife, Corinne, a native Texan, he produced a spectacular variety show. Athletes from twenty-one North and South American nations competed in boxing, track and field, soccer, and football. There was an automobile race through Dallas streets, a reenactment of historical events in the Western Hemisphere at the Cavalcade of the Americas, and nightly wining, dining, dancing, and music at the Casino, a makeshift nightclub in the Dallas Auditorium. The event was so successful that, according to the *Washington Post* society editor, Marshall was being considered for a job as a producer of a Hollywood movie.

During the Expo, Marshall also entertained his top pick in the 1937 NFL draft: Samuel Adrian Baugh. Born in Temple and raised in Sweetwater, Texas, Sammy Baugh was a gifted athlete whose throwing prowess in baseball and football had earned him the nickname "Slingin' Sammy." Marshall, following the advice of the *Boston Post*'s Bill Cunningham, selected the rangy Texan with the sixth pick in the draft. After rejecting Marshall's initial offer of $5,000, Baugh eventually signed for $8,000, nearly double the average player salary. "When I found out what the rest of the players were making," he said after signing, "I felt badly about asking for so much money."

Perhaps owing to his experience on the stage, Marshall was obsessed with presentation and showmanship. Pittsburgh Steelers owner Art Rooney told Bob Addie of the *Washington Post* that he and Marshall once spent the afternoon drinking alcohol in Marshall's suite at the Shoreham Hotel. "Finally, I told George that I was hungry. He said he didn't have a thing in the house. So he sent down the street for some of those nickel hamburgers—they were only a nickel in those days. But George had to make a production of everything. He served those nickel hamburgers on fancy gold plates—but they were still nickel hamburgers."

Marshall used his considerable marketing skills to promote his new sports venture in Washington. "They're here for keeps, not for just 1937," he told the *Evening Star*. The Redskins rented Griffith Stadium for their home games. Named for Clark Griffith, owner of the Washington Senators baseball team, the wooden and concrete structure was constructed in 1911 and held nearly 28,000 fans. Besides the Redskins, Griffith rented the facility to black baseball teams like the Homestead Grays. The stadium was located on Georgia Avenue in a neighborhood known as Shaw, located in the northwest quadrant of the city. Named for Robert Gould Shaw, the white officer who led the heroic black 54th Massachusetts regiment during the Civil War, the neighborhood was becoming increasingly black in the 1930s and 1940s. Besides middle-class residences, it included Howard University and U Street, sometimes called the "Black Broadway" owing to its cluster of nightclubs, theaters, and restaurants. Across the street from Griffith Stadium, a charismatic black evangelist named Elder Solomon Lightfoot Michaux established the Church of God, with a forty-member "Happy Am I" choir, to minister to the spiritual needs of the black community; he would also rent Griffith Stadium for spiritual revivals and mass baptisms. With Marshall footing the $25,000 bill, Griffith installed new lights, a modern sound system, and more seats in Griffith Stadium. Marshall made himself visible by establishing team headquarters on Ninth Street NW with a cigar-store Indian in the window fronting the street. He saturated the city with yellow leaflets announcing the arrival of the team and the onset of the football season. He offered an attractive package of six home games for $9.90, but only 950 customers bought season tickets that first year. Over the next twenty years, however, only once did season ticket sales fall below 13,000.

Marshall also marketed Baugh as a young Texas gunslinger who would come out of the West to lead the Redskins to glory. When he introduced Baugh to Washington fans, he insisted that the player wear Western garb, including a wide-brimmed hat, checkered shirt, and cowboy boots. "He looked," Marshall said later, "like the personification of every cowboy star who ever saddled a bronc, only more so."

In all, Baugh played sixteen seasons (1937–52) with the Redskins and became a legend. An excellent passer, place-kicker, punter, and defender, Baugh became the league's best player and primary gate attraction. He also got along with Marshall. "I liked him," he declared. "He was a good businessman, but I couldn't depend on his word. I thought the world of him. I didn't like lots of things he did, but he was fair with me." To Marshall, no other player, before or since, could measure up to Baugh in ability, star power, and field leadership.

For Marshall, a football game meant more than athletic competition; it also meant pageantry, drama, and thrilling family entertainment. Women, he condescendingly asserted, would likely not attend games just to watch football. "I always try to present half-time entertainment to give them something to look forward to—a little music, dancing, color, something they can understand and enjoy." Moreover, if women went to games, he continued, so would men. "The women will bring them. And the women add class to a sports gathering. They'll discourage a rowdy element." Marshall was receptive when Barnee Breskin, the bandleader at the Shoreham Hotel, offered a team song, "Hail to the Redskins," as a homecoming gift.

Marshall's wife, Corinne Griffith, contributed the lyrics, the first stanza reading:

> *Hail to the Redskins,*
> *Hail victory,*
> *Braves on the warpath,*
> *Fight for old D.C.*

The song became a hit, and it has been used ever since. However, its original, demeaning lines such as "scalp 'um, swamp 'um, we will take 'um big score," have been rewritten. Marshall formed a 150-piece band to march and play music and often participated in planning halftime extravaganzas. Besides the marching band, entertainment over the years included the National Symphony Orchestra, swing bands, "bare-legged dancing girls," and Santa Claus, who made special appearances by sleigh, dogsled, horseback, fire truck, ambulance, Brinks armored truck, and helicopter, out of the middle of a cake, and, on one unhappy occasion, via a parachute that sent him soaring beyond the stadium onto a neighboring housetop.

George Marshall displays his penchant for publicity posing with twins in Native American headdresses. (Star Collection, DC Public Library, © Washington Post)

Corinne Griffith (no relation to the Senators' owner) also contributed to her husband's success. The star of more than forty silent films, she was a talented woman who wrote four books, one of which, *Papa's Delicate Condition,* was made into a Hollywood movie starring Jackie Gleason. She not only wrote the lyrics to the Redskins theme song, but she helped persuade Marshall to relocate from Boston to Washington, assisted with planning halftime shows, and, always glamorous and stylish, turned heads when she accompanied Marshall to games.

The Redskins season opened at home with a Thursday-night game against the Giants on September 15. To Marshall's delight, the game drew 24,000 fans. Not surprisingly, Marshall had prepared a pregame ceremony featuring the playing of the "Star Spangled Banner," the introduction of players on both teams, and Jesse Jones, a prominent Southern personality who was head of the Reconstruction Finance Corporation, to throw a special white football as a ceremonial first ball. During the game, Baugh completed a few passes, but quarterback Riley Smith was the star, scoring all the Redskins' points in a 13–3 victory. After the game, a *Washington Evening Star* reporter wrote: "Offhand, I would say that Mr. George Preston Marshall's enterprise in the Capital is off to a flying start."

Getting dazzling season performances from Baugh and Battles, the Redskins, with a record of 7 wins and 3 losses, prepared for the final game of the year in New York against the Giants, who had a record of 6 wins, 2 losses, and 2 ties. As in the previous year, a win against their despised rivals at the Polo Grounds would clinch the division and the right to play the Bears for the NFL championship. Thousands of devoted fans traveled by bus, car, and train to support the Redskins. "I never saw a town go so football mad in my life," Coach Ray Flaherty told the *Washington Evening Star.* Marshall also brought the band. Dressed in burgundy-and-gold uniforms with Indian feather headwear, the band marched up Fifth Avenue to Columbus Circle playing "Dixie" and "Hail to the Redskins." Bill Corum of the *New York Journal-American* observed: "At the head of a one hundred and fifty piece brass band, and ten thousand fans, George Preston Marshall slipped unobtrusively into New York today."

Actually, Marshall had roared into town the day before and was promptly ambushed by New York writers. As usual, they mocked "Gorgeous George" for overdressing (he had bought a new raccoon coat for game day). Cognizant of his oversized ego, they used laundry humor to belittle his team. The Redskins needed to "iron out" some issues, otherwise they would be "washed up." They were, in fact, the "Washing Done" Redskins. Marshall relished the attention and used what later generations would call "trash talk" to hype the game and the gate. Brashly, he predicted an easy victory. The Redskins had beaten the Giants in the previous year and again in the first game of the current season, and they would do so again. "It's a habit, a custom with us to beat those fellows. It's becoming a tradition. I'm strong for tradition in football. . . . We'll sweep those fellows aside like rubbish." He concluded by saying that the game against the Giants would just be a tune-up for the Redskins. "Better come out to Chicago and see the big game later. Watch us win the national title."

Marshall did not have to eat his words. "For once in his life," wrote John Kieran of the *New York Times,* "the Magnificent Marshall was conservative in his speech." Before 55,000 fans, the second-largest crowd in NFL history up to that time, the Redskins overwhelmed the Giants, 49–14. In what Kieran called the "Massacre at Coogan's Bluff," Battles ran for 170 yards on twenty-four carries and ran back an intercepted pass for 76 yards while Baugh connected on eleven passes, setting a then-NFL record of eighty-one completions in a year. In the locker room after the game, according to the *Washington Evening Star,* former Giants quarterback Benny Friedman pointed to Baugh and Battles and said: "There are the two greatest backs I ever saw. . . . I thought I could pass until I saw Baugh today, and I thought Red Grange was a runner until I saw Battles."

After the game, the Redskins celebrated at the restaurant of former heavyweight champion Jack Dempsey and then boarded a train for Washington, D.C. Arriving at about 11:30 p.m., they were met by five thousand rabid fans. "It exceeds anything I ever imagined," Marshall remarked to the *Evening Star.* From Union Station, Marshall tried to trumpet the victory by having the band march up Pennsylvania Avenue, but he was halted by police due to the late hour and lack of a permit. Marshall ordered the band to proceed. When the police heard the first toot of a horn, Corinne Griffith recalled, they arrested the drum major, rather than the entire group, and hauled him off to jail. In the wee hours of the morning, Marshall paid a $25 fine to spring him.

The following Sunday, December 12, 1937, before fewer than 16,000 fans, the Redskins confronted the Bears at Wrigley Field for the NFL title game. The frosted turf, which necessitated the wearing of tennis shoes, hampered the running attack of both teams. But Baugh put on a sensational aerial performance, completing seventeen passes for 352 yards, including touchdown strikes of 55, 77, and 35 yards, for a 28–21 win. The Bears could not stop Baugh "any more than they could winter's icy hand," wrote Allison Danzig of the *New York Times*.

Baugh had become a national football phenomenon. Not only had the rookie led his team to the national championship, but he had set a league pass-completion record with 81 and drew new fans to the sport, the low turnout for the Chicago title contest notwithstanding. "He's the best I've ever seen," remarked Cliff Battles. Neutral observers expressed similar sentiments. Danzig of the *Times* pronounced him "the hottest thing professional football has known since Red Grange" and the "greatest passer of all time." Bostonians must rue the departure of the Redskins to Washington, he said, like they did the loss of Babe Ruth to the New York Yankees.

During the championship game, Marshall leaped to the field to protest rough play against Baugh, who had been slammed into the Bears' bench. Marshall and George Halas almost got into a fight at that point. Corinne Griffith recalled Halas saying:

> "You dirty ———, get up in that box where you belong. It's too bad it ain't a cage."
>
> [Marshall yelled,] "You shut that ——— mouth of yours, or I'll punch those ——— gold teeth right down that red throat!"
>
> Marshall stormed back to his box seat to rejoin Corinne.
>
> "What's the matter with you? You look white as a sheet."

"Oh! That was *awful!*"
"What was awful?"
"That horrible language. We could hear every word."
"Well, you shouldn't listen."
"And as for that man *Halas!* He's positively revolt—"
"Don't you *dare* say anything about George Halas," Marshall responded. "He's my best friend!"

Grateful Washington fans, including the press, embraced the team and its volatile owner. While Marshall's flamboyance and outlandish behavior did not play well in Boston, it did in Washington, at least for a while. Thomas Sugrue in the *American Magazine* wrote that in Washington in the late 1930s, "George Preston Marshall is the third most interesting sight, preceded only by the Washington Monument and the Lincoln Memorial. Any Washingtonian would rather watch Marshall go berserk at a baseball or football game, especially when his team is losing, than see the best stage or screen show." In their first season in Washington, the Redskins drew 120,000 fans, compared to 57,000 during their last year in Boston. "It's not merely the contrast between Washington and Boston fans," declared Coach Flaherty, "it's the fact that the sentiment in Washington is a thing apart, something that couldn't have been imagined."

Oddly enough, the Redskins attracted a sizable black following despite the league color ban. Dan Burley of the *Amsterdam News* wrote that the Redskins would travel to New York "with a special train full of Negroes waving flags and miniature footballs and ready to take your head off about Slingin' Sammy Baugh and the rest of the Redskins ménage." Upscale black Washingtonians, he speculated, had "plenty of ready cash to spend on bigtime sports, night life, theatre, and bigtiming," but why they would rabidly support teams like the Senators and Redskins that refused to hire African Americans was beyond his comprehension.

The team disappointed its fans in 1938. Cliff Battles, upset at Marshall's meager contract offer, left to help coach the football squad at Columbia University for what he saw as more fitting compensation. During the entire 1937 season, the Redskins' payroll, according to treasurer Milton King, was $2,969.82 a month, and Battles earned $210.00 per game for an eleven-game season. Battles received a salary of $4,000 at Columbia.

Marshall did not take the defection lightly, blasting administrators for luring professional players, like Battles and later Riley Smith, into college coaching. "I'm appealing," Marshall told the press, "to the sportsmanship of college presidents to protect us from the commercialism of their institutions." NFL owners could not sign players while they were in school, so he argued that colleges should reciprocate by not hiring pro players until they retired from the game. Marshall replaced Battles in the backfield with their top draft pick, Andy Farkas from the University of Detroit.

Besides Battles, Marshall also had difficulties with Coach Flaherty and Sammy Baugh. Exasperated with Marshall's incessant interference, Flaherty threatened to quit unless Marshall agreed to stay off the bench and cease recommending plays. Marshall relented. Baugh wanted more money and refused to sign, threatening to give up football for a professional baseball career. He had signed with the St. Louis Cardinals, and during his holdout, he went to spring training with them and played in their minor-league system, but eventually he signed a three-year football contract for $10,000 per year and gave up baseball.

Although Baugh was injured periodically, he nearly led the Redskins to another division title in 1938. For the third consecutive year, the final regular-season game between the Redskins and the Giants would be the gate to the NFL championship game. As in 1937, Marshall, dressed in a raccoon coat, invaded New York with his band and fervid supporters. Once again he predicted victory, but this time, the Redskins, if not Marshall, were humbled, 36–0.

The scenario was repeated yet again in 1939. With a record of 8–1–1, the Redskins traveled to New York to play the Giants for the right to meet the winner of the Western division for the championship. On this occasion, the game against the Giants, played before 50,000 fans, was marred by a controversial official's call. Marshall had long been critical of NFL officiating and seldom hesitated to challenge their decisions, often running onto the field to do so.

Officials, he once told the *New York Times'* John Kieran, were neither objective nor competent. "Why shouldn't I argue with them when they are wrong? Of course, it keeps me pretty busy. They're always wrong."

With the Giants ahead 9–7 late in the fourth quarter, the Redskins lined up on the Giants 15-yard line for what appeared to be a winning field goal kick. But referee Bill Halloran ruled the kick wide, and the Redskins lost. He said afterwards: "It was just like an umpire calling a ball or a strike, it was that close." The disputed call resulted in bedlam. Fights broke out in the stands and on the field, and one Redskins player tried to pummel Halloran. "If that Halloran has a conscience, he'll never have a sound night's sleep again," Coach Flaherty said. Enraged, Marshall declared to writers that Halloran would never referee another NFL game, and he did not, thanks to Marshall. But the fact that Redskins kicker Bo Russell said that the kick "could have gone either way" indicates that he probably narrowly missed.

Marshall had trouble putting the controversial call behind him. The following spring, at the annual meeting of NFL owners, he snidely recommended widening the distance between the goalposts by twenty feet.

In spite of the heart-wrenching loss on the disputed field goal, the Redskins and their fans were optimistic about the 1940 season. After all, they still had talented players, a superb coach, and fervid followers who would probably top the peak attendance of 130,000 in 1939. The optimism was justified. The Redskins won seven consecutive games before narrowly losing to the Dodgers, 16–14. They lost one more game, against the Giants, but they won the division handily.

With a record of 9–2, they hosted the 1940 championship game against Chicago, "the Mastodons of the Midwest." The teams appeared to be evenly matched, but Marshall was a wild card who could do or say something to affect the outcome. Earlier in the season, he had run onto the field to protest the officiating in a game against Detroit, and the Redskins were assessed a fifteen-yard penalty. A similar display of emotion in the championship might be game-deciding. Marshall's outspokenness also could be a factor. Indeed, after squeaking by the Bears 7–3 in November, Marshall in effect called them losers and whiners who could not handle the pressure. "The Bears are a team that must win by a big score. Don't ask me why they lose the close games, except that they do." Marshall continued to put down the Bears before the championship game. "Washington has a confidence that borders on overconfidence," *New York Times* reporter Arthur Daley ominously warned. Coach Halas fired up the Bears by reading and posting on the bulletin board some of Marshall's provocative statements. Some Redskins, like Baugh, wanted Marshall to stop talking. "We're getting ready to play the championship game," he said, "and Mr. Marshall called them cry-babies. That's the way to get a team ready for you; you don't want to say things like that. A lot of the boys hated that. They hated what Mr. Marshall was putting out."

The title game sold out in three hours, drawing 36,000 fans for a then-record gate of $102,000. The crowd included representatives from Congress, the cabinet, the diplomatic corps, and the military. As the "showman supreme," wrote Arthur Daley of the *New York Times,* Marshall would give spectators "a show they never will forget. But will the Redskins contribute their share on the field?"

They did not. In the game's first minute, the Bears scored a touchdown and went on to tally ten more, crushing the Redskins 73–0, in the worst defeat in the history of the NFL championship games. During the game, fans jeered when, with the score 54–0, they were informed by the public address announcer that they could buy season tickets after the game. At another point in the game, a fan shouted: "Take the bums back to Boston." Unhinged, Marshall bolted from his box and confronted the heckler. There was no violence, but Marshall told the press afterward that the fan would not be attending Redskins games next year. When the gun finally sounded at the end of the game, one wag said: "That's George Marshall shooting himself." Baugh told the *Washington Post*: "That's the most humiliating thing I've ever gone through in my life."

Despite the lopsided score, some reporters believed there was a turning point. Shortly after the Bears' first touchdown, the Redskins drove down the field, and Baugh hit the normally sure-handed Charley Malone with a pass that would have knotted the score—but he dropped it. Asked what the outcome of the game might have been had Malone caught that pass, Baugh responded: "73–7."

After the game, Marshall barged into the dressing room and, according to Bill Dismer in the *Washington Evening Star,* screeched: "They quit! Some of our players were yellow. There were too many high-paid players on our club trying to get by on their reputation. There'll be plenty of new faces next year." The next day, having cooled off, Marshall credited the Bears with having played an outstanding game. He did not blame them for running up the score, either. Professional football was no gentleman's game, after all, and he would have done the same to the Bears if he could. Although Redskins fans had been "stunned into dumb silence," they had time to recover. As the *Evening Star* put it: "[N]ine months will intervene before the 1941 edition of the 'Skins will appear. In that time lots of things can happen."

Some of those "things" propelled the United States into war. The Roosevelt administration had gone on high alert when war broke out in Europe in September 1939. While sympathetic with the Allies, especially Great Britain, Roosevelt and most Americans hoped to avoid the war. Some citizens, who organized the Committee to Defend America by Aiding the Allies, believed that the best hope of avoiding American involvement in another European war would be to provide the Allies with all military aid short of troops. Other Americans like Sen. Robert Taft, aviator Charles Lindbergh, and George Preston Marshall supported the America First Committee, a group that wanted to make the United States so strong militarily that Hitler would never dare to attack. Roosevelt tried to satisfy both groups by declaring American neutrality, and obtaining congressional approval for a draft, increased defense spending, and a Lend-Lease bill that would extend military aid to Britain, and later to the Soviet Union.

By the summer of 1941, the United States appeared to be hurtling toward war with either Germany or Japan. Sports were a comfortable diversion. The Redskins lost their opening game against the

Giants, won their next five, and then lost four games in a row. Their record stood at 5–5 when 27,000 fans, including Navy ensign John F. Kennedy, thronged into Griffith Stadium on December 7 to watch the last game of the season against the Philadelphia Eagles. During the game, the press corps received the news that the Japanese had bombed the U.S. naval base at Pearl Harbor. Marshall received the news in his box by telephone. Perhaps to avoid panic, the Redskins made no public announcement of the attack, but fans must have wondered why many military, diplomatic, and political officials were asked by the PA announcer to report to duty. Soon, as Corinne Griffith has written in *My Life with the Redskins,* small clusters of empty seats became noticeable, and the crowd was abuzz with the word-of-mouth news. The 20–14 victory seemed insignificant.

In early September 1942, before the start of the football season, Arthur Daley of the *New York Times* predicted that the Redskins and Bears would meet in the championship game, in large part because neither team had lost many players to the war effort. His prediction was on the mark. The Bears completed the regular season 11–0, while the Redskins lost only one game, setting up a repeat of the 1940 championship game. Even though the game would be played at Griffith Stadium, the Bears were prohibitive favorites to win their third consecutive championship. They had won twenty-four games in a row and thirty-nine of their last forty. They had mauled the Redskins in a preseason exhibition and in the NFL title game two years earlier, but they had not faced them in the regular season. In addition, the Bears had two skilled quarterbacks, Sid Luckman and Charlie O'Rourke, who operated out of the T-formation. Initiated by the Bears in 1940, the "T" had the quarterback take the snap directly behind the center. By contrast, the Redskins used the single-wing formation, with a tailback, usually Baugh, taking the snap several yards behind the center. Gamblers established the Bears as 7–1 favorites and gave twenty points to bettors who laid money on the Redskins. What the Bears would do to the Redskins, said Daley of the *Times,* "makes strong men shudder."

The game sold out just three days after the Redskins had clinched the division on November 22. Marshall said that he could have sold

150,000 tickets, but had to settle for a capacity crowd of 36,000. Counting the sale of radio rights, the gate of $113,000 established a new NFL record for a title game. Having learned his lesson from 1940, Marshall made no brash pregame predictions of victory. Instead, he devoted his attention to a halftime extravaganza honoring U.S. military personnel.

In a bruising game, the Redskins defeated the Bears 14–6 to win their second world championship. Although the score was close, the Redskins dominated the game. "The only thing the Bears won," said one reporter "was the coin toss." Baugh threw a touchdown pass, made a key interception on defense, and punted brilliantly for a sixty-two-yard average.

The game would be Coach Ray Flaherty's last. Two days later, he joined the Navy and never coached the Redskins again. After the war, he would coach the New York Yankees to two division titles in the All-America Football Conference league. In his seven NFL seasons, one in Boston, he had won four division titles, two world championships, and established a record of 54 wins, 22 losses, and 3 ties. "He had a brilliant football mind," recalled Redskins tackle Jim Barber. "He developed the screen pass. He could handle players. He knew when to kick you in the fanny and pat you on the back. Everyone respected him." He was arguably the most successful coach in Redskins history.

Marshall hired Arthur "Dutch" Bergman to succeed Flaherty. The Redskins won their first four games, including a victory over the Dodgers in which Baugh threw six touchdown passes. During the season, Baugh added to his reputation as the sport's star attraction by leading the league in punting with a 45.9 average, passing with 1,754 yards and twenty-three touchdowns, and defense with eleven interceptions. With a record of 5–0–1, the Redskins appeared certain to capture the division with only three games left to play. But they proceeded to lose those three games, including their last two against the Giants, and the Redskins and Giants ended up tied in the division.

The Redskins' woeful finish to the regular season necessitated a playoff game with the Giants at the Polo Grounds, which the Redskins won handily 28–0. Once again, they would confront the Bears in Chicago for the NFL title. Early in the battle, Baugh received a concussion and sat out most of the game. A poignant *Washington Evening Star* photograph shows a parka-draped Baugh on the bench crying because he could not get into the game. Sid Luckman tossed five touchdown passes in the Bears 41–21 victory.

As usual, Marshall made a spectacle of himself. Shortly before the half, with his team losing 14–7, he strolled down to the field behind the Bears bench. Bears president Ralph Brizzolara, who ran the team while Halas was in the Navy, accused Marshall of trying to listen to the instructions given to Bears players. Marshall lamely denied the charge of snooping and entered into a shouting match with Brizzolara. The exchange became so heated that security guards had to escort Marshall from the field. Although it was fairly obvious that Marshall was spying, those charges could not be proved. Both Marshall and Brizzolara, however, were each fined $500 by the league for their unbecoming behavior.

Regardless, Marshall was obsessed with winning and not above using underhanded methods, including spying, to do so. Rival coaches and owners accused him of trying to peek at their player rating lists on NFL draft day. Chicago Bears assistant coach Carl Brumbaugh recalled in Bob Curran's *Pro Football's Rag Days* that when Chicago played the Redskins in Washington, Marshall situated the band behind the opposing team and ordered it to play loud music when the rival coach used the telephone to communicate with an assistant high above the field.

But Marshall needed more than dirty tricks to win in 1944. The 1944 Redskins, wrote Arthur Daley of the *New York Times,* were like the "old Gray Mare. They ain't what they used to be." They had hired a new head coach, Dudley "Dud" DeGroot, to succeed Dutch Bergman, who had resigned to enter broadcasting. A Stanford University graduate, where he had played football and earned Phi Beta Kappa honors, DeGroot understood that working for Marshall would be challenging, and he tried to make light of it. The headstrong owner would be sure to lend "plenty of assistance," he told the press, but "I want to go on record right now that whenever we fail to score while he is on the bench, the responsibility will be Mr. Marshall's and not mine." Although he produced two winning seasons, including a division title, DeGroot lasted only two years before, in effect, being fired in the middle of a championship game.

In 1944, DeGroot installed the T-formation, even though that system would be new to Baugh and curtail his ability to quick-kick from the single wing. But Baugh's playing time was limited because, to retain his draft deferment, he needed to be on his Texas ranch to oversee the production of beef that was essential to the war effort. Baugh's draft board did give him permission to fly to Washington to play on weekends, but Frank Filchock, the backup who practiced with the T-formation, would get most of the playing time. The season came down to the last two games against the Giants, as it had the year before. Once again, the Redskins lost those two games, but this time a playoff was unnecessary because the Giants won the division outright.

During the 1944 season, Washington's "man-in-motion play," as *Washington Post* writer Shirley Povich labeled Baugh's shuttle between Dallas and the District, rankled many citizens. "We got thousands of protesting letters from fathers and mothers of boys in the service asking how Baugh could be permitted to use essential transportation to fly more than half way across the country for the Redskins' games. They were hard to answer," a War Department official told Povich. Those letters, coupled with the pivotal Battle of the Bulge in Europe from December 1944 to January 1945, triggered a government crackdown over all sports. The War Department instructed draft boards not to give prominent individuals special treatment in terms of military deferments and discharges without the approval of the federal government.

The Redskins flaunted voluntary restrictions against travel more than most teams. Not only did Baugh fly hundreds of round-trip miles each weekend of the season, but in 1942, Marshall had transferred the Redskins' training facility to San Diego, 3,000 miles away. Not complying with travel restrictions looked worse when Eddie

Kahn, a guard on the title-winning 1937 Redskins team, was killed in action during an invasion of the Philippines, the nineteenth NFL player to die in the war. Marshall moved the training facility to Georgetown for the 1945 season.

With the conclusion of the war in August 1945, the Redskins could rely on Baugh for the entire season. Having familiarized himself with the T-formation, he enjoyed a successful season, leading the Redskins to their sixth Eastern Division title. The championship game against the Rams in Cleveland was marked by freak plays and fateful decisions. Expecting subzero temperatures and a frozen field, the Redskins brought sneakers to grip the slick turf better. The Rams were not similarly equipped, so their coach, Adam Walsh, asked DeGroot not to have the Redskins wear sneakers, in the interest of good sportsmanship. DeGroot agreed.

Freaky plays ensued almost from the beginning of the game. In the first quarter, Baugh threw a pass from his own end zone to receiver Wayne Millner, who was wide open. Instead of resulting in a long gain or perhaps even a touchdown, the pass hit the goalpost and plopped into the end zone for an automatic safety. (At the time, the goalposts were located on the goal line, not on the end line as they are today. Marshall had that rule changed soon after this game.) The Redskins countered, however, when Filchock, substituting for an injured Baugh, threw a touchdown pass for a 7–2 lead. The Rams regained command when their gifted quarterback, Bob Waterfield, connected on a touchdown pass of his own. Then the kick for the point after touchdown squarely hit the crossbar but freakishly tumbled over, for a 9–7 Rams edge at halftime.

In the locker room at halftime, according to the account of the incident that rookie center Al DeMao later gave to author Thom Loverro, Marshall instructed DeGroot to have the team wear sneakers for the second half. DeGroot informed him of the gentlemen's agreement. Marshall replied: "This is no gentlemen's game. That's the last decision you will ever make as coach of the Redskins."

In the second half, the Rams went ahead 15–7, but the Redskins responded with a touchdown and extra point to make the score 15–

14. (The two-point conversion was not adopted by the NFL until 1994.) In the fourth quarter, Redskins kicker Joe Aguirre attempted a thirty-one-yard field goal, but it narrowly failed, and the team lost 15–14. The team would not make another title appearance under Marshall, in large part because the bigoted owner refused to change with the times.

CHAPTER 4

Leveling the Field

In a tactic that foreshadowed integration developments with the Washington Redskins, *Los Angeles Sentinel* sportswriter Halley Harding, representing more than two dozen black newspapers, appeared before the Los Angeles Memorial Coliseum Commission in January 1946 to protest the ban against African American players in professional football. At that meeting, he traced the early history of black players in the game, blamed George Marshall for initiating the ban against them, and reported about several players, including Kenny Washington, who possessed the talent to play professionally. The commissioners, he boldly suggested, should not lease their facility to any team until it agreed to field a qualified black athlete. When he completed his remarks, said one observer, "you could have heard a rat piss on cotton."

After their momentary silence, the commissioners agreed to consider Halley's suggestion because the world had been transformed. World War II was a powerful engine for social change in both the United States and the world. Fought to preserve democratic ideals against totalitarian oppression, the war challenged traditional attitudes and practices toward colonial subjects, women, and minorities. In the United States, it helped propel the civil rights movement, in part through desegregation.

Combating entrenched racial intolerance was no easy task. According to a classic 1944 study by Swedish scholar Gunnar Myrdal,

Americans suffered from a societal bipolar disorder that he gave to the title of his book *The American Dilemma*. At their best, Myrdal wrote, Americans avowed their belief in liberty, equal opportunity, and justice for all; at their worst, they practiced racial discrimination and denied one-tenth of the population their constitutional rights. Myrdal expected Americans to resolve their dilemma in favor of racial justice because of their traditional democratic idealism, but African Americans were less optimistic. Walter White, executive secretary of the National Association for the Advancement of Colored People, told the *Washington Post* in 1949 that the war "revealed the national schizophrenia which enabled us to embark on a crusade to end racism as preached by Hitler and practiced by the Nazi State, while at the same time adhering to equally as vicious practices of racial discrimination and segregation in our own country." Coping with a schizophrenic nation at war was indeed a dilemma. Guardedly, black leaders decided to fight racial discrimination at home without disrupting the battle against dictatorship abroad.

When the United States entered World War II, African Americans were hesitant to lend their support and involvement. The previous world war had not delivered on its promise to make the world safe for democracy. True, gains had been made during the New Deal, but racial justice appeared to be a distant reality. "We are not exaggerating when we say that the American Negro is damned tired of spilling his blood for empty promises of better days," declared the *Chicago Defender* one month before the attack on Pearl Harbor. "Prove to us," said Walter White, "that you are not hypocrites when you say this is a war for freedom. Prove it to us." Right after the December 7 bombing of Pearl Harbor, "a date that will live in infamy," according to FDR, the NAACP advocated a "Double V" policy of defeating tyranny abroad and racism at home.

African Americans seethed at the idea of fighting for freedom in segregated military units. When the war began, the Army Air Corps, Marines, and Coast Guard did not accept blacks. They could join the Navy, but they were relegated to food service duties. Historian John Hope Franklin—author and Harvard scholar, who in the

1990s was awarded the Presidential Medal of Freedom, the nation's highest civilian honor—tried to join the Navy but was told by the recruiting officer that there was no position for him because he was black. The War Department recruited white historians, many without advanced degrees, to prepare studies of the global conflict but ignored Franklin's application.

Blacks could be drafted or join the Army, but they served mainly in support roles—guards, porters, manual laborers—and lived separately from whites, as they did in all military branches. Blacks who had demonstrated collegiate athletic success often escaped menial duties in the military by playing sports. While Kenny Washington's bad knees exempted him from military service, his UCLA teammate, Woody Strode, was drafted. Former NFL coach Paul Schissler, who before the war had coached Strode with the independent Hollywood Bears team, told him that if he was ever drafted, get in touch and he would have him assigned to the March Field Fliers, an Army Air Corps football team in California.

As a young man in California, Strode had not experienced much racial discrimination, and he was appalled by the extent of the segregation he encountered when he reported for duty at the Army base. "They assigned me to a black outfit that lived in Dusty Acres," he wrote in his memoir, *Goal Dust.* "They worked in the mess hall, cleaned the latrines and the officers' quarters. They were the service unit. And the base was like a little Southern town. The black soldiers lived in separate quarters, rode segregated buses, and went to a segregated theatre and PX. What a slap in the face that was."

After living apart from his white teammates for six months, Strode escaped army apartheid when Coach Schissler persuaded the commanding officer to permit all football players to live together. Cases of booze were served as an initial interracial icebreaker. "Everybody got falling down drunk," Strode wrote, and his white teammates "saw I wasn't any different." In addition, "if you're white and rooting for your team and one of the guys on the team is black, well then, he's one of yours and he's all right." Strode served the bulk of the war with the Fliers, playing football games against other service and college teams and one exhibition versus the Washington Redskins, a 7–3 loss. After the war, Strode went on to enjoy a long career as a film actor.

During the war, some college-educated African Americans became officers. However, the prevailing attitude of the time held that they nevertheless lacked the intellectual necessities to command ships, aircraft, and white men. That same attitude would later thwart efforts of black athletes to become football quarterbacks, centers, linebackers, coaches, and front-office executives. Jackie Robinson, the former UCLA star athlete, became an Army lieutenant, but his military experience was not a happy one because he was court-martialed for insubordination when he refused a Southern bus driver's directive to sit in the back of the vehicle (though he was acquitted and ultimately exonerated).

Segregation was so rampant that the American Red Cross had to separate black and white blood donations, an ironic policy given that a black physician (and former college player) named Charles Drew had developed the process of isolating and storing plasma from blood. When the NAACP complained about the racial profiling of blood, Mississippi representative John Rankin took to the House floor to denounce efforts of Communists and other organizations "to mongrelize the nation." When blacks protested military segregation, General-in-Chief George Marshall (no relation to the Redskins owner) said racial discrimination had existed for decades, and the army would not become "a sociological laboratory."

African Americans also were initially denied equal access to jobs in the booming defense industry. In 1941, black leader A. Philip Randolph proposed a march on Washington to protest discriminatory hiring practices and the segregation of the military service. That proposed action eventually prompted President Roosevelt to issue an executive order prohibiting racial hiring discrimination in defense industries. The order made no mention of military desegregation. Lured by economic opportunity, 700,000 blacks migrated to Northern and Western cities to work in defense plants. In some cities, such as Detroit in 1943, race prejudice provoked deadly riots.

Increasingly, blacks criticized FDR for being too cozy with Southern racists. He failed to endorse a federal anti-lynching measure or the elimination of the poll tax, a law in Southern states requiring the payment of a fee before voting. They were also frustrated by Jim Crow policies in schools and the close association of FDR and the armed forces with "conspicuous Negrophobes" such as senators Theodore Bilbo of Mississippi and Walter George of Georgia. In February 1945, Ralph Mathews editorialized in the *Baltimore Afro-American* that "after our armies have marched on Berlin and Tokyo, if the GI Joes, both colored and white, don't turn and march on Washington and drive out the Fascist coalition of Southern Democrats and Republicans who are trying to Nazify America, they will not have learned what they were fighting for."

The threat of belligerent action was just talk. Above all, blacks did not want to be considered disloyal or a threat to national security. They were well aware that more than a hundred thousand Japanese Americans had been rounded up and placed in internment camps because they were considered potential security risks. Black wartime dissent was also restrained by economic and social gains. More than two million African Americans worked in desegregated defense plants and another 200,000 took jobs with the federal government. Slowly, segregation began to fray in the military service. The Navy officially ended segregation in 1945 and graduated its first black officer from the Naval Academy four years later, and the Marines began recruiting blacks in 1942 but kept them in segregated units, commanded by whites. The Army sent a few black units into combat and also agreed to accept a few black fliers who had trained at the Tuskegee Institute in Alabama.

World War II also proved a major boon to sports integration. Not only did the war promote the ideals of democracy and fair play, it also gave blacks a chance to showcase their talents on college, semipro, and service teams. Football, like other aspects of American life, had to endure wartime hardships. Manpower difficulties forced NFL teams to reduce their rosters from thirty-three to twenty-five players. Most college players had their education and playing days interrupted by wartime commitments, and some colleges ended football programs altogether for the duration.

Bill Willis, a native of Columbus, Ohio, was an exception. He entered Ohio State University in 1941 and graduated four years later. A 212-pound tackle, nicknamed the "Cat" for his quickness, he played three varsity seasons. At OSU, Willis has related, he never experienced a racial slight from a teammate. "I always attempted to show respect and conducted myself in such a way as to demand respect from my fellow players." Ohio State won conference titles in 1942 and 1944. As a senior, Willis was regarded as "one of the greatest tackles in football history" and was named to several All-America and All-Star teams. Although the NFL was desperate for competent players, it bypassed Willis. Upon graduation, he took a football coaching position at Kentucky State.

There was also Claude "Buddy" Young, perhaps the most sensational college gridiron star during the war years. A freshman running back at the University of Illinois in 1944, he captured national attention. "Not since the days when Red Grange was ripping up the sod . . . for Bob Zuppke and the Illini has there been so much pigskin excitement on the University of Illinois campus," wrote one sports columnist. A native of Chicago, the five-foot five-inch "Bronze Bullet" had exceptional quickness and acceleration. A track star, he won the national collegiate championships in the 100- and 220-yard dash, tied the world record for the 45- and 60-yard dash, and was the Amateur Athletic Union's 100-meter champion.

Young was equally impressive on the gridiron. In his first game against Iowa, he scampered 64 yards for a touchdown on the first play from scrimmage. On his second carry, he ran for a 30-yard touchdown. In all, he gained 139 yards on seven carries—an average of 19.7 yards. Before the season concluded, he had touchdown runs of 93, 92, 74, 64, and 63 yards. He averaged 8.9 yards per carry and scored 13 touchdowns, equaling the Big 10 Conference record established by Red Grange in 1924. Sportscaster Bill Stern called him "the fastest thing in cleats and the runner of the year." Ray Eliot, Young's coach, referred to him as "the best running back I have ever seen." Only a freshman, Young was named to several All-America teams.

In late January 1945, Young was drafted by the Navy instead of the NFL. Initially, he reported to the Great Lakes Naval Training Station, but he was eventually transferred to the naval base at

Fleet City, California. Like many star athletes, Young played football for the service team. Coast service teams, one writer claimed, "unquestionably played the toughest football extant during the war. The personnel of the league was 30 percent All-America, 30 percent professional, and 40 percent better than the average college squad."

Coached by Bill Reinhart, the Fleet City Bluejackets was the best football team on the coast in 1945. Besides Young, the squad consisted of such NFL stars as Charlie O'Rourke (Bears), Aldo Forte (Bears), and Frank "Bruiser" Kinard (Redskins). Games were scheduled against other service teams and one semipro team, the Hollywood Rangers. After games, O'Rourke recalled, players would go to their lockers to find envelopes stuffed with $300 or $400 from unknown donors.

The Bluejackets' toughest competitor was the Marines team from El Toro, California. Like the Bluejackets, the El Toro team was brimming with talent. In mid-December, the two teams met for the championship. In an earlier contest, the Bluejackets had prevailed, 7–0. The championship game was played in Los Angeles at Memorial Stadium before 65,000 fans. It was one of Buddy Young's greatest games. After a scoreless first quarter, he returned a kickoff for a 94-yard touchdown, ran back another kickoff for an 88-yard touchdown, and took a handoff from O'Rourke and scampered 30 yards for yet another score. The Bluejackets won the game, 45–28, to complete an unbeaten season. They challenged the unbeaten West Point team, but the cadets refused the invitation. Young's performance won accolades from players, coaches, writers, and fans, and rumors circulated that once Young fulfilled his service obligation, he would be drafted by the NFL or lured to UCLA to play for the Bruins. Neither proved true. Young returned to the University of Illinois and helped the Illini win the 1947 Rose Bowl.

Minority athletes who had fulfilled or escaped their military commitment had an opportunity to play minor-league professional football on the West Coast. In 1944, both the American Professional League and the Pacific Coast Professional League fielded desegregated teams. Kenny Washington played for the San Francisco Clippers, and Ezzrett Anderson for the Los Angeles Mustangs. The Los

Angeles Wildcats and San Diego Gunners also had black players. In the Pacific Coast League, Jackie Robinson represented the Los Angeles Bulldogs, and Mel Reid was one of twelve blacks on the Oakland Giants. The following year, the two leagues merged into the Pacific Coast League. The Hollywood Bears, with Kenny Washington, Woody Strode, and Ezzret Anderson, dominated play and won the title.

African Americans denounced the lack of opportunity in professional sports. For them, the desegregation of Major League Baseball during the 1930s and 1940s was of ultimate importance. The national pastime was extremely popular among minority athletes, and dozens of qualified blacks played in the Negro Leagues. Unlike football, however, blacks had never participated in Major League Baseball in the twentieth century. Indeed, when professional football was desegregated during the early 1930s, minority writers condemned baseball for being the "only national sport that bars Race players." Even after the color barrier was established in professional football, blacks were slow to attack it because they were reluctant to admit that it existed.

The African American press, led by Wendell Smith of the *Pittsburgh Courier,* worked diligently for the desegregation of Major League Baseball. Some writers urged blacks to boycott games until the ban was lifted. Others wondered why owners would forgo able-bodied, honorably discharged minority athletes to sign disabled white veterans. Finally, in November 1945, Branch Rickey, the owner of the Brooklyn Dodgers, broke the color ban by signing Jackie Robinson to a minor-league contract.

Blacks also expected the fulfillment of the American ideal in professional football. In 1944, two leagues were created to compete with the NFL: the U.S. Football League (USFL) and the All-America Football Conference (AAFC). Red Grange, the president of the USFL, announced that "our new league has set up no barriers. Any athlete, regardless of color, will be invited to try out for our teams, and if he has the ability, he will be welcomed. The Negro boys are fighting for our country; they certainly are entitled to play in our professional leagues." Unfortunately, the USFL didn't become a reality; it never played any games at all.

The AAFC, organized by Arch Ward, sports editor of the *Chicago Tribune,* was more successful than the USFL. Franchises were created in New York, Chicago, Cleveland, Los Angeles, San Francisco, Buffalo, Brooklyn, and Miami. The fledgling league, which existed only on paper until 1946, drafted Frankie Albert, LeRoy "Crazylegs" Hirsch, and several other college stars who had played on service teams. African Americans, however, were initially ignored. Buddy Young was bypassed, perhaps because he still had college eligibility. But to the dismay of blacks, the AAFC overlooked Kenny Washington and Woody Strode.

Only a few weeks after Jackie Robinson crashed baseball's color line, African American sportswriter Don Deleighbur launched a campaign to break the barrier in professional football. "Every red-blooded sports fan with a desire to see justice done should sit down and start writing letters to newspapers and to the owners of the clubs in the national professional football league and demand that democracy be led into those lily-white ranks." Desegregation hopes flagged, however, when the Miami Seahawks entered the league in January 1946. Miami, wrote Wendell Smith, was the most "Nazified of all the cities in the world on matters of racial equality." AAFC officials, like their NFL rivals, denied the existence of a color barrier. African Americans had had hopes that the AAFC would be "operated by more liberal men—men who wouldn't draw the color line as the NFL has been doing for years. But it's the same old story. Negroes won't be permitted to play."

Expectations ebbed, but blacks pushed for desegregation. In Los Angeles, two teams, the Rams of the NFL (recently transferred from Cleveland) and the Dons of the AAFC, hoped to use spacious Municipal Stadium (also known as the Coliseum). At a Coliseum Commission meeting, several black writers, including Halley Harding of the *Los Angeles Tribune* and Herman Hill, the West Coast correspondent of the *Pittsburgh Courier,* objected to the use of the Coliseum by any organization that practiced racial discrimination.

Because both leagues banned blacks, they argued, they should be denied the use of the facility. Representatives from the Rams and Dons promptly announced their intent to sign black athletes and the Coliseum Commission allowed both teams to use the stadium.

The breakthrough came in late March 1946, when the Rams signed Kenny Washington. Not surprisingly, the black press hailed the signing of Washington. "Rams Sign Kenny Washington: 1st Negro in Pro League," blared the *Los Angeles Sentinel*. The Hollywood Bears' Paul Schissler, who had witnessed the play of Joe Lillard, Cliff Battles, and Bronco Nagurski in the NFL, told the *Sentinel* that Washington "is not only the greatest all-around football player I have ever coached, but the greatest I have ever seen." Parallels were drawn with Jackie Robinson. "Both athletes had performed brilliantly at UCLA. Both became pioneers for their race in professional sports." In mid-May, the Rams purchased the contract of Woody Strode from the Hollywood Bears. But Strode was thirty-one years old and beyond his peak. And Washington was hampered by an injured knee. Neither excelled. And Strode did not relish being a racial pioneer. As Washington's roommate on the road, he had to share the humiliation of eating and staying overnight at separate establishments from their teammates. "If I have to integrate heaven," Strode once told a reporter, "I don't want to go."

The AAFC delayed signing blacks. To obtain its lease from the Coliseum Commission, the Los Angeles Dons had agreed to provide blacks an opportunity to play. The Dons, however violated that pledge. Sharply criticized by the black press, the Dons eventually relented, but not until the following year. Meanwhile, AAFC Commissioner James Crowley reminded fans that the league had no restrictions against black players. The AAFC, he informed a black newspaper, "is just what the name implies; it is All America in every respect." The Cleveland Browns, however, was the only AAFC team to prove that point, in 1946.

In mid-August, Paul Brown, coach and part-owner of the Cleveland franchise, invited Bill Willis and Marion Motley to tryout camp at Bowling Green University. From the moment he was appointed coach in 1945, Brown has written, he was determined to sign the best athletes available, regardless of color. He was aware of the unwritten black ban, but he had no intention of adhering to it. Both athletes impressed the coaches and were signed to contracts. Only a few owners, Brown recalls, took exception to his actions.

The invitation to training camp caught Willis by surprise. Due to the black ban, it was "inconceivable to me that I would play pro ball." In camp, he encountered few difficulties. He demanded respect, and Brown insisted that all players be treated fairly. Invited to camp a few days after Willis, Motley ran the fastest times in the sprints and left little doubt that he had the ability to play professional football.

Motley and Willis were well-liked and got along with teammates. "It's too bad the whole world couldn't participate in athletics, because if they did, there would be no racial or religious prejudice," Browns quarterback Otto Graham once told me. "On the playing field, it doesn't matter whether you are Protestant, Catholic, Jew, Muslim, white, black, or brown. You are judged on talent and performance." Of course, not all athletes were as open-minded as Graham. Motley and Willis often encountered racial prejudice from opposing teams. Neither athlete was allowed to play in the game against Miami because Florida law forbade integration. Rival players sometimes taunted them with racial slurs and provoked them by stepping on their hands with their cleats. Usually, their teammates "took care" of the offending parties because Coach Brown warned the black players to be thick-skinned and composed themselves. "If Willis and I had been anywhere near being hotheads," Motley recalled, "it would have been another ten years till black men got accepted in pro ball." Motley and Willis excelled throughout the season and helped lead the Browns to a conference title and the first of four consecutive league championships. Both athletes were named first-team All-Pros, an honor that became perennial.

The black press considered the desegregation of professional football one of the top stories of 1946. Only the debut of Jackie Robinson with the Montreal Royals was regarded as more important in the sports field than the signing of Strode, Washington, Willis, and Motley. According to *Pittsburgh Currier*'s Wendell Smith, Paul

Brown "automatically becomes one of the 'men of the year' in sports because he voluntarily signed Motley and Willis." The Rams, on the other hand, "are not to be congratulated with the same enthusiasm as Brown" because they hired minority athletes only under pressure.

Many black Americans believed that desegregation in the sports field would promote the spirit of equality in other aspects of American life. "It has been proven time and again," wrote Bill Nunn of the *Pittsburgh Currier,* "that the athletic field has been the front line in this continued battle for racial tolerance." And Dan Burley of the *New York Amsterdam News* beamed, "It's a helluva feeling, folks, to know that you're an American. Yep. In spite of all they're doing in Louisiana, Georgia, Mississippi, and right in Washington." Racists the world over, he continued, "are falling by the wayside or into public disfavor, and those who are foolish enough to declare themselves openly against the manifestations of progress are being driven to cover in the world of sports." And Wendell Smith believed that athletic success was an "effective slap" at "racial mobsters" who claimed that blacks were inferior.

The success of the Cleveland Browns, on the field and at the gate, led to the desegregation of other teams. In addition, the replacement of the financially troubled Miami franchise with the Baltimore Colts also somewhat facilitated desegregation in the AAFC. Baltimore resisted signing blacks until it joined the NFL in 1953, but it had no objection to playing against minority athletes. In 1946, AAFC teams added more blacks to their rosters. The Browns signed Horace Gillom of the University of Nevada, the Buffalo Bisons selected Dolly King, and the Chicago Rockets took Bill Bass and Bernard Jefferson.

The Los Angeles Dons, who shunned blacks in 1946 in part because they wanted to avoid racial problems with the Miami team, offered contracts to Ezzert Anderson, John Brown, and Bert Piggott. Not to be outdone by the baseball team with the same name, the Brooklyn Dodgers signed Elmore Harris. And, with considerable fanfare, the New York Yankees football team offered a multiyear contract to Buddy Young. A Rose Bowl hero and the most valuable player in the college All-Star game against the Bears, Young had a successful rookie year. He finished fifth in the league in rushing and helped lead the Yankees to a division title. "The limitations have been lifted and, now, the sky's the limit," wrote an enthusiastic black sportswriter in 1947. "Come to think of it, that's all a plain Negro citizen needs in this country—a chance to get to the top."

Yet not all blacks were optimistic. Some worried that the signing of black players, especially by the AAFC, was done mainly to boost minority attendance and establish the viability of the league. The NFL had only two African American athletes, and they rarely played. Were they just tokens? The legendary Fritz Pollard, a star player with the Akron and Hammond teams in the 1920s, reminded Dan Burley of the *New York Amsterdam News* that the NFL employed blacks at first, and yet once the league had become established, it shunned black players. The same pattern might be repeated in the late 1940s or 1950s. Overall, Pollard "was pessimistic" about the permanence of racial integration in professional football.

Fortunately, Pollard's pessimism turned out to be wrong. In 1948, the San Francisco 49ers, the only lily-white AAFC team besides Baltimore, signed Joe Perry. In its four years of existence, the AAFC helped pave the way for desegregation by signing more than one dozen minority athletes. Not only did AAFC coaches seek talent in "white" schools, but they pursued athletes from black colleges as well. A sure sign of progress, noted the *New York Amsterdam News,* was the fact that "Negro stars are being added to or lopped off pro football squads so fast one cannot tell who's where these days."

Unlike baseball's Jackie Robinson, professional football had no single integration pioneer. Californians looked to Kenny Washington and Woody Strode. Ohioans touted Bill Willis and Marion Motley, with Paul Brown serving as the counterpart to baseball's Branch Rickey. And at least one African American New York writer, perhaps unwilling to see beyond the Hudson River, lionized Buddy Young as well as Dan Topping, the New York Yankees owner who signed him. The main heroes and gate attractions of black sports fans, argued Dan Burley of the *New York Amsterdam News,* were Joe Louis in boxing, Jackie Robinson in baseball, and Buddy Young in football. Young, more than any other black football player, he said, symbolized what he called the "New Thought"—a disregard for "color, race, and national origins" as hiring considerations. The youthful and wealthy Dan Topping, Burley continued, was an owner who embodied the new era of progressive thinking. Like Rickey and Robinson, Topping and Young were collaborators in racial integration. Yes, Paul Brown had signed Willis and Motley earlier, but he did not have a close relationship with those two players, and after all, Cleveland was a much smaller stage than New York. Although Young was a superb athlete, he never lived up to Burley's expectations as the Jackie Robinson of pro football integration. Burley also overstated Topping's commitment to racial equality and flattered him, hoping that the baseball Yankees, a team Topping co-owned, would hire a black player, too. The baseball Yankees did sign some black players to minor-league contracts, but their major-league roster was not integrated until Elston Howard was added in the mid-1950s.

With the exception of the Detroit Lions, who signed two blacks in 1948, NFL owners did not pursue black players actively until the early 1950s. With the collapse of the AAFC in 1949, the NFL added new teams, including the Baltimore Colts, San Francisco 49ers, and the Cleveland Browns. Cleveland was nearly as successful in the NFL as it had been in the AAFC. Following Paul Brown's example, NFL owners, with the notable exception of the Redskins, gradually added black players.

The democratic idealism sparked by World War II, the protest of writers and fans, the emergence of the AAFC, and the success of several minority athletes in college football all account for the collapse of professional football's racial barrier. In the eyes of most fans, owners who claimed that blacks were not qualified to play in the NFL had been discredited. But even as NFL team rosters revealed that complete integration was being achieved in the late 1940s, such opportunities to excel with the Washington Redskins would still be years away.

CHAPTER 5

The Washington Whiteskins

On November 23, 1947, the Washington Redskins held a fan-appreciation day for their iconic quarterback, Sammy Baugh. They presented him with a glistening maroon car with wide, white-walled tires, the number "33" on the front bumper plate, and a door panel reading "Slingin' Sam—the Redskins Man." On that special day, before more than 30,000 fervid fans, Baugh had one of his best games, rifling six touchdown passes to down the defending league champion Chicago Cardinals, 45–21. After the game, he drove his sister and brother-in-law to Philadelphia. On his return to Washington that same evening, an oncoming vehicle forced him into a skid that demolished his spiffy new automobile. Baugh was unhurt, but the car wreck would come to symbolize the Redskins' football fortunes in the years following World War II. From 1946 through 1961, the Redskins enjoyed only three winning seasons, appeared in no title or championship games, and amassed a record of 69 wins, 116 losses, and 8 ties. They devoured eight head coaches and played no black athletes.

The most obvious reason for the Redskins' futility is that they did not have enough skilled players, and for that crucial shortcoming, George Marshall must be held accountable. His skill at promotion did not extend to the building of a winning franchise. His monumental ego, and perhaps the team's past success under Sammy Baugh, gave him an exaggerated sense of his understanding of the game and his ability to assess talent. Arrogant, autocratic, meddlesome, bigoted, and caustic, he also failed to establish a comfortable work environment for his players and coaches.

By the mid-1940s, if not earlier, Marshall had developed an obsession with football that bordered on the pathological. To paraphrase *Washington Post* writer Richard Coe, George Marshall not only owned the Redskins, but the Redskins "owned" him. "I've never found anything I enjoyed more," Marshall said of football. "If I get out of football, I'll retire; there's nothing else I'd want to do. To do anything well, you have to enjoy it first. And not just for the money, either. Anything else is just another form of prostitution." In 1946, he sold his laundry business to devote more time and attention to football. Aside from football, only the theater captivated him. When he went out on the town, which was often, he did so mainly for self-aggrandizement and promotion of the Redskins.

Marshall's preoccupation with football strained his family life. He rarely saw his two children from his first marriage, and his union with Corinne became a sham. "How anyone can be interested in football when he's married to Corinne Griffith is one of the great mysteries of life," wrote one baffled sportswriter. She lived most of the year in Beverly Hills, California, where she sold real estate. Marshall saw his wife occasionally when the Redskins travelled to Occidental College in southern California for training camp, but mostly the couple lived separate lives. Corinne moved west because she resented subordinating her life to football. On a local 1953 television program called *The Redskin Show,* Marshall said of Corinne: "She used to be the Corinne Griffith of the movies until she became more famous as Mrs. George Preston Marshall."

Corinne did try to take an interest in football. She wrote the lyrics to "Hail to the Redskins," helped choreograph halftime shows, initially attended games, and plugged the team in a 1947 book, *My Life with the Redskins.* But she never developed any affection for the game. After twenty-two years of marriage, the couple divorced in 1958. Commenting to the press on the breakup, she said: "Please don't blame George. He just couldn't love me. It's that simple." There was, she continued, "[n]o other man. No other woman. Just things that got in the way. And as hard as I tried, I just couldn't learn football."

As Corinne intimated, Marshall let nothing get in the way of football. Yet, in spite of his passion and commitment, he could not field a winning team. The Redskins still had some talented athletes following their 1945 championship appearance. Even in decline, Baugh was an effective quarterback, and he had a sure-handed receiver in Hugh "Bones" Taylor. But, after sixteen seasons, Baugh retired in 1952, and Taylor left two years later after an eight-year career. Finding an adequate replacement for Baugh proved especially difficult. Eddie LeBaron, a diminutive sixteenth-round draft choice, was arguably the team's best quarterback in the decade following Baugh's retirement.

After Dick Todd retired in 1948, the Redskins scrambled to find a durable running back. They obtained Bill Dudley in 1950 from the Detroit Lions, and he offered some flashes of brilliance with the Redskins, but the future Hall of Famer was past his prime. The team drafted Charlie "Choo Choo" Justice in 1950, but the two-time runner-up for the Heisman Trophy got injured and never lived up to expectations. Vic Janowicz, who won the Heisman Trophy with Ohio State University, signed with the Redskins in 1954, but his promising career ended two years later when he was paralyzed in an automobile accident. Eventually the University of Oregon's Dick James performed productively at running back from 1956 to 1963, but the team had no winning seasons during his tenure.

Although Dick McCann carried the title of general manager, Marshall,effectively had total control over the personnel decisions. Coaches had input, of course, but Marshall prided himself on evaluating talent and always got his way on trades and draft selections. The Redskins and most NFL teams did not have the elaborate scouting and assessment systems that prevail in the twenty-first century. "They used to say the Redskins scouting budget was 50 cents, the cost of *Street and Smith* and another football magazine," said Eddie LeBaron. The Redskins did so little preparation for draft day that some owners accused them of cheating. "At the player draft meetings," recalled Paul Brown in *PB: The Paul Brown Story,* "we all sat at separate tables with our lists spread before us, and Marshall inevitably made the rounds of each table, coming up from behind, leaning over and giving the big hello. At the same time, he would look over our shoulders at our lists, trying to get some information. After a while, it became so obvious that everyone just closed his book when he saw Marshall coming." Some owners, said LeBaron, exposed lists of players that they did not want, hoping Marshall would take them.

Some of the Redskins' draft picks made it seem like Marshall was taking the bait. With their first pick in 1946, the Redskins selected UCLA running back Cal Rossi, but he was ineligible for the draft because he was only a junior. Stubbornly, they selected Rossi again the following year, even though he had no intention of playing pro football. Looking for another Baugh, Marshall used the first overall choice in the 1948 draft to select Alabama's Harry Gilmer instead of future Hall of Famers Y.A. Tittle and Bobby Layne. In fairness, it should be pointed out that Gilmer was an excellent prospect, and six other teams also bypassed Tittle and Layne. In the draft, Marshall was partial to quarterbacks, choosing seven with the team's first pick between 1948 and 1960—Gilmer, Larry Isbell, Jack Scarbath, Ralph Guglielmi, Don Allard, Richie Lucas, and Norm Snead.

"Marshall was a showman first of all. He wanted entertainment. That's how I looked at his draft picks," recalled LeBaron. "We never had very good defensive teams when I was there, but we kept drafting offensive players. He wanted big names, people who would draw fans and bring excitement. It was like treading water." Arkansas native Hugh "Bones" Taylor, one of Baugh's favorite receivers in the postwar years, also was baffled by Marshall's player personnel decisions. "It was weird. If Marshall could get a big name or some player from Maryland, Virginia, or North Carolina, he did, even if it didn't help us," he complained. "We should have been signing blacks. Len Ford grew up in the shadow of the stadium in D.C. and never had a chance to play for us. Why? What difference did it make if he was black?"

Like all teams, the Redskins made some regrettable transactions. Against the advice of Baugh, Marshall traded quarterback Frank Filchock to the Giants after the 1945 season. He also lost two future stars. Considering Harry Gilmer a can't-miss prospect, he dealt quarterback Charley Conerly to New York, where he excelled for fourteen seasons, winning three division titles and the NFL championship in 1956. The Redskins in 1954 also sent defensive tackle Dick Modzelewski to the Steelers, who, in turn, traded him to the Giants. Winner of the 1952 Outland Trophy as the nation's top collegiate lineman, Modzelewski anchored the Giants defensive line from 1956 through 1963.

Blinded by racism, Marshall refused to tap into the pool of African American talent. "There were only so many good players anyway," said former Redskins running back Jim Podoley, "and when you eliminate half of them, it was tough. Very tough." Podoley's teammate Joe Tereshinski was certain that the black ban "was a very important reason we did not reach ultimate success."

Meanwhile, teams like the Cleveland Browns, using gifted blacks such as running back Marion Motley and guard Bill Willis, dominated play, first in the All-America Football Conference (AAFC) and then in the NFL. The Browns won the title from 1946 through 1949, every year of the AAFC's existence. During those years, they also drew more fans than every team in the NFL.

Named coplayer of the year in 1949 by the Washington Touchdown Club, Otto Graham surprised his audience by addressing the issue of racial intolerance and taking an indirect shot at George Marshall. "I wish the people of this country and the world had the philosophy of our Cleveland football team," Graham began. "We don't rate our fellows on their background or the[ir] religion or parentage or color. We have Protestants, Jews, Catholics, white players and Negro players in our gang, and it's a happy one. The prejudiced people could take a tip from our success. Our coaches are interested chiefly in what we can do on the football field and rate us on that. It's the best spirit on any team I've ever played with and it would be truly wonderful if that view of men were world wide."

After joining the NFL, the Browns appeared in seven championship games, winning titles in 1950, 1954, and 1955. After Marion Motley retired in 1953, they added Syracuse University running back Jim Brown, who arguably became the game's greatest player. During his brief, nine-year career from 1957 to 1965, he led the NFL in rushing eight times, appeared in nine Pro Bowls, won the Rookie of the Year Award and three Most Valuable Player awards, averaged 5.2 yards per carry, and never missed a game.

The Browns played particularly well against the Redskins, winning nineteen of twenty-three contests between 1950 and 1961, including drubbings of 45–0 and 62–3. In Cleveland's first appearance in Washington, in December 1950, a black health educator cringed as fans abused Marion Motley with racial epithets. Residents of Cleveland, he said in a letter to the *Cleveland Call and Post,* had integrated African Americans into their community, whereas Washingtonians had not. "Residents of Cleveland," he continued, "could be a vital force for good if they could each pen a letter to George Preston Marshall . . . and ask him to give racial tolerance a chance by following Cleveland's example of Democracy in sports."

Following the successful example of the Cleveland Browns, NFL owners—except for Marshall—gradually added black players. To avoid offending some white fans, owners established unofficial quotas of no more than eight minority players per team. Those few pioneers paved the way for additional African American players and often made a difference between winning and losing seasons. The New York Giants won the 1956 NFL championship with the help of linemen Roosevelt Brown and Roosevelt "Rosey" Grier, running back Mel Triplett, and defensive back Emlen Tunnell. The Baltimore Colts, who defeated the Giants for the title in 1958 and 1959, attributed much of their success to defensive tackle Eugene "Big Daddy" Lipscomb, offensive lineman Jim Parker, and running back/flanker Lenny Moore, who was Rookie of the Year in 1956, a perennial Pro Bowl selection, and, like Parker, a future Hall of Famer. Other heralded African American players of the 1950s included lineman Lamar Lundy, defensive backs Abe Woodson, J.C. Caroline, Johnny Sample, and Dick "Night Train" Lane, and running backs Willie Gallimore, Ollie Matson, John Henry Johnson, and Joe Perry, the first runner to record consecutive thousand-yard rushing seasons.

African Americans also made gains outside the lines, despite scant leadership from the White House. (Although President Dwight

D. Eisenhower disavowed racial intolerance, he did not believe that federal laws and dictates could "change people's hearts." (If General Eisenhower had pursued the enemy with the same vigor that he pursued racial equality as president, said one black leader, "we'd all be speaking German now.") In the 1954 *Brown* decision, the U.S. Supreme Court unanimously ruled against segregation in public schools. The following year, the court mandated the speedy integration of all public schools. In 1955, Rosa Parks refused to surrender her seat to a white man, triggering a boycott that led to the integration of the bus service in Montgomery, Alabama. When a truculent mob in 1957 tried to prevent nine courageous black students from attending Central High School in Little Rock, Arkansas, Eisenhower (however reluctantly) sent federal troops to protect them. Major strides for racial justice prompted Lillian Smith, a white Georgian, to predict to the *New York Times* that Jim Crow would end in Dixie by the mid-1960s: "Although signs will still be nailed to a few people's minds and hearts, the signs over doors—those words 'White' and 'Colored' that have challenged democracy throughout the world—will be down. A prophet is not needed to make this forecast. Anyone who looks closely at recent events in the South . . . will know that the future holds no place in it for the philosophy and practice of segregation."

George Marshall did not get that message. Like other strident segregationists, he bristled at federally directed desegregation efforts and resisted integration. Adding blacks to the team, he reasoned, would offend white Southern racial sensibilities and his profit margin. Marshall, said a *Cleveland Call and Post* writer, was "an unreconstructed grid rebel" and the only thing he "likes about Negroes is the color of their money."

Marshall also appeared to be bigoted toward Jews. As a guest on the *Oscar Levant Show,* he repeatedly disparaged the physical appearance of his host. When Levant said, "I hear you're anti-Semitic," Marshall replied, "Oh no, I love Jews, especially when they're customers." The insensitive remark brought a flurry of protests, and Levant apologized to his audience for inviting Marshall on the show. "I shouldn't have done it. *Variety* raised hell with me. Marshall kept saying how ugly I was—right there on the show. He said, 'What an ugly fellow you are, Oscar.'" The flap left Marshall unabashed. "If I'm doing a show that's supposed to be amusing and entertaining, and if Levant asks me a facetious question, I'll give an amusing answer," he told a *Sports Illustrated* writer. "The audience laughed like hell. No one of intelligence has ever questioned my theories on race or religion. Ah is an independent boy!" In fairness, it should be pointed out that during Marshall's decades with the Redskins, his vice president and treasurer was Milton King, who was Jewish.

For racial and commercial considerations, Marshall took pains to curry favor with his mainly white, Southern fan base. At halftime, he had the band play "Dixie," "The Eyes of Texas," and other songs with Southern appeal. In the NFL draft, he went out of his way to select players from Dixie schools, bypassing not only blacks, but sometimes more qualified non-Southern whites as well. Not only did he hold a fan appreciation day for the legendary Texan Sammy Baugh, but in 1954, before a packed stadium, he honored "Choo Choo" Justice, a North Carolinian who played only four mediocre seasons for the team.

Besides his bigotry and limited ability to assess athletic prowess, Marshall had an exaggerated sense of his command of the game. Former player Joe Tereshinski said that Marshall longed to be a coach: "I always firmly believed that his life would have been complete if he could have coached the team for one season. He was always competing with George Halas, and it made Mr. Marshall jealous because Halas would be on the field and Marshall would have to sit up in the stands."

From the stands, he telephoned plays and player substitutions to the head coach. On one occasion, according to Arthur Daley of the *New York Times,* one of the owner's recommendations brought victory when substitute quarterback Jim Youel scampered for a forty-yard touchdown. Marshall said afterward: "There's nothing difficult about coaching." On occasion, when he found it too time-consuming to travel by train to Texas or the West Coast, he watched games on television from home. But he could still meddle. "I'm plugged into the bench," he told Bud Shrake, a Dallas reporter. "I can call the coach from my living room and tell him what to do. Sometimes the coach doesn't do it, and that's how we lose." Marshall made light of his interference. One year after the team started with two wins and two losses, a fan asked him if it was true that he was coaching the team. "Partially," Marshall responded. "I coached them in the two they won, and the other coaches were in charge in the ones they lost."

Players resented Marshall's meddlesomeness, and during games, they tried to sabotage communication between the owner and the coach. Redskins running back Jim Podoley recalled that on one occasion, they draped heavy parkas over the phone at the bench. "When Marshall saw what was happening, he'd send his chauffeur down there to take the cape off the phone." Unlike Redskins players, rival coaches took comfort in Marshall's meddling. New York Giants coach Steve Owen told a *New York Times* reporter, "One thing we're sure of, and pleased about, is that George Preston Marshall will be there in a raccoon coat. He will start looking at the game from the stands but before long, he'll be right down on the bench sending in substitutes, and we like that. The subs George sends in always help us very much."

Ray Flaherty, who had guided the team to two world championships during the late 1930s and early 1940s, would not tolerate game-calling interference from Marshall. But subsequent coaches were less confident and insistent. In a twenty-year stretch from 1943 through 1963, Marshall went through ten head coaches. Coaching the Redskins, wrote the *Washington Post*'s Shirley Povich, "has all the permanency of a soap bubble."

After burning through Dudley DeGroot and Turk Edwards, Marshall in 1949 turned to U.S. Navy admiral John Whelchel to bring strict discipline to the team. He promised the commander full authority over the team, saying, apparently in all seriousness, "I never wanted to interfere in the coaching of the Redskins. But I felt it was necessary. I'm glad I can turn everything over to my new coach." The new coach was fired after seven dismal games. Herman Ball, Dick Todd, and Curly Lambeau followed Whelchel in brief coaching stints.

Hired in 1952, Lambeau was an icon who had founded the Green Bay franchise and had coached the Packers to six NFL championships in his thirty-one-year career. Like Marshall, he was a volatile personality, and there is little wonder that the two men soon had a blowup. After a hot and grueling 1954 exhibition game in Sacramento, California, some Redskins players brought beer to their rooms at the Senator Hotel. Marshall did not condone players drinking alcohol in the hotels where they were staying. Tipped off to the infraction, Marshall confronted Lambeau. Former Redskins guard Gene Pepper related the exchange to writer Thom Loverro: "'Do you know these boys are drinking beer? What are you going to do about it?' Curly answered, 'George, it's no problem. We lost a lot of weight out there today. It was hot. Let them drink a beer.' But George raised hell, and Curly wasn't about to take that. He was an equal—both of them were legends in the game. He didn't have to take a step back from Marshall. He did Marshall a favor by coming to Washington to coach. It got pretty nasty in the hotel lobby between George and Curly, and at one point, Curly grabbed George and put him up against the wall and said, 'You can't talk to me like that, you son of a bitch. I don't have to take that from you. If these guys want to drink beer, they can drink beer.' I was watching the whole thing, and I said to myself, 'Oh, shit, another new coach.' I knew Curly was gone." When the players next reported for practice, assistant Joe Kuharich had been elevated to head coach. In a marvelous understatement, Kuharich told the press: "Naturally, a sudden, unexpected development like this throws things into confusion."

Initially, Marshall refused to discuss the abrupt coaching change. "I have no statement, no comment of any kind to make on the incident. I won't discuss it," he told the *Washington Post.* But he did not remain silent for long, saying that he fired Lambeau because he was "too easy" on the players. After posting one winning season in five years, Kuharich obtained Marshall's consent to void his new-five year contract to become head coach at the University of Notre Dame. Asked why he allowed Kuharich to void his contract, Marshall responded: "I didn't want the Catholics to get mad at me. I've got enough enemies."

In an interview with *Sport* in 1957, Marshall provided a brief evaluation of each of his coaches up to that time, except for DeGroot. Flaherty was intelligent but money-hungry. Bergman failed because he was resistant to the introduction of the T-formation and advice from Shaughnessy. Edwards was too cozy with the players. Herman was not tough enough. "I should have never given him the job," Marshall declared about Herman. Dick Todd was "a wonderful boy," but he didn't like to release anyone. Whelchel had an exceptional football mind, but his war service sapped his energy and spirit. Lambeau was "an old friend," but he had to be fired after their fight. Kuharich had potential for greatness, but he left to coach at Notre Dame.

Excitable and combustible, Marshall agonized over every loss and sometimes took out his frustration on the players. Arthur Daley of the *New York Times* described him as "the most vibrant figure in professional football," but he is "just too enthusiastic and his enthusiasms just carry him away on occasion." After a tough loss to the Giants, Marshall barged into the locker room, threatening to fine any player who dared crack a smile. On another occasion, at halftime during a 1950 game against the Chicago Cardinals, he berated linebacker Pete Stout, who was unable to cover a speedy receiver. Recalling the scene to writer Thom Loverro several years later, Redskins end Joe Tereshinski said that when Marshall began swearing, Stout leaped up and grabbed him by the throat, saying, "My father never talked to me that way, and I won't let you." Although woozy from nearly being asphyxiated, Marshall hopped on a footlocker and barked to the team: "Now that's the kind of fight I want to see from you fellows. Go out there and give me that kind of spirit and fight and I will be proud of you." The Redskins lost 38–28.

While bigoted, tyrannical, and overbearing, Marshall was a driving force among NFL owners. Art Rooney recalled that during Bert Bell's commissionership from 1946 to 1960, he, Marshall, Halas, and Mara dominated the league. To garner publicity, Marshall persuaded owners to adopt Major League Baseball's tradition of giving U.S. presidents free passes to NFL games. Marshall also initiated a rule change in 1946 mandating an incompletion, rather than a safety, if an end zone pass hit a goalpost. The new rule, he joked, should be made retroactive, thus making the Redskins, not the Rams, winners of the 1945 championship game. In 1951, he pushed successfully for the reintroduction of the Pro Bowl game, dormant since World War II. He was unsuccessful in his efforts to improve the quality of officiating by making NFL referees full-time employees. With characteristic hyperbole, he claimed that local high school referees were more competent than part-time NFL officials.

Although Marshall generally got along with old-guard NFL titans like Rooney, Halas, and Mara, he incensed some of the younger owners. "He was obnoxious; he insulted your intelligence and had a great habit of sleeping most of the day and showing up at meetings late in the afternoon," Paul Brown has written. "We then had to stop the proceedings to brief him on all that had been accomplished. By that time, all of us were pretty tired and ready to adjourn, but he was rested and mentally sharp. That was when he tried to work some of his little deals."

Marshall also exasperated Philadelphia Eagles owner Alexis Thompson, who wanted to end the so-called cold war between the AAFC and the NFL. Competition between the leagues for players, Thompson argued, was swelling salaries and shrinking revenues. He proposed a merger between the leagues to reduce costs. Only a few AAFC teams were moneymakers, so representatives of the two leagues proposed a settlement, adding the Cleveland Browns, San Francisco 49ers, and Baltimore Colts to the existing ten-team NFL. Marshall balked. He wanted to be paid a "nominal fee" for allowing the Baltimore franchise to encroach within the seventy-five-mile territorial moat encircling Washington, D.C. Asked by a reporter for his definition of "nominal fee," Marshall said, "[A]nything under one billion dollars is considered nominal in this town." The merger was consummated in January 1950, when the Colts agreed to pay Marshall an encroachment fee of $150,000. He celebrated the deal for reporters by smoking an Indian peace pipe.

While unenlightened on racial issues, Marshall, in some ways, was visionary on matters of business and entertainment. He foresaw the day when teams would build domed stadiums with retractable roofs. He also took advantage of the revenue potential of television. "In this business," he once said, "it isn't the number of fans, but the money you take in that counts." He championed selling broadcast rights to radio and television to enhance revenues. In 1950, he became the first NFL owner to have his team's road games televised. Purchasing television and radio stations throughout the South to broadcast games brought in added revenue and reinforced the idea that the Redskins were Dixie's team. He also initiated an NFL rule prohibiting the broadcast of any other professional football contest into the territory of a team playing a home game.

Marshall also worked to reduce expenses. He kept salaries low and was the only league owner who refused to pay players for exhibition games. When his players protested not getting paid for six or seven exhibition games per season, he told them to quit if they did not like the policy. When running back Vic Janowicz became paralyzed from a 1956 car accident during training camp, Marshall dropped him from the payroll.

Given the flintiness and callousness of Marshall and other owners, it is not surprising that players sought reforms. In 1956, they formed the NFL Players Association, but owners refused to recognize the union for more than a decade. Marshall also led the battle, which he eventually lost, against a players' pension plan. He called the proposal a "ridiculous" demand that would financially ruin owners. Individual players, he said, could always buy retirement plans from insurance companies. He said that Norm Van Brocklin, who headed the players' pension movement, should devote more attention to playing football than playing labor leader—otherwise he would be seeking a pension sooner than expected. Van Brocklin portrayed Marshall as a miserly owner who did not want players to share in the growing wealth of the league. "The best thing for pro football," he told the *New York Times,* "would be for Marshall to walk in front of a taxi-cab."

Marshall also saw himself as a guardian defending the league against other threats besides unions. When the U.S. Justice Department challenged the NFL's television broadcast rules as a restraint of trade, he appeared in court as a witness, defending and ultimately preserving the restrictive policy of blacking out home games. When Congress considered legislation during the Korean War requiring all athletes with physical deferments to undergo basic military training, Marshall denounced the proposal as "the rankest sort of discrimination against a small minority." When college presidents eliminated or downsized football programs, especially in the East, he called them "idiots and screwballs" because they were ruining college football and crimping the player pipeline to the NFL. He also denounced Congress and the federal courts for not giving professional football the same exemption from antitrust law that Major League Baseball had.

Marshall relentlessly promoted his team and sport. Football, not baseball, he told the press, was the national pastime. The Redskins, he bragged, made more money in six home games than the Senators baseball team did in seventy-seven home games. He also made insulting or outlandish statements to boost ticket sales. Disappointed by soft ticket sales for an exhibition game against the Green Bay Packers, he called the host city of Winston-Salem, North Carolina, a "lousy town." Stung by the criticism, the Rotary Club invited him to take a tour of the city. He accepted, only to ridicule the R. J. Reynolds tobacco factory, the Western Electric plant, and the airport and people who enjoyed flying. At an underwear plant, he said: "I haven't worn an undershirt in twenty five years. Only wear shorts. Guess I cut your business in half." "Winston-Salem turned the other cheek to critic George Preston Marshall," wrote the *Winston Salem Journal*, "and he managed to slap it too."

Marshall employed a similar tactic when ticket sales sagged in New York. That city, he declared, was a dying sports' town. As in Boston two decades earlier, he said, the media did not provide enough hype and support for professional baseball and football teams. Franchise owners worked maniacally to boost their teams, he contended, but media representatives were either critical or indifferent toward them. Soon, he predicted prophetically, New York would lose some of its hallmark sports franchises. New York writers like Red Smith pooh-poohed Marshall as just another arrogant owner who believed taxpayers owed him a living. But in 1957, the baseball Giants and Dodgers moved to California.

Marshall attributed much of his success with the Redskins to showmanship. Like the popular *Ed Sullivan Show,* he offered fans variety—football, a popular fight song, a first-rate marching band, and captivating halftime entertainment. "It could be said that when George Marshall put on a football game," wrote one journalist, "the two halves were merely bookends to keep the halftime show standing tall." Even after limiting his direct involvement in planning halftime shows, Marshall continued to dote on the band. One year, so the story goes, Washington was surprised by a blizzard that cloaked the city in snow. Marshall scurried to find equipment to clear the field. Shortly before the game, Giants owner Tim Mara gazed upon the snow-clad field with a worried look. Marshall said: "Don't worry. They're coming. They'll be here any minute." "You mean the snowplows?" asked Mara. "No," said Marshall, "I mean snow boots for the band."

In spite of the team's abysmal record, Washingtonians developed a love affair with the Redskins. Washington had some awful teams, Marshall once confessed, "but I never had a losing season at the gate." Bob Addie of the *Washington Post* speculated that the "enduring romance," at least with white fans, began with the first home game in September 1937, or else in December of that same year, when thousands of Redskins fans paraded through New York streets to back the team. The Redskins might not have a winning record in 1957, wrote *Post* sports editor Bus Ham, "but the team nevertheless has a firm grip on the community's affection." Fans flocked to games even though they had to endure civil-defense bomb drills and the prohibition of beer sales by Clark Griffith, the stadium's owner. The team was so popular that restaurants, taverns, clubs, business groups, and fraternal organizations often sang "Hail to the Redskins" at their functions. When throngs of people attended President Eisenhower's outdoor inauguration in 1957, Bob Addie said facetiously, "This was the first time so many people were gathered outdoors without 'Hail to the Redskins' being played." When the prestigious, tuxedo-clad

National Symphony Orchestra once performed at halftime, it began with the patriotic "Stars and Stripes Forever," shifted next to the contemplative "Prelude to Lohengrin, Act Three," and closed with a snappy rendition of "Hail to the Redskins."

The fight song was even used as a bargaining chip in a dispute over the expansion of the league. In 1959, two Texas oil tycoons, Lamar Hunt and Bud Adams, announced the establishment of a new professional football league. With teams in Dallas, Houston, Denver, Los Angeles, Buffalo, Boston, Minneapolis, and New York, the rival American Football League (AFL) scheduled play to begin in 1960. To avoid the appearance of restraining competition, the NFL initially welcomed the new league. Soon, however, NFL owners moved to cripple the AFL by poaching two of its cities: Dallas and Minneapolis. Marshall denounced the proposed raid as a violation of the antitrust laws. "The only reason for expansion I've heard from the other owners is that we could destroy the new league," he told the press. "If that is the only reason, then we are guilty of monopolistic practices." Marshall preferred to give the new league three years to establish itself before intruding upon its territory.

George Halas and Art Rooney, who favored expansion, conceded that Marshall had enough influence to round up other owners for the three votes necessary to block expansion. But Marshall suddenly reversed his position when he learned that Clint Murchison, principal owner of the proposed NFL Dallas franchise, had acquired the rights to "Hail to the Redskins." To obtain the song rights, Marshall agreed to support expansion. So, in a sense, Murchison got his NFL franchise in Dallas for a song. Just as important (and probably even more so), the other owners agreed to pay Washington's share of the financial damages if the NFL was sued for restraint of trade. In January 1960, NFL owners, with the Chicago Cardinals alone dissenting, awarded franchises to Dallas and Minneapolis.

Marshall used fan devotion and the fact that Eastern sport franchises were relocating to the West to seek a new publicly financed sports facility for the Redskins and Senators. Other cities, such as Baltimore, had constructed municipal stadiums; the nation's capital deserved nothing less, he said. Although he didn't say so,

Marshall also wanted to move because Griffith Stadium was located in a heavily black area of the city. Eventually, Congress authorized the District of Columbia Armory Board to construct and manage a 54,000-seat oval stadium located on Interior Department land at 2201 East Capital Street, S.E., near the National Guard Armory. The Armory Board would be granted parking and concession fees, plus 12 percent of the gate receipts. In 1959, Marshall signed a thirty-year lease, to take effect in 1961. "With this stadium," he declared, "both big-league baseball and big-league football will be guaranteed in the future of Washington." What was not guaranteed, however, was the policy of business as usual. Marshall's new federal landlords would have a big surprise for him when they took control of the new stadium in 1961.

CHAPTER 6

The Owner, the Journalist, and the Hustler

George Marshall had an edgy relationship with representatives of the mainstream Washington, D.C., media. They found him overbearing but also entertaining. With Marshall as the owner of the beloved Washington Redskins, his unabashed behavior and controversial stewardship demanded attention. And Marshall thrived on attention. "I don't mind being disliked or even hated but I can't stand to be ignored," he once huffed to a *Washington Star* reporter. *Washington Post* columnist Bob Addie summed up the attitude of the local press when he wrote of Marshall in 1954: "He's irascible, violent, opinionated, a dictator, and completely uninhibited. . . . But he's colorful and good copy. I like him—but I wouldn't want to work for him." Shirley Povich was one Washington journalist who neither liked nor ignored Marshall. Neither did broadcaster and Redskins stockholder Harry Wismer. Both men despised Marshall and feuded openly with him, decrying his micromanaging style and racial bigotry, and insisting that the team's on-field performance would improve if Marshall hired African American players.

The son of orthodox Jewish immigrants, Povich was born in Bar Harbor, Maine, where his father ran a furniture store on Main Street. Shirley lived above the store with his parents and eight siblings. A few other boys in the area shared his first name, so he never became self-conscious about it. Later in life, having achieved acclaim as a sportswriter, he found humor in being named to *Who's Who Among American Women.* As a youngster, Povich developed a love for baseball and followed the Red Sox in Boston newspapers that were delivered evenings by boat. But it was golf, not baseball, that transformed his life. During the summers, he caddied at Kebo Valley, a posh private course that attracted elite summer tourists such as the Rockefellers, Vanderbilts, Pulitizers, and McLeans.

A multimillionaire who owned the famous Hope Diamond and the not-yet-famous *Washington Post,* Edward B. McLean developed a fondness for the hustling teenager, making him his personal caddy and transporting him to and from the golf course in a Rolls Royce. Upon Povich's graduation from high school, McLean offered him an entry-level position at the *Post* and a job caddying on his eighteen-hole golf course at his estate, Friendship, in Washington. At the end of the summer season, in September 1922, McLean asked the seventeen-year-old to accompany him to Washington in a private railroad car, but Povich's parents forbade him to travel during the Jewish holy days.

Using his own meager funds, he wrangled a car ride to Boston (where he slept on the Common to avoid the expense of a hotel), and then he took a boat to New York, where he watched a 1922 World Series game from Coogan's Bluff outside the Polo Grounds. After that, he bought a train ticket for Washington, where he stayed with an older brother. The next morning he traveled by streetcar to Friendship. When he arrived, McLean was drinking illegal Prohibition-era whiskey with his golf partner. "Shirley," he said, "I'm so glad you're here. Just in time too. I want to introduce you to the man whom you'll be caddying for. Shirley, I want you to meet the president of the United States, Warren G. Harding. Mr. President, I want you to meet Shirley Povich, of Bar Harbor, Maine, the best caddie in the United States."

The following day, McLean sent Povich to the *Post* for a job. He was hired as a copy boy at $12 per week, plus he earned another $20 per weekend caddying for McLean. He eventually moved up to reporter, covering crime and then sports. In 1926, McLean named the twenty-one-year-old as sports editor, a position Povich would hold for nine years. Crushed by the 1929 stock market crash and the ensuing Great Depression, McLean sold the *Post* and spent his remaining years in a mental institution.

As sports editor, Povich launched a column, "This Morning," that ran five or six days per week until he retired in 1974. He soon "retired from retirement," as he put it, and periodically contributed "This Morning" columns until 1998. He submitted his last column the day before he died of a heart attack that year, at age ninety-two.

A spare man of 5'7", at 140 pounds, Povich was passionate about his work. He delighted readers with stories about quirky topics like the gasoline station on the St. Lawrence River in upstate New York that dispensed fishing worms from a vending machine. Baseball was always his primary love, but he also enjoyed covering football, horse racing, boxing, and golf. Basketball was about the only sport he did not enjoy because it was dominated by "carnival freaks" that "don't shoot baskets any more, they stuff them, like taxidermists." He also had a gift for writing memorable leads, like the one following the perfect game that Don Larsen pitched for the Yankees against the Dodgers in the 1956 World Series: "The million-to-one shot came in. Hell froze over. A month of Sundays hit the calendar. Don Larsen pitched a no-hit, no-run, no-man-reach-first game in a World Series." A writing dynamo, with laserlike wit, he contributed more than 17,000 columns during his career and was Washington's most widely read and respected columnist. Like the Redskins, Povich became a community institution. Katharine Graham, who would take control of the *Post* in 1963, credited him with being "responsible for about a third of our readership. He's one of the cornerstones on which today's *Post* was built." Native Washingtonian Robert Kaiser, who became an associate editor with the *Washington Post*, remembered reading Povich's "This Morning" column as a teenager. "It was the first journalism that spoke to me in a direct, personal way, and it made a permanent impression," he said. "Povich brought the race issue home in a way that a white kid could understand. He devoted many columns to a crusade against George Preston Marshall."

Povich worked at the *Post* for seventy-five years, relished his craft, and inspired younger writers like Tom Boswell, Tony Kornheiser, and Michael Wilbon. "There he was, day after day, in what seemed to me an elegant suit, treating everyone in a gentle, friendly manner," Boswell has written. "Though he was in his sixties at the time, he was clearly having a ball. He didn't think the games were dumb or boring. . . . He liked his colleagues and they liked him."

Povich was also a dedicated family man. He smoked, drank whiskey, and gambled, but he deplored immoral behavior, preferring to spend his private time with Ethyl, his wife of sixty-six years, and their children. David (a lawyer), Maury (a television personality), and Lynn (a magazine editor) remember being pulled from school for six weeks to accompany their father, who was covering the Washington Senators spring training baseball season in Florida. Sports were the main topic at home as well. "Dinnertime was taken up talking plays, players, teams, and stats," daughter Lynn wrote in a tribute to her father.

He deplored racial injustice but had to tread lightly because he lived and worked in a segregated city. For decades, mainstream newspapers, including his own, carried "For Colored" and "For White" want ads, hired no black reporters, and generally ignored law-abiding African American residents. But as the civil rights movement gained traction, especially after World War II, Povich became more outspoken about racial intolerance in sports.

Before World War II, he hailed the boxing prowess of Joe Louis and the record-setting track achievements of Jesse Owens. He blasted Hitler and the Nazis for snubbing African American athletes at medal award ceremonies during the 1936 Olympics. At the same time, he ripped the U.S. track and field coach for pulling two Jewish athletes, Marty Glickman and Mark Stoller, from the 400-meter relay race for fear of offending the Nazis.

He also took Major League Baseball to task for its racial ban and advocated its desegregation shortly after attending a 1939 spring training Negro League baseball game in Florida with his friend Walter Johnson, formerly of the Senators and arguably baseball's greatest pitcher. They were especially impressed with catcher Josh Gibson, deeming him superior to Bill Dickey of the New York Yankees. In early April 1939, six years before Jackie Robinson signed with the

Brooklyn Dodgers, Povich urged Major League Baseball owners to sign Negro stars like Josh Gibson and Satchel Paige. "There's a couple of million dollars' worth of baseball talent on the loose, ready for the big leagues yet unsigned by any major league clubs," he wrote. "Only one thing is keeping them out of the big leagues—the pigmentation of their skin. They happen to be colored. That's their crime in the eyes of big league club owners."

Sam Lacy, the respected black writer for the *Washington Afro-American,* recalled that in 1942, when he tried to cover a boxing match at Griffith Stadium, he was denied a seat in the whites-only press area. Povich saw him standing apart and insisted that he sit next to him. "That was the beginning of press seat integration, he recalled. "When somebody like Shirley would support you, all of them started to accept you." In his own column, Lacy also commended Povich for being one of the very few daily journalists who since 1946 had been condemning "the Redskins ownership for its lily-white policy."

While personally gracious and well-mannered, Povich could play rough in his columns. The *Washington Post*'s Tony Kornheiser wrote, "When he took you apart in print, he did it so skillfully you never felt the blade, you just watched your blood run down the page." Some of that blood belonged to George Marshall. "Marshall was easy to dislike," Povich once wrote. "He bullied many people. He bragged about being big-league, but he deprived his players of travel comforts to save expenses while reaping huge profits. He refused to let Negroes play for the Redskins and thus watched other teams pass him by while he presented the fans of later years with all-white losers." The public feud between Marshall and Povich entertained *Post* readers for decades. "Povich's running battles with George Marshall," wrote *Post* guest columnist Bob Considine in 1957, "have made some of the drollest talk and writing that has enlivened the local scene for a generation." The quarrel "has been out in the open, with neither side yielding. Brother Marshall will sound off on our man at the drop of a mangle, and vice versa."

Like most Washington sports fans, Povich heralded the transfer of the Redskins to the District. The addition of a division-winning professional football team, along with the existing Senators, would make Washington a major sports town, he said. In typical booster fashion, he predicted that Washington fans would embrace the new team. In that maiden 1937 Washington season, Povich wrote positive stories about the team and its owner, portraying Marshall as a shrewd business executive who was passionate about the sport and about winning. He also hailed him for having the foresight to draft college star Sammy Baugh. And when the team defeated the Bears for the NFL championship, he commended Marshall, in that bygone era before Super Bowl rings, for generously rewarding players with team sweaters and windbreakers.

After that initial storybook season, Povich began to look more critically at Marshall, especially after he lost star running back Cliff Battles in a salary dispute. One of the league's premier players, Battles sought a raise from $2,800 for the 1938 season. When Marshall refused, Battles left to coach at Columbia University for $4,000 yearly. "Why on earth do you insist on putting the Redskins' salaries in the paper? It only embarrasses me and the players," Marshall griped to Povich. "A half-dozen $200-a-game-men playing in front of a halfback who's dragging down $500 a game can make him look awful bad if they resent his salary—awful bad." When Marshall complained about colleges raiding professional football for coaches, Povich publicly advised him to solve the problem by raising player salaries. Periodically during the 1938 season, especially as losses mounted, he chastised Marshall for being cheap and for saying the team would not miss Battles. He ripped him for charging admission for intrasquad practice games and for not paying players for exhibition games. Stung by the criticism, Marshall declared: "I have never done any chiseling or cheating, in football or out, and I stand by that." Dutifully, Coach Flaherty added: "In all my experience in pro football, I have seen no team better treated by the ownership than the Redskins."

Povich tore into Marshall again in 1938, after an embarrassing 31–7 loss to the Bears in mid-November in Chicago. The players engaged in fistfights, and the owner leaped onto the field to confront officials for not penalizing the Bears for roughness. Even though the team lost, Marshall bragged about the size of the gate receipts, claiming a record profit for a visiting team. Despite a handsome financial gain, Povich reported, Marshall would not pay for his players to travel in sleeping cars on the return train trip. Irate, Marshall banned Povich from the Redskins locker room and demanded that the *Post* fire him. Managing editor Casey Jones told Marshall: "You run your Goddam Redskins and I'll run the *Washington Post*." Povich was not intimidated, and after a 36–0 loss to the Giants in the final game of the season, he wrote that the Redskins were made "chumps of." When Marshall objected to that negative characterization of his players, Povich "apologized," saying: "I never meant to end a sentence with a preposition."

During World War II, Povich further infuriated Marshall by accusing him of chiseling a charity. The Redskins played an exhibition game against a U.S. Army team in Los Angeles in August 1942, with gate receipts going to benefit needy families of U.S. soldiers. Minus the federal tax and stadium rental fee, the game raised more than $76,000 for the Army Relief Fund. Povich reported that Marshal "pocketed" $13,000 of the gate proceeds. "By what right the Redskin owners took $13,000 out of that gate before the Army Relief Society was paid off, we don't know. The game wasn't advertised as for the Redskins' benefit, if we remember rightly." He presumed that the Redskins would claim the $13,000 as "training expenses," but that would be "strictly malarkey." The team was already in southern California and had earlier played an exhibition game that would pay their expenses. He also pointed out that the Green Bay Packers had played a similar Army charity game in Milwaukee with all proceeds designated for the fund, including use of the stadium. Similarly, Major League Baseball owners took no money from sixteen Army Relief games and even had the players and umpires pay admission to the games.

Povich's column brought an immediate, angry response. Marshall assailed him for maligning the Redskins. The scurrilous column, he thundered, would discourage additional athletic contests to benefit Army relief. Yes, the Redskins claimed $13,608 for training expenses, but the army had agreed to the team taking 20 percent of the gate receipts for that purpose. The net contribution of $53,000 to the fund, he concluded, was larger than any other charitable football game. Povich refused to let up, apologizing only for underreporting the size of Marshall's "cut" from the fund. "We add that the financial success of his Redskins is due in part, . . . to the $13,608.75 the soldiers' relief fund did not get."

Marshall demanded a retraction. When the *Post* and Povich refused to oblige, he sued, seeking $100,000 in libel damages from each party. A year later, after a two-day trial, a jury ruled in favor of Povich and the *Post*. "I guess I won't be needing that $100,000 I have been trying to scrape together for the past 12 months," Povich told his readers. In reporting the results of the trial, he reiterated the charges that Marshall had chiseled Army widows and orphans. "The column rests," he concluded, "but only until there is occasion for further fair comment."

Povich found plenty of opportunity for "further fair comment." As he wrote in a 1969 memoir, "I used to wake up, every morning of my life with two questions immediately on my mind: What day is it, and what am I going to write about Marshall?" Eventually, he claimed to have put aside his malice when he stumbled upon a bit of Eastern wisdom: "He who bears a grudge digs a grave for two."

Yet there is little merit to his claim of philosophical enlightenment. For two decades, his *Post* columns were peppered with unflattering and caustic remarks about Marshall. It was no coincidence, he wrote in 1949, that the team's performance declined shortly after Marshall sold the laundry stores to devote his full attention to football. Not only did Marshall recruit poor players and pay his few good ones poorly, he also emasculated his head coaches by sitting on the bench, recommending plays, undercutting their authority, and hiring advisers to guide them. Sarcastically, he referred to Marshall as "Coach Emeritus," "Co-Coach," "eminent football authority," and "beloved figure of pro football." If Marshall, when pacing the sidelines, happened to step onto the field, Povich predicted that the Redskins would be penalized for having "eleven and a half men on the field." Marshall telephoned his coaches during games so frequently that Povich dubbed him "Chief of Communications." The Redskins, he wrote, were considering dropping the "T-formation" in favor of the "AT&T formation." Povich suspected that something was wrong in 1953 because three days had passed without Marshall firing a coach. He was the only coach, Povich wrote, who could get along with the owner.

Nor did Povich spare Marshall's wife. When she published *My Life with the Redskins* in 1947, he trashed it. He described the bulk of the book as sappy and self-serving. The book's appendix, however, was worthwhile because it provided valuable team and player statistics. "This was one operation in which they should have thrown away the body and preserved the appendix."

Povich also lampooned the 1953 launch of Marshall's television program about the Redskins. "You could see television on your screen the other night," he remarked, "and also smell it." The thirty-minute *Redskin Show* was an "insufferable presentation" and "unabashed corn" that glorified Marshall and his effort to sell season tickets. "The Marshall show was a turkey from the opening theme, a recording of 'Hail to the Redskins.'" The lyrics to that song—"Scalp 'um, swamp 'um, We will make 'um big score," were "pure gibberish." While viewers were provided with some entertaining football film clips, they also had to endure some of Marshall's absurd generalizations, such as "Communism never affects men who play football" and "Men who don't like football are no good for America." His feud with Marshall, he claimed, did not bias his review. "After all, you had to start feeling a bit more kindly toward a man who hasn't sued you for 10 years."

Povich slammed both the Senators and Redskins for being slow to use black athletes. In football, he extolled the talents of black standouts like Ollie Matson of the Chicago Cardinals, who ran for touchdowns of 75, 62, 15, and 5 yards against the Redskins in a 1954 game. Two years later, Matson burned the Redskins with a 105-yard kickoff return. Marion Motley, Mel Triplett, Lenny Moore, and Jim Brown were other African American players who had made their marks in the league. Blacks who picketed outside Griffith Stadium to protest the Redskins' racial barrier made a good point, he wrote in 1957. "How come the Redskins are the only team in the pro league that doesn't sign a Negro football player?" The woeful Redskins, he repeatedly stated, were missing an opportunity to improve by excluding black players. Both coaches and fans, he wrote, "are losers in Marshall's refusal to hire colored players. His passion for identifying the Redskins as the South's team, even to rewriting the lyrics of the team's song to make them read 'Fight for Old Dixie' instead of the original 'Fight for Old D.C.' is bewildering." The Redskins' colors, he lamented, "are inflexibly burgundy, gold, and Caucasian."

Privately, Marshall bristled at Povich's barbs, suspecting him of being a Communist. Once at a restaurant, he encountered Ethyl Povich and asked her how such a delightful woman could be married to such a disagreeable person. Publicly, after losing the libel suit, Marshall rolled with the Povich punches. "Let him rap me," he told Ed Linn of *Sport* in 1957. "The problem is when you're left out. I get more publicity from Povich—even if it's in reverse—than from any other writer in the city." Povich saw to it that Marshall continued to get "publicity," especially on the issue of racism.

Harry Wismer was another Marshall nemesis. An established radio sportscaster, Redskins minority stockholder, and cofounder of the AFL, Wismer despised and feuded with Marshall.

Like Marshall, Wismer was egotistical, brash, unpredictable, and a self-described hustler. "I always have been a hustler and I'm proud of it," he wrote in a 1965 memoir, *The Public Calls It Sport*. "No one ever gave me anything; what I made I made through my own efforts. I broke some rules, trod on some toes, gambled and risked. I thought I had all the answers. I hadn't learned that no matter how good you think you are, how shrewd you are, there is always someone down the block, across the street, in the next town, who is a little bit better, shrewder, more ruthless."

Born and raised in Port Huron, Michigan, Wismer was a talented athlete who played baseball, football, and basketball at St. John's Military Academy in Delafield, Wisconsin. After graduation in 1932, he received an athletic scholarship to play freshman football at the University of Florida, where he ingratiated himself with Coach

Charles Bachman. When Bachman took the head coaching job at Michigan State University, he took Wismer with him. When Wismer became injured and could no longer play football, Bachman got him a job broadcasting football games for the college radio station. That job morphed into an association with George "Dick" Richards, a wealthy Detroit auto dealer who owned the Detroit Lions and several radio stations.

Richards offered Wismer a job reading the late-night sports at his WJR radio station in Detroit. After his classes, Wismer would hitchhike 170 round-trip miles between Lansing and Detroit. Eventually, he dropped out of Michigan State to pursue radio work full time. Besides his ten-minute nightly sports program, he did play-by-play for the Detroit Lions and Big Ten football games, and by age twenty-five, during the heart of the Great Depression, he boasted yearly earnings of $100,000. He also enjoyed the heady experience of accompanying Richards to NFL annual meetings, where he associated with owners like George Halas and George Marshall. "Marshall, along with Halas, dominated the league," he wrote several decades later. "He is a most complex person, and anyone who one day thinks he knows the real George finds himself facing a new George the next time they meet." About the only constant in Marshall's life, Wismer maintained, was his passion for football.

Like Bachman and Richards, Marshall initially liked the young, brash, self-promoting radio announcer. Wismer provided a memorable demonstration of his hustling skills the evening before the 1940 NFL championship game between the Bears and the Redskins, when he strolled uninvited into the Griffith Stadium press room. Marshall, announcer Red Barber, and an advertising representative with the Gillette Razor Company were having a drink. "He just sat down, ordered a highball, rolled his cigar around, and started hustling," Barber recalled in his book *The Broadcasters.*

He first tried to convince the Gillette executive to permit him to join Barber for the broadcast. When that failed, he turned to Marshall, asking him if he thought it would be permissible for him to broadcast a quarter or two. Marshall answered: "It's not my decision. I've got enough problems without worrying about who's going to broadcast." Wismer next put the squeeze on Barber. "What would you say, Red—would it be all right with you if I had two quarters . . . if I had one quarter. . . . Say yes, Red." Barber gave an emphatic "No!" With a "nothing-ventured, nothing-gained" shrug, Wismer ordered another drink and dropped the issue. But two years later, Marshall hired him to broadcast Redskins games. "Washington was the seat of power and influence in the nation," Wismer once wrote, "and I wanted to be part of it."

Although criticized for talking too much during broadcasts, dropping the names of celebrities he associated with, and announcing that famous people were at the games when they were actually miles away, Wismer served as the voice of the Redskins from 1942 through 1951. During that time, he and Marshall expanded the Redskins radio network throughout the South and as far north as Albany, New York. Wismer had married Betty Bryant, the niece of Henry Ford, and he used his family connections and gift for hustling to help Marshall obtain advertisers for the games. Although he was affiliated with the Redskins, Wismer also used his family influence to obtain a minority interest in the Detroit Lions for $20,000.

In 1950, after a falling-out with Marshall over the direction of the team, tax attorney Leo DeOrsey, who had acquired a 25 percent interest in the Redskins, sold his stock to Wismer for $44,000. Wismer now held a 15 percent interest in the Lions and a 25 percent interest in the Redskins. (He would assign his Lions stock to his father-in-law and latter battle him legally for its return.)

After leaving the Redskins (he was replaced in 1952 by New York Yankees announcer Mel Allen), Wismer moved to New York, where he continued to do radio, later transitioning to television. In 1957 alone, he broadcast the NFL championship, the Pro Bowl, the Sugar Bowl, and the Masters golf tournament. "In a 20-year period I broadcast more sporting events than all other network guys put together," he told Ted Patterson, who wrote *The Golden Voices of Football*.

As the voice of the Redskins, Wismer had always put a positive spin on the team's performance and leadership. "I was one of the first of the broadcasting shills and one of the biggest," he once stated. But after leaving the Redskins and moving to New York, he refused to pull his punches. "The Redskins are the worst team in pro football history," he told listeners on his radio show over the Mutual Broadcasting System in October 1954. He lambasted the team, he told the Washington press, because as a part-owner, he wanted "to see them win more games."

As a minority owner and one of the team's three directors of the board, he personally brought his principal concerns to Marshall. First, he recommended reinstating Red Flaherty as head coach. Marshall would not consider it. Second, he decried the decision not to pay the salary of Redskins running back Vic Janowicz. Marshall refused. Third, he lamented the fact that dividends weren't paid to stockholders and accused Marshall of using team revenues for personal expenses. Marshall said revenues were not sufficient to pay stock dividends. "Our receipts are not as high as other clubs in the league," he informed the press, "but we manage to eke out a profit. Sometimes it surprises even me."

He also criticized Marshall for not hiring black players. On several occasions, according to his memoir, he advised Marshall to sign African American athletes. But Marshall was worried, Wismer asserted, about upsetting white Southern fans who might stop attending games. "He was wrong, refused to admit it, and blames all the Redskins' failures on everyone but himself." Prone to exaggeration and overstatement, Wismer's memoir must be treated cautiously. But, on at least one public occasion, in remarks before the all-black Washington Press Club in January 1957, Wismer ripped Marshall for not hiring African American players. Asked by the Press Club for a reply, Marshall refused to publicly engage "Mr. Wismer on this or any other issue. The sentiments expressed by him have no connection whatsoever with this organization."

Wismer going public with his criticisms enraged Marshall. "To be critical of Marshall in the press or over radio was to create an enemy," Wismer has written. In 1956, Marshall had him ousted as a Redskins director and demanded that Wismer sell his stock in the Redskins. Wismer not only refused, but he sued Marshall for $500,000, claiming that he had illegally used that amount of money over the years on personal expenses. Marshall labeled the charge "ludicrous." Wismer also claimed that Marshall used his influence with Tom Gallery, sports director of NBC, to sabotage his career in television sports broadcasting.

Marshall ripped into Wismer, portraying him as an ingrate, in a 1957 issue of *Sport*. Wismer was broadcasting Detroit Lions football when Redskins games "went on a national network," Marshall informed readers. "I had the choice of naming anyone I wanted and I chose Wismer. Well, I inflicted him upon the public so I'm probably only getting just retribution. For nine years, he got all the championship games, solely through me. . . . I made him a big shot and he turned around and bit me."

In 1959, Wismer further infuriated Marshall by cofounding the AFL. Not only did he own the New York Titans franchise, but he hired Sammy Baugh and other former Redskins players—Dick Todd, "Bones" Taylor, and John Steber—to coach the new team. "Harry Wismer's New York Titans of the new American Football League are taking on a deep burgundy tinge," wrote the *Post*'s Jack Walsh. Wismer riled Marshall again by saying that the AFL was considering locating an expansion team in Washington, D.C. He told the Washington Touchdown Club that the Redskins were so awful, the team theme song should be changed from "Hail to the Redskins" to "Never on Sunday." He also blasted Marshall's exclusionary racial policy. When he suggested drafting African American players once, he told *Sports Illustrated* writer Robert Boyle, Marshall allegedly replied: "I was born in West Virginia . . . and I will never play a Negro on the Redskins."

Marshall also bore a nearly homicidal hatred for Wismer because he believed his ex-wife, Corinne, had a romantic interest in him. He wrote to Corinne that Wismer, having disassociated himself from the Redskins through the sale of stock and the dismissal of the lawsuit, "is available to you for parties or anything you see fit."

Marshall's letter brought a sharp reply and some words of advice from Corinne: "I have always kept myself unspotted from any gossip because I have led as clean a life as *anyone* [is] leading, and I am certain that you, above all people, know just how decent I am. So, don't say again I can do 'anything with Wismer I see fit.' I am not interested in Harry, and Harry is not interested in me." She advised him not to let hate be his ruination. "Hate always does. But heaven knows there is no reason to hate *me*. When you insisted I marry you, I married you. When you insisted for years on a divorce, I divorced you. What more can you ask? And may I repeat, please get someone around you whose thinking is correct. With your ability and my right thinking, you became a success. Now you are surrounded with such degenerate, unprogressive thoughts that [you] are fast becoming a failure. Come on now, get your good thinking cap on and do the things you are capable of doing—now!" She concluded by instructing him to never "again accuse me of chasing with Wismer. To begin with, I don't 'chase.' I'm the old-fashioned type that believes in letting men chase me. Remember?"

Unfortunately for Wismer, the infusion of capital from the stock sale was insufficient to retain control of his financially troubled expansion football team. After three years, he lost nearly $2 million and was forced to declare bankruptcy. In March 1963, he sold the Titans to David "Sonny" Werblin for $1 million. Renamed the Jets, Werblin's team benefited from a new AFL television contract and from the transfer of its home games from the Polo Grounds to the newly constructed Shea Stadium in Queens.

Wismer, Povich wrote, was hardly a "titan of finance." But "without him there would have been no AFL. He conceived it, promoted excellent radio-tv contracts, enlisted wealthy owners for franchises in other cities, and got the league off the ground. Lacking the wealth of many of his colleagues, Wismer unfortunately could never get his own team off the ground."

Broken financially and emotionally (he would also lose his Navy pilot son in a flight-training exercise), Wismer spent his remaining days battling health problems and alcohol. Drunk, he tumbled down a set of stairs at a New York City restaurant in 1967 and died of a fractured skull at age fifty-four.

Both Povich and Wismer were openly critical of Marshall's ban against African American players; however, their efforts alone were not sufficient to effect a policy change. A hidebound racist, Marshall blithely ignored appeals for social justice and arguments that integration would improve the team's performance. Eventually, there were appeals from other influential sources, however, that Marshall could not simply ignore.

CHAPTER 7

The Black Blitz

At the conclusion of the momentous March on Washington, in August 1963, Martin Luther King Jr. confided to Bob Addie of the *Washington Post*: "I wish that I had a lot more time for sports. You people in sports have done a great job in giving the Negro equal rights, and you have achieved that without bloodshed. . . . I hope you sportswriters will remember us and help our cause." Unlike Addie, black journalists needed no reminder about a cause for which they had been fighting for decades. Writers like Sam Lacy, Wendell Smith, and Joe Bostic had been instrumental in the integration of professional baseball, while Halley Harding and Herman Hill prompted the reintegration of professional football. As victims of intolerance themselves, they championed racial equality in all sports and all facets of American life. And, as historian Jules Tygiel has pointed out in *Baseball's Great Experiment,* those and other African American writers, like the pioneering black athletes, "were victims of Jim Crow. . . . Segregation hid their considerable skills from the larger white audience and severely restricted their income-earning potential. Yet they rarely mentioned their own plight. Indeed, the barriers for black journalists lasted long after those for athletes had disappeared."

While baseball, as the then-more-popular sport, drew most of their attention, black journalists also pushed hard for the reintegration, as they put it, of professional football. Having achieved that goal in the years after World War II, several writers were incensed that the last team to desegregate was located in the democratic capital of the United States. Journalists Sam Lacy, L. I. "Brock" Brockenbury, and Brad Pye, as well as Washington community leaders E. B. Henderson and Lawrence Oxley, spearheaded the black effort to integrate the Washington Redskins.

According to journalist Michael Wilbon, Shirley Povich and Sam Lacy "were the clearest and sharpest voices in demands for racial justice on and off the field." Both men were gracious, unassuming, and approachable. Both were devoted husbands and fathers. Both were dedicated to their newspapers, worked into their nineties, and contributed columns just before dying. Both were inducted into the writer's wing of the Baseball Hall of Fame. Having access to the cultural memories of both icons, wrote Wilbon, was the "sportswriting equivalent of having Babe Ruth and Josh Gibson alive and well, writing, reporting, teaching, mentoring right up until the time they died. They are the only men before whom I genuflect as an adult."

John "Jake" Oliver, publisher of the *Baltimore Afro-American,* where Lacy worked for nearly sixty years, called him "the father of modern-day African American sportswriters." He served as a role model and inspiration for Wilbon, Ralph Wiley, Robin Roberts, William Rhoden, and dozens of others. A Lacy protege before moving to the *New York Times,* Rhoden recalled his first day of work at the *Afro-American.* He arrived at 8:30 a.m., early by his reckoning, but discovered that Lacy, always dressed in a coat and tie, had been there for three hours, as was his custom. "That was my introduction to a journalism work ethic," Rhoden wrote in a Lacy tribute. "Someone asked whether Sam showed me the ropes, but he essentially told me that there were no ropes, just a long, hard road littered with challenges. . . . If you have one great mentor in your life, consider yourself lucky. I was blessed. I had Sam Lacy."

Lacy also enjoyed the respect of most white sportswriters, especially those at East Coast dailies. When he was denied access to the press box and forced to sit on the stadium roof during a late 1940s spring training game in New Orleans, several Eastern sportswriters joined him, on the pretext that they had to improve their tans. Lacy also became the first black sportswriter to be admitted to the Baseball Writers Association in 1948. Lacy's death brought tributes from the *Washington Post*'s William Gildea and George Solomon, with Gildea calling him "one of the greatest sportswriters in American history."

Although there is some disagreement about the date and location of Lacy's birth, he was raised in the early 1900s with three siblings in an upper-middle-class neighborhood near Griffith Stadium. Short and slender, he "was built to carry a pen," wrote one of his colleagues, "but wanted to carry a football." At Armstrong High School, he played baseball, football, and basketball. He also worked an assortment of jobs—waiter, bowling alley pin setter, shoeshiner, and golf caddy. In 1921, he shouldered the bag of Jim Barnes, who won the U.S. Open.

During the Washington Senators' baseball season, he worked at Griffith Stadium as a batting practice ball retriever, vendor, and general errand runner for the players. Like his father, he became an avid fan of the Senators, but being a black fan came with indignities, like having to sit in segregated seating in right field; or having to listen to Arch McDonald, a racially insensitive Senators radio broadcaster, saying, "there goes one into the coal pile," when a home run or foul ball was hit into the black seating section. On another occasion, during a parade for the Senators before the 1924 World Series, Sam's father stood on a street corner displaying a badge given to him years earlier by Walter Johnson. It read: "I saw Walter Johnson Pitch His First Game—1907." A passing Senators player, pitcher Nick Altrock, looked at Lacy Sr. and spit in his face. That humiliating incident, however, did not keep father and son from Senators games. "One thing I never quite figured out about my father," Lacy wrote in his autobiography, *Fighting For Fairness,* "was why he refused to go see the all-white Redskins play but was a regular in the Jim Crow Pavilion to take in games of the all-white Senators." (Historian Brad Snyder, in *Beyond the Shadow of the Senators,* says that the elder Lacy grew weary of the Senators' ban against blacks and stopped attending games in 1946.)

After his high school graduation, Lacy spent the next two decades working as a sports journalist for several black newspapers. He joined the *Baltimore Afro-American* in 1944 and remained there as sports editor until his death in 2003. Established in 1892, the *Afro-American* controlled sister papers in Washington, Philadelphia, Newark, and Richmond, and was one of the most respected and widely read black weeklies. Lacy's chatty "A to Z" column was read by thousands of readers each week for decades.

During the late 1930s and through the war years, Lacy pushed hard for the integration of Major League Baseball. Having played sandlot and semipro baseball himself, and having watched the Homestead Grays play rivals in the Negro Baseball League at Griffith Stadium, he realized that several black players were capable of playing in the big leagues. He urged Clark Griffith, owner of the Senators, to hire black athletes. When that failed, he asked baseball commissioner Kennesaw Landis and all major-league owners to integrate the game. And when the Brooklyn Dodgers' Branch Rickey sought his input on qualified black players in 1945, he recommended Jackie Robinson. Lacy and most other African American journalists relegated football to secondary status. Professional baseball had far more historical and social standing. It appeared to be more economically stable than football and paid its players higher salaries. There was even some doubt among the black press that professional football would ever rival college football in popularity. There was also no real equivalent in football to the Negro Leagues in baseball for showcasing black talent. Baseball, too, had a longer tradition of segregation, so toppling that racial barrier seemed a loftier goal. And, once the barrier in baseball fell, those in football and other professional sports would eventually follow.

The *Afro-American* gave scant attention to the Senators and Redskins, preferring to cover the Homestead Grays of the Negro Leagues and the blacks who played football at the local high school, semipro, and college levels. Black weeklies in cities such as Pittsburgh, Philadelphia, Chicago, and New York followed a similar pattern. When the Redskins announced the move to Washington in 1936, the black press ignored the story because black players had been banned from the NFL. Instead of reporting on the Redskins, Lacy heralded the success of blacks like Brud Holland and Ozzie Simmons, who played at predominantly white colleges. If whites and blacks could get along on the field, he reasoned, they could get along off the field. Moreover, if blacks could excel in mainstream college programs, they might gain a shot in the NFL someday.

In the late 1930s, Lacy gained some notoriety when he divulged that Syracuse University quarterback Wilmeth Sidat-Singh was black, not East Asian. Sidat-Singh, he reported, was born to African American parents in Washington, D.C., but he took the name of his adopted father when his widowed mother remarried. When the University of Maryland learned that Sidat-Singh was black, it asked Syracuse to bench him for their game. Syracuse complied and lost its first game of the season. Some blacks argued that Lacy should have waited until after the game to break his story. But to Lacy, "[S]uch a contention seems to be a weak-livered admission that we're willing to see our boys progress under any kind of masquerade; that we agree with the Nordic observation that ANYTHING BUT A NEGRO is okay."

Following the fall of the "Nordic Curtain" in professional baseball and football after World War II, Lacy worked to integrate all sports at all levels of play. He praised major colleges that preferred to cancel games rather than bench black players against Southern opponents. In a weekly autumn column, "On the Mixed Grids," he familiarized readers with black college stars, like Levi Jackson, Emlen Tunnell, and Buddy Young, who deserved to play professionally. He was especially high on Young, whom he helped persuade to turn professional rather than return to the University of Illinois. "The 21-year-old comet from Chicago is, perhaps, America's No. 3 athlete," he wrote. "Next to Joe Louis and Jackie Robinson, no other competitor in the nation commands the headline respect that goes to Buddy. . . . If his skin were of a different hue . . . he could write his own ticket."

Citing the success of the Brooklyn Dodgers in baseball and the Cleveland Browns in football, Lacy pushed for the inclusion of more blacks in those and other sports. Teams with African American players, he noted, generally outperformed those without. With more black players, the All-America Football Conference (AAFC) drew far more attention than the NFL from Lacy and other African American journalists. Lacy expressed skepticism when the AAFC's Miami franchise was transferred to Baltimore in 1947. The Colts agreed to play against black players, unlike the Miami team, but Lacy feared they would never have an African American on their roster because Baltimore was as racially intolerant as Miami or Washington, D.C. He was encouraged when Colts owner Abe Watner committed to hiring a black player for the 1950 season. When he had failed to honor that commitment by the start of the season, Lacy took him to task. Watner claimed that he had wanted to obtain Marion Motley, George Taliaferro, or Buddy Young, but couldn't arrange a deal. There were no other qualified players, he claimed. Lacy was incredulous. What professional team wouldn't want three of the most talented players in the league? he asked. Surely, the hapless Colts could set their sights a bit lower. Eventually, in mid-October, the team signed guard Ollie Fletcher.

Fletcher's signing pleased Lacy, but not some Colts fans. Watner told Lacy that news of the contract "brought a flood of blasphemous telegrams, letters, and phone calls" from incensed white patrons who "cussed me out for, as they put it, trying to change the Maryland way of life." A few, he continued, "warned me that for every additional colored fan the Colts picked up as a result of the move, we would lose ten white patrons." With a dismal record and declining fan base, the Colts disbanded after the 1950 season.

But the team resurfaced in 1953 when Carroll Rosenbloom acquired the lapsed Dallas team and transferred it to Baltimore. Unlike Marshall, Rosenbloom was progressive on racial matters, recruited African American players, and transformed the team into an NFL powerhouse. Rosenbloom also fought to protect black players from indignities. In 1954, when the Lord Baltimore Hotel refused to seat four of his players for a team dinner, he had the team headquarters switched to another hotel.

During the late 1940s and early 1950s, Sam Lacy did not cover the Redskins, probably hoping that Marshall would integrate the team without prodding. When Lacy did speak out publicly in the mid-1950s, he chastised black fans more than Marshall. "Isn't it about time colored fans were waking up to the Washington Redskins?" he wrote in a September 1956 column. "Wonder whether those tan folk who flock to Griffith Stadium to see the town's pro gridders in action, are aware that theirs is the only team in the National Football League that has NEVER shown any inclination whatsoever to pick up one of the many colored players who each year become eligible for professional contracts." "There was a time when this column was proud of its Washington D.C. birthright," he wrote three months later, "but not anymore. Washingtonians who used to look down their noses at people who made themselves content with indignities of the deep South should now hang their heads in shame. . . . Alabama and Florida and Texas colored folk would no more continue patronizing a football club whose membership acted as do the Washington Redskins, than they would flap their arms and try flying to Catalina."

When the Philadelphia Phillies baseball team announced its intent to sign a black player, Lacy scoffed. "It is hard to say which is worst," he wrote, "to brag year in and year out that you're anxious to integrate, or just ignore the subject completely and not bother to even suggest that a qualified colored player would be acceptable . . . like the Washington Redskins."

Harry Wismer's public protest against the Redskins' hiring policies prompted a response by Lacy. When Marshall refused to meet with him, he sent a telegram asking if Wismer's allegations were true and if the owner was concerned that blacks might boycott games at Griffith Stadium. Marshall said that Wismer "simply is not telling the truth" and dismissed the threat of a boycott, saying that "any citizen has a right to avoid any event he does not care to attend."

Marshall's indifferent response infuriated Lacy. "Marshall's team is the ONLY ONE in the National Football League that has NEVER shown interest in qualified colored players," he fumed. He informed readers that he had not attended a Redskins game since 1950, "NOT EVEN FOR FREE." And he would not attend games in the future until the team was integrated. He also announced plans to boycott the Palace Laundry, apparently unaware that Marshall had sold the business a decade earlier. Throughout the 1950s, Lacy berated blacks who continued to pour into Griffith Stadium. True, some attended games to watch visiting black athletes, but their purchase of tickets gave Marshall the economic wherewithal to maintain his racial barrier.

Almost always shrewd when it came to making money and promoting his product, Marshall understood that in Washington in the fall, he had the best show in town. In addition to a professional football game, fans were entertained by a variety show at halftime. And from the beginnings of the team, in 1937, black fans could avoid the humiliation of segregated seating. Griffith Stadium was one of the few public entertainment arenas in Washington and in the entire South that was completely open to African Americans, and they took advantage of it.

Lacy once asked an old family friend, a season ticketholder, why he continued to attend Redskins games. The friend said that he loved football and rooted for the opposing team, and staying away would do no good. "If I didn't go to the football games, what would I do for enjoyment?" That response probably reflected the attitude of most black fans. But that position troubled Lacy. Fans, he said, could listen to the games on radio and watch away games on television without supporting Marshall. And what if black bus commuters in Montgomery, Alabama, had taken that approach instead of opposing segregated seating with a boycott? What if those seven black teenagers who integrated the public school system in Little Rock, Arkansas, had put convenience ahead of principle and dignity?

Lacy sought reader input on the Redskins' color ban. Published over a month in four installments, the letters comprised four categories. A few defended Marshall on the grounds that, in a free-enterprise economy, an employer could hire whomever he pleased. Others castigated Marshall for clinging to outdated racial views. Besides excluding black athletes from the team, wrote one man, "His frequent use of black-faced comedians in his halftime shows, the singing of 'd. . . . y' [darky] songs by his choral group, his employment of white vendors instead of regular Griffith Stadium employees for the relatively lucrative sale of programs, and his game-opening format which consists of the playing of 'Hail to the Redskins,' 'Dixie,' and the 'National Anthem,' in that order, are among the other ways in which his racial attitudes are expressed." Others, like Lacy's friend the season ticketholder, claimed that staying away would not force Marshall's hand. And still other readers demanded a boycott of games until Marshall integrated the team. "Why would any self-respecting person support a team that will not use a colored player, regardless of how well he is qualified to play?" wrote a Virginian. "If I were still living in Washington," wrote United Nations undersecretary Ralph Bunche, "I would . . . studiously avoid giving my patronage to any of Mr. Marshall's enterprises."

Frustrated by Marshall's "inscrutable, bigoted, rude affronts," other letter writers wrote the owner directly to ask if he ever planned to hire minority athletes. Marshall's reply to one such inquiry, which Lacy quoted in a September 1957 column, was not encouraging. "Your problem seems to be not that there are colored football players appearing at Griffith Stadium, but that there are none on the Redskins," Marshall wrote. "We have never shown any discrimination against anyone regarding tickets or who appears there. . . . That attitude, I think, would be satisfactory to most people. Tickets are on sale. . . . If you or any of your friends are interested, we would be glad to accommodate you." In other words, blacks should be content to watch visiting African Americans play at an integrated venue.

By the late 1950s, Lacy, like Povich, grew more strident in his attacks on Marshall. Learning that fans at home games burst out with rebel yells after the playing of the Redskins fight song, he shared one New York writer's opinion that the nickname of the team should be changed to the "Washington Confederates" or the "Washington Lily-Whites." When the mainstream press reported that Joe Kuharich had been given a five-year coaching contract with expanded powers, Lacy learned from the coach that increased authority did not include hiring minority players. He was also astounded when Marshall told *Sport* that he didn't hire minority athletes because he did not want to "exploit" them as Major League Baseball did. In an article entitled "Million Dollar Exploitation," Lacy pointed out that in 1958 major-league African American baseball players collectively would earn approximately $630,000 and minor-league black players would earn another $370,000. If that was "exploitation," he concluded, "here's my plate. Please pass some morsel."

In 1958, after the Redskins lost to the Cleveland Browns in a game in which Jim Brown set the NFL single-season rushing record, *Washington Post* sports editor Bus Ham observed: "Too bad . . . there's only one Jim Brown in professional football and the Redskins can't get him." Lacy jumped on that comment, pointing out that with the second overall pick in the 1957 NFL draft, the Redskins could have taken Brown of Syracuse or Ohio State guard Jim Parker, but the team passed on both in favor of Don Bosseler, a white fullback from the University of Miami. "The fact that Brown and Parker were All-Americans didn't mean as much to the Skins' owner as did the fact that they were colored." Both black players became transcendent at their positions and were inducted into the Pro Football Hall of Fame.

Lacy also pointed out that, in 1958, the Redskins invited University of the Pacific tackle John Thomas, an undrafted free agent, to a tryout at their camp at Occidental College, in California. When Thomas showed up and the coaches discovered he was black, they informed him that they had no openings. Thomas went on to play ten years for the San Francisco 49ers.

When Jackie Robinson ripped the Boston Red Sox in early 1959 for never having hired a black player, Lacy used that attention-grabbing moment to criticize Marshall further. While the Red Sox front office had clearly practiced racism, he said, at least it had belatedly come around to the idea of integration. "There is only one difference between the Redskins and the Red Sox as we see it from here. . . . The Washington hierarchy of George Preston Marshall makes no pretense of desiring tan athletes."

With tongue in cheek, Lacy gave credit to Marshall in early 1961 for getting choice draft picks each year because his team had performed poorly. His early picks did not worry other owners, however, because they knew he would never select a premier black player. They, in turn, were busy scouting African American players at predominantly white colleges, and increasingly from black colleges as well. Fifty-five black athletes played professional football in 1960, Lacy noted—none with the Redskins. "This column has never advocated suicide, but in GPM's [Marshall's] case, it would be readily forgivable."

Edwin Bancroft (E. B.) Henderson, a respected black Washington community leader, also began speaking out against Marshall's racist hiring policy. Henderson spent his life teaching, coaching, refereeing, and advocating for racial toleration. The grandson of a slave, he was born in southwest Washington, D.C., in 1883. After a brief move to Pittsburgh, his middle-class parents returned to Washington, where E. B. was raised and educated. A precocious, talkative, athletic child with a sunny disposition, he was popular among schoolmates and teachers.

He spent his summers with his former slave grandmother in Falls Church, Virginia, about ten miles from Washington. There, he witnessed a confrontation that inspired him for a lifetime. While seated on the steps of the town feed store, he recalled to the *Afro-American* fifty years later, he saw a black cavalry officer ride by toward Fort Alger. At the same time, a white Virginia enlisted man said to a companion: "I'll never salute a damned Nigger." The cavalry officer turned his horse around and ordered the white soldier to salute, reminding him that he was honoring not a man, but the U.S. Army. The white soldier obeyed, and Henderson went home a proud young boy.

After graduating from the M Street School (later Dunbar High School), Henderson went to college at the Miner Normal School to become a teacher, and later he attended Harvard, where he learned that Massachusetts was not free from racial discrimination. Ostensibly free to go wherever he wanted, he once made the mistake of entering a white-owned barbershop in Harvard Square. There, as a joke, a Southern-born barber cut a wide furrow from the back of his skull to his forehead. Henderson never went to another white barber. Soon after his 1910 marriage to schoolteacher Nellie Meriwether, Henderson moved to Falls Church, where he spent most of the rest of his life. As an educator, coach, and NAACP member, Henderson devoted himself to combating what he called "racial fascism," especially in the nation's capital. In speeches and in hundreds, if not thousands, of letters to the black and mainstream press, he lashed out at segregated District schools, department stores, trade unions, transit companies, the fire department, the National Theatre, Uline Arena, playgrounds, boys' clubs, and swimming pools. Henderson insisted that the best way to achieve racial toleration was through interracial sports competition. "More than any other factor it is the field of competitive sports that American youth learns the true spirit of America," he once wrote. "Millions of people on Saturdays and Sundays as spectators of major college and professional football learn vicariously the lessons of tolerance and fair play."

With World War II shadowing the United States in 1940, Henderson, curiously enough, saw signs of racial progress during a Redskins game at Griffith Stadium. While glancing at the somber faces of fans during the playing of the national anthem, "one could not help thinking that every man, woman, and child sensed the oncoming possible destruction of civilization," he wrote in a letter to the editor of the *Washington Post* headlined "Democracy and Football." Henderson continued, "In this setting, we have democracy at its best. Crowded and packed together, Jew and Gentile, black and white, thrilled and slumped with the fortunes of Marshall's Indians. That's how it is not in Germany and Italy." Yet, Americans should not feel too superior to Nazis, he wrote. "This country must soon realize that until discrimination based on color, creed, or race in all public relations are abolished, we, too, are but a little better off in our practices than those of the condemned totalitarian regime abroad." While sharing Henderson's positive sentiments about the integrated crowd, a fellow letter writer reminded him, "Democracy will be at its best only when you can look down on the playing field and see Jew and Gentile, black and white, playing side by side. When we witness that spectacle we will have reached a level of democracy of which we will be proud."

While pleased by the desegregation of professional baseball and football, blacks after the war experienced mixed results in their struggle for racial equality. In Washington, D.C., Swedish actress Ingrid Bergman was shocked to learn in 1946 that blacks could not attend her stage performance at George Washington University. "And this in the Capital City, too," she said.

Like Lacy, Henderson grew exasperated with black fans who supported Marshall's lily-white team. Writing as a special correspondent for the Negro Press Association in October 1952, he urged Washingtonians to boycott both the Senators and Redskins. He repeated the call for a boycott against the Redskins a decade later. "It seems to me that it is high time for colored fans to stop paying money into the white-Redskins treasury," he wrote the *Baltimore Afro-American* in January 1961. Marshall, he said, had made it clear that he did not intend to sign African American athletes. In the recent draft, thirty-eight black players had been selected; the Redskins took none. "I realize that many of us like football and some go these Redskins home games mainly because they want to see colored boys play on the visiting teams. To refrain from attending would be a genuine hardship for them," he continued. "But when we note the thousands of young people throughout the South risking life and limb and going to jail rather than submit to the indignity of racial discrimination, why should we not be able to deny ourselves the luxury of supporting Marshall's racism? . . . To me it is a tragedy when intelligent people, in this day of moving forward, persist in buying humiliation with their hard-earned dollars."

Another black community leader who decried Marshall's racial intolerance was Lawrence A. Oxley. A social worker from Raleigh, North Carolina, Oxley established a model program in the mid-1920s to help blacks deal with unemployment, poverty, child abuse, and other social problems. In 1934, he joined the Department of Labor to focus on finding jobs for unemployed African Americans. In the 1950s, Oxley served as president of the Washington Pigskin Club, the black counterpart of the Washington Touchdown Club. Organized in 1938, the Pigskin Club was made up of former football players, mostly African Americans, who loved the sport and honored contributions to it at an annual awards dinner in Washington. E.B. Henderson was a charter member and the longtime club archivist.

As Pigskin Club president, Oxley censured both the Washington

Senators and Redskins for their "disgraceful anti-racial policies." He had spoken with Marshall, he reported to Sam Lacy in 1957, but had come away exasperated. "I realized I was insulting my intelligence in talking with him." He continued, "There is no question in my mind that the Redskins and the Senators do not want colored players . . . and that they do not want my money . . . yet I love sports." He recommended a black boycott against the team similar to the successful one used by Rosa Parks's supporters to combat the segregated bus service in Montgomery, Alabama. He also issued public statements denouncing Marshall. "When Dixie is played instead of the Star Spangled Banner at a football game or any other place," he declared, "we know what the score is. We await the day when Marshall comes to a realization of what democracy in sports means."

While a general black boycott of Redskins games was slow to materialize, in 1957 the Washington, D.C., chapter of the NAACP initiated a two-day protest against Marshall's discriminatory hiring policy outside the Philadelphia hotel where the NFL held its annual meeting. Several picketers also carried signs outside Griffith Stadium denouncing Marshall's racism, but without much effect. Lacy reported that some black players, led by Ollie Matson, were considering demonstrating against Marshall's hiring policy at the NFL owners' meeting in Philadelphia. But that rumor proved false. The players in 1959, white and black alike, were far more interested in getting the owners to recognize their union and in obtaining a more equitable share of income, especially from the Pro Bowl.

The strongest protest against the Redskins occurred on the West Coast. African American writers, particularly those with the *Los Angeles Sentinel,* pummeled Marshall. *Sentinel* sportswriters took an interest in the Redskins because the team trained at nearby Occidental College and played an annual charity exhibition game against the Rams. Moreover, in 1946, journalists for the *Sentinel,* in concert with civic officials, had forced the Los Angeles Rams to integrate to play games at the Los Angeles Coliseum.

But Marshall did have his defenders, in a "damning with faint praise" kind of way. *Sentinel* sports editor Halley Harding maintained that Marshall hated just about everyone, not just blacks.

Marshall's West Coast defenders, like Melvin Durslag, the white writer with the *Los Angeles Examiner,* portrayed Marshall as a colorful nonconformist. "Marshall, to start with, is no bigot," he wrote in 1961. Rather, he was an independent-minded owner who would not be told how to run his business. Harding painted him as mulish and mean. He told the story of a farmer who advertised a prize mule for sale. A prospective buyer visited the farm to inspect the animal. When the farmer opened the gate, the mule bolted through, crashing into a fence, then off a stone wall, and finally into a big tree. "I can't purchase that mule," said the buyer, "he's blind." "He's not blind," the farmer responded. "He just doesn't give a damn." Harding concluded that "those people we thought were prejudiced were probably just ornery to start and end with. We gave them too much credit for having real brains and the ability to be reasoned with. Now it turns out that most of those cats just don't like anybody."

Harding's sportswriting successors at the *Sentinel,* L. I. "Brock" Brockenbury and Brad Pye, gave Marshall no quarter, painting him as a racist and a scourge on the game. A native of Plain Dealing, a one-traffic-light town near Shreveport, Louisiana, Pye ran away from home at the age of twelve. He paid an older acquaintance $5 to drive him to southern California, where he was raised in East Los Angeles by kind-hearted strangers. After graduating from Thomas Jefferson High School, he attended college, first East Los Angeles College and then, after a stint in the Marines, California State College. He played football at both schools. After graduating from college, he was hired by the *Sentinel,* eventually launching a column called "The Prying Pye," and rising to sports editor in the mid-1950s. His associate, L. I. "Brock" Brokenbury, was a tax accountant who also contributed columns to the paper. The two colleagues were contrasts. Pye was slight of frame; Brock was a mountainous man weighing more than three hundred pounds. Pye was quiet and reserved. "I was afraid of white folks," he told me. Brock, on the other hand, was brash, assertive, and intimidating.

But the men were equally assertive in their newspaper columns. They lambasted the Rams for scheduling charity exhibition games against the team of "Negro hater" Marshall. Not only did the Rams have to play the snow-white Redskins in Los Angeles, but they also scheduled games in Southern cities like Mobile, Alabama, where African American Rams players could not stay or eat with their teammates. "Why in the hell did the Rams agree to this game in the first place?" asked Pye. "They bring these Washington Redskins here every year to insult their Negro customers in the first game of the season."

When shaming did not bring results, Brockenbury and Pye considered proposing a boycott of the charity game in 1958. But Paul Schissler, the director of the charity game, who had coached Joe Lillard with the Chicago Cardinals, convinced black community leaders to forgo a demonstration. A boycott, he said, would mainly hurt the poor children, black and white, who would benefit from the proceeds of the charity game. Schissler would meet with Marshall, he said, to try to get him to hire a black player. When Pye asked him if he believed Marshall would ever hire a black athlete, he said, "I would think so. He once told me to 'Get me another Kenny Washington and I will have him right on this team.'" Of course, the year previously, Marshall had a chance to draft Jim Brown and had refused. Black leaders voted to let Schissler try to reason with Marshall, but they felt guilty for doing so. "We hope that members of our ethnic group in Washington D.C. and other cities around the league where the Redskins have been picketed don't think we are letting them down." Brockenbury summed up the view of most community blacks when he wrote that Schissler "knows that George Preston Marshall is plain no-good on the Negro question and that all the talking to Marshall he has promised to do will avail nothing as far as getting that gentleman (?) to use Negro players." There is no evidence to indicate that Schissler ever approached Marshall about integration.

Hopes climbed for Redskins integration in 1959, when the Boston Red Sox, the last Major League Baseball team without a black player, signed Pumpsie Green. "Will the lilywhite Washington Redskins follow suit?" asked Pye. The answer was no. Marshall, contended Brockenbury, "has made it clear that he doesn't intend to hire Negroes so long as there is breath in his body" and "has already resigned himself to never winning the championship S.I. (since integration)."

Like black fans in Washington, D.C., African Americans in Los Angeles wanted to watch a professional football exhibition game, but they felt guilty about condoning racism. "Because George Preston Marshall, the confirmed hater of Negro football players, brings his Redskins here Friday night, I want to stay home," wrote Brockenbury in August 1959. "But I want even more to see what the 'new' Rams are going to look like against some opposition."

Pye and Brockenbury hoped that Pete Rozelle, who was named NFL commissioner in 1960, might "shake Marshall loose from his pre–Civil War beliefs." When Rozelle refused to intervene, they urged direct action by the black community. They recommended finding a legal loophole to break the annual charity game contract, or else conducting a boycott and donating to charity the money that otherwise would have been spent on tickets and concessions. "There should be no place in the 20th century for people who will deny any American, no matter what the pigmentation of his skin might be, the right for equal employment," wrote Pye in August 1960. Two months later, the American people elected a president who shared that sentiment. But would he take action against Marshall's Redskins?

CHAPTER 8

The New Frontier

Despite frigid temperatures and a heavy blanket of snow, Washingtonians were flush with Potomac fever in mid-January 1961. They, as well as their fellow Americans, anxiously awaited the inauguration of their newly elected president, John F. Kennedy. He was charismatic, handsome, and young, the first president born in the twentieth century and the youngest elected to office. During the campaign, he had pledged a New Frontier–a promise to get the nation moving again after eight years of Republican inertia. Abuzz with excitement, citizens looked forward to learning how JFK proposed to move the country forward during the next four years.

In early 1961, however, Washington Redskins fans and blacks in general had little reason to believe that the incoming Kennedy administration would challenge George Marshall's racial hiring policy. The previous Eisenhower administration had taken few executive initiatives in the area of civil rights. And given the conservative, conformist thrust of the 1950s, there was scant support for federal interference in social or economic affairs. Moreover, there was little in Kennedy's background to give civil rights leaders much hope for federal action.

Born to privilege in Brookline, Massachusetts, John Kennedy had little contact with African Americans at the Choate preparatory school, at Harvard University, in the U.S. Navy, or in the U.S. Congress. *New York Times* columnist and family associate Arthur Krock observed that he "never saw a Negro on level social terms with the Kennedys. And I never heard the subject mentioned." When Kennedy was elected to the House of Representatives in 1946, he hired George Thomas, Krock's black valet, who remained with Kennedy until the end. Kennedy also employed a black office secretary, Virginia Battle. That appeared to be the extent of JFK's familiarity with blacks.

As a presidential candidate in 1960, JFK was initially suspect among black leaders because of his undistinguished civil rights record. But he courted their support by adding black advisers to his campaign staff and by giving exclusive interviews with black newspapers. The next president, he told the *Pittsburgh Courier* in late June, must exert moral leadership. "This means achieving equal opportunity in all parts of our public life for all Americans regardless of race or color. This requires equal access to the voting booth, to the schoolroom, to jobs, to housing—and to lunch counters."

At their July convention in Los Angeles, Democrats sanctioned nonviolent demonstrations against racial injustice and crafted a strong civil rights plank that called for executive action against discrimination in hiring and housing and legislation against voting literacy tests and segregation in public places. "Above all," the plank read, racial progress "will require the strong, active, persuasive, and inventive leadership of the President of the United States."

Once nominated, with Senator Lyndon Johnson of Texas as his running mate, Kennedy sought to balance doing the right thing with doing a thing right. Advocating racial equality would be morally correct and would appeal to blacks whose votes might be decisive in a close election. But would it be politically expedient? Pushing too hard might alienate white voters, especially in the traditionally solid Democratic South. Indeed, Senator Richard Russell of Georgia said: "I devoutly hope and pray that Divine Providence will give us the strength and wisdom to save our Southland from the evil threat of the Platform adopted at Los Angeles."

In his first televised debate with his Republican opponent, Richard Nixon, JFK pointed out the social, economic, and political hurdles facing black citizens. "We can do better," he asserted. Racial discrimination also bruised our image abroad, he insisted. How could the United States win the ideological battle against communism, especially in Africa, when it clung to a form of apartheid in the American South? Why were there only twenty-three African Americans among six thousand U.S. Foreign Service employees? Through executive action, he said, more minorities could fill positions in the federal government. The president's authority could also be used to end discrimination in federally assisted housing.

To blacks, Kennedy seemed more interested in attracting their votes than Nixon was. Unlike Nixon, JFK campaigned in Harlem, where he reiterated his call for executive action. He pointed out that no matter how intelligent or well-schooled, a black child had little chance of being a federal appeals court judge because none had ever been appointed. He also demonstrated concern for the safety of Martin Luther King Jr. who had been jailed in Georgia for civil disobedience and a minor traffic violation. Kennedy called King's wife, Coretta, to express his concern, and Robert Kennedy, the president's brother and former federal attorney, used his influence with Georgia's governor, Ernest Vandiver, to gain King's release. JFK's telephone call to Coretta King was cheered in the black press. Kennedy's campaign staff distributed a pamphlet to black churches and other organizations that contrasted JFK's sensitivity to civil rights with Nixon's indifference. Kennedy's humane act also won over Rev. Martin Luther King Sr., who earlier had announced his support for Nixon because Kennedy was a Catholic. JFK later expressed his annoyance with King's anti-Catholicism to campaign adviser Harris Wofford. "He said that he was going to vote against me because I was Catholic. Now he is going to vote for me just because I called his daughter-in-law. That's a helluva bigoted thing to say, wasn't it?" Wofford concurred. Smiling, JFK then said: "Well, we all have fathers, don't we?"

While Nixon received public support from Jackie Robinson, Kennedy was backed by Willie Mays, Hank Aaron, Elgin Baylor, and Bobby Mitchell. "What I want to see in the White House," said Chicago Cardinals running back Willie Gallimore, "is a man who can score for our side. . . . Kennedy is that man."

Blacks, with good cause, attributed Kennedy's narrow victory to their votes. Consequently, they had high expectations for his presidency. Blacks had supported the Democratic candidate, the *Baltimore Afro-American* editorialized, because "we confidently believe that under Mr. Kennedy America will at last come of age, making a reality the long promise of the democratic ideal." Most African Americans, wrote Simeon Booker in *Ebony,* "look to the Kennedy era to become the most hopeful, the most encouraging period for racial progress in U.S. history." Martin Luther King Jr., addressing an Emancipation Day rally in Chattanooga, Tennessee, pointed out that "we are expecting him to use the whole weight of his office to remove the heavy weight of segregation from our shoulders." Lincoln's Emancipation Proclamation, he continued, was an executive order. "We must remind Kennedy that when he gets the pen in his hand, we expect him to write a little with it."

Presidents, as historian Thomas Sugrue reminds, "do not govern alone." Preoccupied with foreign policy, JFK left most domestic matters, including civil rights, in the hands of his White House staff and cabinet. One cabinet member, Secretary of the Interior Stewart Udall, did not figure to be a significant player in the drive for racial justice because his responsibilities dealt principally with national parks, Native Americans, and public lands. So when he confronted George Marshall about his racist hiring practices, it came as a jaw-dropping event.

Stewart Udall, the man responsible for the sudden move against the Redskins, was himself a bit of a surprise choice as interior secretary. Although the post typically went to a Westerner, Udall was not especially well known among senior Democratic officials, and his home state of Arizona had voted for Nixon in the 1960 election. But he was young, liberal, and gung-ho for Kennedy and the New Frontier program. A forty-one-year-old Democrat from St. Johns, Arizona, Stewart Udall had been elected to four terms in the U.S. House of Representatives prior to his appointment as secretary of the Interior. As a member of Congress, he had endeared himself to many Washingtonians by championing home rule—an elected government for the District. Although that legislation failed, mainly because Southern legislators recoiled at the prospect of African Americans governing the capital, home-rule supporters appreciated his effort. "The hard-fighting legislator from Tucson," the *Washington Post* editorialized in June 1960, "might be designated public servant of the year in the District." The following year, the *Post* hailed his appointment as interior secretary. "Washingtonians have a particular interest in Mr. Udall—first, because of his valiant work on behalf of home rule; and second, because the Department of the Interior is intimately involved in park and other programs."

Udall descended from a pioneering Mormon family dedicated to public service. His father, Levi, an elected Arizona supreme court justice, left his children "with the feeling that the finest thing a person could do was render public service," Udall informed a *Detroit News* journalist. His father also instilled in him a belief that the right to vote took precedence in a democracy because it protected all other rights. That belief prompted his support of home rule for Washington, D.C., and federal protection of black voting rights in the South. He interrupted his college education to perform two years of service as a Mormon missionary in Pennsylvania, and then he joined the Army Air Corps, serving as a gunner on a B-24 in Italy during World War II. After the war, he returned to the University of Arizona, where he completed his bachelor's degree and, as a 5'11" guard, helped lead the basketball team to a successful season. One of eight teams invited to participate in the 1946 National Invitation Tournament at Madison Square Garden in New York, the Arizonans lost in the first round to the University of Kentucky, the eventual tournament winner.

After graduating, Udall obtained a University of Arizona law degree, married Ermalee Webb, fathered six children, opened a Tucson law practice with his younger brother Morris, and made a successful run for the U.S. House of Representatives. He also lapsed in his religious faith, becoming a self-described "Jack-Mormon," who did not adhere to the dictates against alcohol and caffeine consumption. Udall's commitment to racial equality also ran counter to his church's abysmal civil rights record. That commitment, he informed me, came about when, as a serviceman during World War II, he noted the irony of African Americans in the U.S. military fighting to preserve democracy abroad in segregated units.

In Congress, Udall had enjoyed only a casual relationship with Kennedy, but he was impressed by JFK's intellect, charisma, and grace under pressure. He became an early supporter of Kennedy's bid for the presidential nomination and delivered Arizona's seventeen delegate votes. Grateful, Kennedy rewarded Udall by appointing him Secretary of the Interior.

As a cabinet member, Udall enjoyed a trusted but reserved relationship with JFK. "My relations with President Kennedy and with the White House were not everything, looking back, that I would have them to be," he recalled. Overall, Kennedy provided inspirational leadership, he said, but he wished that the president "had concentrated more on domestic ills and on changing our national priorities—and less on the clashes of the Cold War." Kennedy referred to his presidency as the New Frontier to symbolize his goal of getting the country moving again, meeting new foreign and domestic challenges and fulfilling the democratic ideal of equal opportunity for all.

As the steward of the nation's conservation program, Udall was disappointed that Kennedy was not more enthusiastic about the outdoors and wild landscapes. Growing up in a near-frontier setting, Udall developed a passion for hiking, fishing, camping, and other outdoor activities. In many ways, he embodied the image of the youthful, athletic, vigorous New Frontiersman more than Kennedy did. True, Kennedy loved the sea and sailing, but, at heart, he was a city boy with urbane tastes. "I long for a flicker of emotion, a response to the out of doors and overwhelming majesty of the land," Udall wrote privately about JFK in his journal. "There is such a thing as having a poetic feeling about the land. Even a politician can have it. . . . The chief lacks it, I'm sorry to say." Udall longed to be part of Kennedy's inner circle, but he never was. Kennedy's failure to invite him to socialize, even when they traveled together, caused Udall to wonder privately whether the rumors were true about Kennedy's sexual indiscretions. "Why doesn't he invite me or the senators to come down to his room for a chat or a visit–that would be the normal thing to do," he wrote after one trip to the West. Was it reserve, he wondered, or was "something being concealed?"

President John F. Kennedy and Secretary of the Interior Stewart Udall at the White House in 1961. (Stewart Udall Papers, Special Collections, courtesy of University of Arizona Libraries)

For Kennedy, Udall was too much the Boy Scout, which, in fact, he had been. He was zealous, serious, outdoorsy, and consumed by causes—engaging the outdoors, preserving wild places, expanding the national park system, patronizing the arts, making better use of the cabinet. But Kennedy liked Udall and enjoyed teasing him. When Udall identified a mountain he had climbed as being located in Afghanistan instead of Pakistan, JFK said to a visiting Pakistani dignitary: "That's why I named him Secretary of the *Interior*." When Udall once asked him what his reaction would be if he saw Udall tackle a woman the president wanted to avoid, JFK said: "Don't worry, Stewart, if I ever see you on the ground with a woman, I'll give you the benefit of the doubt."

Udall's youthful zeal, Western informality, and tendency to make gaffes initially put off some of his fellow cabinet members and Kennedy's staff. Presidential assistant Lee White started to record Udall's miscues on a legal pad but gave up when the list became extensive. Working with Udall, Secretary of Agriculture Orville Freeman noted privately, draws "into sharp focus the fact that good-hearted, energetic, knowledgeable, and able as he is in many ways, he is the least mature and effective member of the Cabinet."

Having lived for fourteen years at 3307 N Street in Georgetown, Kennedy understood that Washington, D. C., was a paradox. It was "a city of northern charm and southern efficiency," he said, reversing the stereotypes. It was brutally hot in the summer and nippy in the winter. The capital region enjoyed one of the highest per-capita incomes in the nation, but slums skirted the Capitol. The District's major industry outside politics was history, with statues, monuments, museums, research libraries, and legendary buildings attracting thousands of tourists yearly. Foreign embassies, visiting dignitaries, and diplomatic receptions provided a cosmopolitan flair, but the District also had a small-town feel, being dappled with outdoor parks, hiking trails, and a variety of blossoming trees. It lacked skyscrapers because regulations prevented buildings to overwhelm the Capitol in height. Although the city bustled with tourists, politicians, foreign dignitaries, social hostesses, and diplomats, Washington could be a lonely town. "If you want a friend in Washington," Harry Truman once purportedly said, "get a dog."

Washington was the seat, but hardly the showcase, of democracy. Its residents had no home rule, being governed by a three-person council appointed by the president. Residents paid federal taxes, but they were not represented in Congress, could not vote for a mayor or city council members, and had to rely on congressional appropriations to run the city. Although Washingtonians had no self-government, politics dominated their lives. Washington, wrote journalist Russell Baker, is "more interested in politics than sex." The local and national government was run mainly by faceless bureaucrats, but from the earliest days of the republic, titans battled.

The District had undergone extensive demographic and social change in the decade before Kennedy's inaugural. Schools, movie houses, theaters, churches, and other public facilities had been integrated. Blacks joined the police and fire departments, bar and medical associations, and the Washington Senators baseball team.

Yet problems persisted. Whites fled to segregated suburbs in Maryland and Virginia. In 1950, whites constituted 65 percent of the city's population. Ten years later, whites were a minority of 45 percent. In 1960, six years after school desegregation, 76 percent of the public school system's student body was African American. Private clubs such as the Cosmos and Metropolitan excluded blacks. When four African Americans attempted to enter the National Contract Bridge Tournament in Washington's Mayflower Hotel, they were turned away because their participation might have been offensive to white competitors. The U.S. Supreme Court in 1948 had outlawed property covenants, but realtors still excluded blacks from certain housing developments. The northeast and southeast sections of the city were overwhelmingly black, while the northwest and southwest quadrants were white. The police and fire departments had been integrated, but there were few black officers.

Similarly, blacks were seldom elevated to high-level positions in the federal government. "Opportunities were just dismal for blacks then," said black journalist Louis Martin. "You couldn't really enjoy your own city." Martin recalled taking John Kennedy on a tour of some federal buildings in 1961. "We went to this one building—I can't recall just which one—and on the first floor, we saw a few blacks. On the second floor, there were fewer. On the third floor, fewer still. Finally, when we got to the top, there were no blacks anywhere. Kennedy turns to me and says, 'They get whiter the higher they get.'"

As a city of transients, Washington found a sense of identity in the Redskins. Although the team was inept, having experienced only three winning seasons since 1945, it had not jilted the city like the equally woeful Senators. Fans flocked to games and devoured reports about the team on television, radio, and the daily newspapers. The Redskins also dominated saloon talk.

Saloonkeeper David George "Duke" Zeibert made his restaurant, Duke's, a mecca for Redskins fans and the city's power elite. "If you're not in my joint," he once said, "you're just camping out." Located on the corner of Connecticut and L streets, only a few blocks from the White House, the New York–style steakhouse reminded some people of Bernard "Toots" Shor's establishment in Manhattan. Indeed, when Toots visited the city, he drank brandy sodas and socialized at Duke's. Like Toots, Duke was an outgoing raconteur with a knack for storytelling and remembering names. He was also a big-time gambler and avid sports fan. Just as celebrities, fans, and Yankee players frequented Toots Shor's, bigwigs, fans, and Redskins players patronized Duke's. One of the reasons the Redskins endeared themselves to the capital region, Zeibert once related, was because George Preston Marshall "made it a priority to get local jobs for his players and encouraged them to mix and mingle." In short, they became part of the community.

Although the Redskins were considered part of the community, fans wanted more victories. The 1960 squad had 1 win, 9 losses, and 2 ties. Many critics blamed the abysmal performance on Marshall's discriminatory racial policy. By the mid-1950s, the Redskins were the only NFL team without a black player. Meanwhile a total of 143 African Americans had played in the NFL by the end of the decade. At the close of the 1960 season, there were sixty-one blacks on NFL teams. The following year, that figure jumped to eighty-three, an average of six per team. Blacks constituted 16.5 percent of the players in the NFL, while only 10.5 percent of the nation's population was black. Scores of African Americans also played in the rival AFL. Despite civil rights activists protesting against Marshall's discriminatory hiring policies, Marshall steadfastly resisted desegregation. For Marshall, "NAACP" stood for "Never At Anytime Any Colored Players."

Shirley Povich, Sam Lacy, and other writers mauled Marshall in the press. "Marshall is an anachronism, as out of date as the drop kick," Povich wrote in a December 1960 column. His white supremacist policies, designed to please a predominantly Southern radio and television audience, were a disservice to the players, coaches, and fans. Even Dixie rooters, he argued, should realize that "what is important is how the man plays the game, not the notation on his birth certificate." Gordon Cobbledick, a respected white sports columnist for the *Cleveland Plain Dealer,* also jumped on Marshall, observing that the Redskins' Jim Crow policy was "spotting their rivals the tremendous advantage of exclusive rights to a whole race containing excellent football players." In the past, the Redskins had bypassed black athletes such as Jim Brown, Jim Parker, Roosevelt Grier, Roosevelt Brown, and Bobby Mitchell. Drafting blacks, he cautioned, "is not an argument for social equality. It's a matter of practical football policy."

The criticism was fruitless. To further ally himself and his team with Southern segregationists, Marshall changed the words of the Redskins fight song in 1959 from "Fight For Old D.C." to "Fight For Old Dixie." He also continued to try to improve the team by replacing coaches and drafting only white players. At the NFL player draft in late December 1960, the Redskins pursued "states' rights football" by shunning Elijah Pitts, Irv Cross, and other talented black athletes. Instead, they selected Wake Forest quarterback Norm Snead and seven other whites. "Snead," wrote Ted Maule of *Sports Illustrated,* "faces the blackest future and the whitest huddle in the league."

The December 1960 draft brought another stinging indictment from Povich. "The Redskins had 20 choices in the draft this week. They didn't choose a single Negro player," he complained. "This because the Redskins are playing States' Rights football. Something must be wrong with it. It won them only one game last season. Marshall was born ahead of his time. He could have showed the 10 [in fact, 11] Confederate states that failed, how to make secession stick. Because of Marshall's attitude, his new coach, Bill McPeak, went into the draft meetings figuratively handcuffed. McPeak had to assess the players not only on size, speed and ability, but also on color." Marshall, he concluded, has allegedly shunned blacks to please his mainly Southern television audience. He should be more concerned with paying Washingtonian fans who wanted to see some players "in living color," so to speak.

Meanwhile, African American athletes continued to sparkle at the pro and college levels. Two of the nation's most dynamic players in the late 1950s and early 1960s were Bobby Mitchell and Ernie Davis, a high school phenom who entered Syracuse University in 1958. That same year, the Cleveland Browns paired their punishing running back Jim Brown with Mitchell, a gazelle-like rookie ball carrier.

Robert Cornelius Mitchell was born in Hot Springs, Arkansas, on June 6, 1935. The son of a minister, he was one of eight children raised in a loving but financially strapped home. The Mitchell children were taught to economize and to avoid alcohol, smoking, and cursing, guidelines that Bobby abided by throughout his life. The thermal spring waters of his hometown attracted thousands of patrons, including athletes. "People came from all over the world to take hot baths at Hot Springs," Mitchell recalled to the University of Illinois Alumni Association. "At that time, many of the black athletes were playing baseball. A lot of them would come to my town to work out and get ready for the season." He met former boxing champion Joe Louis and baseball players Roy Campanella, Don Newcombe, and Monte Irvin. "We got to know those guys personally," he remembered. "It was a great situation for all of the young kids. To grow up in an area like that was a great advantage for someone like me." Campanella, in particular, became attached to the youngster, helped out the family financially, and bought Bobby a new suit for his high school graduation.

A resort town, Hot Springs was less segregated than most Southern cities. Mitchell attended a segregated school, but the buses were integrated. "I don't ever remember having to sit in the back of the bus in my town," he told the *Washington Post*'s Ken Denlinger. "Twenty miles down the road, I'd get hanged if I sat in the front of the bus."

A speedy, multisport, high school athlete, Mitchell wanted to attend Grambling College to play football for famed coach Eddie Robinson. But coaches at the University of Illinois also coveted him and convinced his mother that Illinois would be a better fit than Grambling. "So it was a situation where I didn't have much to say about it. I ended up going to the University of Illinois; and it turned out to be a good move." Running backs Red Grange and Buddy Young had starred for the Illini, but those storied players meant little to Mitchell. "I was a young, immature country boy," he related. "In the early years, I was ready to go back home every day."

Fortunately, Mitchell found an upper-class mentor in J. C. Caroline. As a sophomore in 1953, "Mr. Zoom," as Caroline was called, led the nation in rushing, was named a consensus All-American, and finished seventh in the Heisman Award voting. Injured after four games in 1954, he never played another college game, forgoing his senior year to play in the Canadian Football League. Drafted in the seventh round in 1956 by the Chicago Bears (the Redskins passed on him, naturally), he played ten years as a defensive back. "J. C. was a kind of forerunner for most of us, because he was such a great athlete at Illinois," Mitchell recalled. "He helped us to hang in there and fight, because those were not the most happy days for black athletes. There were places we couldn't go and things we couldn't do. J. C. knew where everything was and what we would have to be careful of. He was a great inspiration."

As a sophomore, Mitchell got his chance to run with the ball late in the 1955 season, when the starting halfback, Harry Jackson, was injured. Mitchell entered the game in the third quarter and scurried for 173 yards on ten carries, helping to defeat Michigan 25–6. He also ran for 100 yards in the two remaining games. After those performances he received a telegram: "I am very proud of what you are doing." It was signed Roy Campanella.

Owing to injuries, his junior year was undistinguished. As a senior, though, he earned Second Team Big Ten honors and excelled in the College All-Star game in Chicago. But track seemed to be his first love. In February 1958, he set an indoor world record in the seventy-yard hurdles and also excelled as a sprinter and long-jumper. He was looking forward to trying out for the Olympics when he learned that the Cleveland Browns had selected him in the seventh round of the NFL draft.

Even though Mitchell possessed blazing speed and quickness as a running back, NFL teams were hesitant to draft him because he had a reputation for fumbling, according to Paul Brown. At his son's urging, Brown had attended a track meet in Cleveland and remembered being impressed with Mitchell's "athletic ability as he skimmed over those hurdles. As the draft went on and his name stayed on the board, I kept waiting for someone to make the selection until finally our turn came in the eighth [*sic*] round, and I said, 'I've got to find out for myself.' I was never sorry."

Mitchell also remembered that track meet as pivotal. Brown and other Cleveland coaches watched him perform, he recalled, "and I did quite well. They were impressed with that, and Paul wanted that speed. Later, I was still shocked when they drafted me. They thought I was better than I thought I was." When Brown offered him $7,000 to play football, Mitchell accepted. "When you're broke, it doesn't take much. . . . They convinced me to play football."

As a rookie in 1958, he played in all twelve games, displaying a talent for running, receiving, and punt and kick returning. He ran back one kickoff for a 98-yard touchdown. In four years with the Browns, he scampered for nearly 2,300 yards (averaging 5.4 yards per carry), snagged 128 passes, returned punts for 607 yards, kickoffs for 1,550 yards, and notched 38 touchdowns. He held the Browns record for kickoff touchdown returns (3) until 1990. His most memorable game came in mid-November 1959 against the Redskins. In a stellar performance that George Marshall could not help but notice, Mitchell romped for 232 yards, including a 90-yard touchdown run in a 31–17 victory. Coach Brown pulled him from the game, denying him the chance to top Jim Brown's single-game rushing record of 237 yards. In 1961, New York Giants scout Walt Jowarsky described him as "the most dangerous and exciting player in football today. He can beat you by going 100 yards at least four different ways—taking a pass, returning a kick, going off tackle, or turning an end. He hasn't even reached his peak yet, but is already one of the game's top all-around stars."

Bobby Mitchell as a college halfback at the University of Illinois in 1957. (Image 0002667, courtesy of the University of Illinois Archives)

Ernie Davis was as dazzling on the college gridiron as Mitchell was professionally. Born in 1939 in New Salem, Pennsylvania, he was sent to live with his mother's parents in Uniontown, Pennsylvania, near Pittsburgh, while his mother reconstructed her life following a breakup with her husband. When she remarried and relocated to Elmira, New York, she sent for eleven-year-old Ernie.

Located just across the Pennsylvania border in New York's southern tier, Elmira was a working-class town of fifty thousand in the mid-1950s. Charismatic, easygoing, and a superior athlete, Davis experienced little racial discrimination. He excelled in organized youth sports before entering Elmira Free Academy, where he played varsity baseball, basketball, and football. A member of the Southern Tier Athletic Conference, Elmira Free Academy played crosstown rival Elmira Southside, Ithaca, and several schools in the Binghamton vicinity, some sixty miles away.

As a freshman, Davis made the junior varsity football team, but he snapped a wrist in the opening game, ending his season. With his injured wrist protected by wrapping, he made the varsity basketball team and scored twenty-two points in his first game. He played four years of varsity basketball, with his team going undefeated in his junior and senior years. In his four years, he averaged over eighteen points a game, establishing a conference record with over 1,600 points.

As a sophomore, he played defensive end on an undefeated varsity football team. As a junior and senior, he switched to running back, averaging 7.4 yards per carry. "Having played two sports with him—I didn't play baseball—you could just see he was special," teammate Chuck Prettyman later recalled. Davis made All-Conference in football, basketball, and baseball in all three of his upperclass seasons.

Heavily recruited, Davis had his choice of football programs in Northern colleges. His high school coach, a local attorney, and the famed Jim Brown convinced him to attend Syracuse University. There, he played on an undefeated freshman team before joining the varsity for his sophomore, junior, and senior years.

As a sophomore, he roomed with John Mackey, a freshman who would go on to a Hall of Fame career with the Baltimore Colts. Davis, Mackey has written, was "one of the greatest football players I've ever seen and one of the greatest friends a man could ever have. . . . He was my roommate, my teammate, my friend, my brother." Besides remembering his athletic prowess, Coach Ben Swartzwalder recalled Davis as affable, good-hearted, and enthusiastic: "He had that spontaneous goodness about him. He radiated enthusiasm. His enthusiasm rubbed off on the kids. Oh, he'd knock you down, but then he'd run back and pick you up."

In 1959, as a sophomore running back, Davis helped lead Syracuse to an undefeated season and a national title. The *Elmira Star-Gazette*'s Al Mallette dubbed him the "Elmira Express." In the fight-marred Cotton Bowl, Davis scored two touchdowns, one on a run, another on an 87-yard pass play. He was voted the Most Valuable Player in the 23–14 Syracuse victory. After the post-game dinner and presentation of the Most Valuable Player award, Cotton Bowl officials asked Davis and his two black teammates—John Brown and Art Baker—to leave the banquet. Contrary to myth, their coaches and white teammates did not walk out with them as an act of protest.

As a junior, Davis finished third in the nation in rushing yardage, helping his team compile a 7–2 record. As a senior, he broke all of Jim Brown's Syracuse records, setting career marks in rushing, touchdowns, and points. He became the first African American to win the Heisman Trophy, narrowly outvoting Bob Ferguson, another black running back from Ohio State. Both Davis and Ferguson would be available to the Redskins, who held the first choice in the NFL draft. But would their bigoted owner break tradition by drafting one of them?

Never averse to controversy, and perhaps trying to divert attention from the woeful performance of his football team, Marshall contributed an article to the *Saturday Evening Post* in December 1961 claiming football as America's national pastime. In the process, he trashed just about every other sport. Professional football began its ascendancy over Major League Baseball, he asserted, shortly after World War II with the advent of television and the population shift to the suburbs. Professional football, he maintained, had several advantages over baseball. Compared to football, baseball was "a bloodless, unemotional spectacle." "The very nature of the football uniform is exciting," he continued. "It suggests the gladiator—man-to-man combat." Baseball was slow-moving, and its season seemingly endless. Unable to compete with football at the high school and college levels, baseball tried to capture fan interest through the Little League program. But Little League was "cute stuff" that attracted "overenthusiastic parents who make asses of themselves in the stands." Major League Baseball would be better served, he believed, by adopting an amateur draft system like pro football and ending the season on Labor Day.

Marshall denigrated other sports as well. Only auto racing escaped his withering gaze. Basketball had virtually no public appeal, and not even its point-shaving scandals were interesting. Boxing had become "strictly a freak show for characters in poolrooms, bars, bookie joints, and barbershops." Horse racing only interested gamblers, and tennis was followed and played only by the elite. Golf and bowling were gaining in popularity, he conceded, "although I can't understand why." Golf was a foolish game played by elitists who hit a stationary ball and then walked after it. Golf was a sport of "cocktails and tweeds," whereas bowling was "one of beer and T-shirts." Like golf, it was "a stupid game. You roll a ball down an alley and one of two things happens (a) it knocks down pins or (b) it doesn't. People guzzle beer while they play. The noise is deafening, the atmosphere smoky and the participants wear the shabbiest clothing in sports." Women come to football games fashionably dressed in a new hat or dress, Marshall noted, but in bowling, they "are usually attired in unattractive slacks and gaudy polo shirts that have such inspirational messages as SAM'S AUTO PAINTING." He had difficulty deciding "whether bowlers are duller than golfers. Both species bore you stiff with long, dry accounts of their trials. Only fishermen are less interesting." In short, he said, "no sport can compare with football."

Professional football, in particular the Washington Redskins, was about to receive plenty of interest from the Kennedy White House—and more attention than even a publicity hound like George Marshall wanted.

CHAPTER 9

Showdown

The national capital was splashed by sun and heaped with snow during Kennedy's inauguration. Udall had convinced JFK to invite Robert Frost to read a poem, but the sun's glare caused the esteemed New England poet to stumble over the lines he had written for the occasion. But despite Frost's "fumble" and the winter chill, the Kennedy inaugural was generally well received. Although more blacks were invited to participate in the festivities than ever before, some African Americans were disappointed that Kennedy had not invited Martin Luther King Jr. and had not mentioned civil rights in his inaugural address with its now-famous line "Ask not what your country can do for you—ask what you can do for your country."

Many civil rights activists were also disappointed to learn that Kennedy did not plan to advance the cause of racial justice by asking Congress for more laws immediately. He would shun "the forward pass," grumbled Roy Wilkins of the NAACP, in favor of surer gains through symbolic gestures and limited executive action. When an all-white Coast Guard squad paraded by during the inauguration, Kennedy voiced his displeasure over the absence of African Americans to his aide Richard Goodman. Once in office, he had Goodwin contact the commander of the Coast Guard with instructions to integrate the Coast Guard Academy, as well as future parade groups.

In his first few months in office, JFK appointed more than forty blacks to important federal positions. He also named the first African American, John B. Duncan, to the Board of Commissioners of the District of Columbia. To the dismay of blacks, though, he also named some white supremacists to the federal bench and failed to deliver promptly on a campaign promise to abolish discrimination in federally subsidized housing and to seek civil rights legislation ending discrimination in public places. In early March 1961, he issued an executive order creating the President's Committee on Equal Employment Opportunity, with the aim of ending discrimination in federal employment and federally contracted jobs.

Knowing that JFK and Attorney General Robert Kennedy were committed to ending racial discrimination in hiring, Udall, after consulting with Interior Department lawyers, decided to challenge the hiring practices of George Marshall. He decided to move against the Washington "Paleskins," he later recalled, because he "had personal convictions about civil rights and considered it outrageous that the Redskins were the last team in the NFL to have a lily-white policy." He did not discuss his proposed action with JFK beforehand because he "instinctively felt that JFK and RFK would applaud. To me, it was the kind of stance that was all on the plus side." Besides, he knew that JFK was about to issue the executive order establishing the President's Committee on Equal Employment Opportunity and his action complied with the spirit of that executive order.

Instead of speaking with the president personally, Udall notified him of the proposed action against the Redskins in his "Weekly Report to the President." (JFK detested meetings, preferring to communicate with his cabinet through memoranda.) On February 28, 1961, Udall wrote: "George Marshall of the Washington Redskins is the only segregationist hold-out in professional football. He refuses to hire Negro players even thought [*sic*] Dallas and Houston, Texas have already broken the color bar. The Interior Department owns the ground on which the new Washington Stadium is constructed, and we are investigating to ascertain whether a no-discrimination provision could be inserted in Marshall's lease. Marshall is one of the few remaining Jim Crow symbols in American sports, and we believe such action would have a wide impact in the civil rights field."

Udall understood that civil rights activists would welcome his bold move. But he did not accurately assess the national attention that it would receive, or that it would provoke a showdown with a combative sports owner who was described by one black newspaper as "a throwback to the racial savagery of the early twenties." The eyes of Washington and the nation would be watching to see whether the White House or the Redskins would blink first.

With Kennedy's prior approval, on March 24, 1961, Udall notified Marshall by special messenger that the Interior Department had approved regulations that prohibited job discrimination by any party contracting to use "any public facility in a park area." He went on to say that "there have been persistent allegations that your company practices discrimination in the hiring of its players." Without prejudging the owner, he nonetheless warned him "of the implications of this new regulation—and our view of its import."

At a news conference that same day, Udall explained that the new guidelines were designed to conform to the administration's recently announced antidiscrimination policy. "It is certainly our feeling that here in the Nation's Capital, with the marvelous new facility being built on property owned by all the people of the country that we ought to set the very highest of standards in terms of adhering to the policies of this Administration with regard to treating everyone in this country equally." If Marshall continued his ban on blacks, he would be denied the use of D.C. Stadium. "I think it is quite plain that if he wants an argument, . . . he is going to have a moral argument with the President and with the Administration." He cautioned the headstrong owner to heed the antidiscrimination guidelines.

Pressed by reporters for more background, Udall divulged that when the Armory Board and Marshall negotiated lease terms in 1959, the board inserted in the contract nondiscriminatory hiring language pertaining to the use of the stadium. Marshall had no problem with the provision as it pertained to stadium and concession employees, but not his players. At Marshall's insistence, the nondiscrimination clause relating to Redskins players was removed. But couldn't Marshall cry foul? a reporter asked. After all, he negotiated a lease in good faith, and now the terms were being altered. Udall pointed out that the lease also contained language stating that the

Redskins would comply with all Interior Department regulations. "He knew that when he did it. So we are proceeding completely in accord with the contract that he signed."

Udall's ultimatum immediately gained nationwide attention. The *New York Times* and *Washington Post* featured the story on the front page. Not surprisingly, the black press also gave the story prominent coverage. The *Chicago Defender* headlined: REDSKINS TOLD: INTEGRATE OR ELSE." A headline in the *Pittsburgh Courier* read: "Washington Redskins Told to Integrate: Govt. Does What NFL Wouldn't."

"I don't know what the hell it's all about," Marshall told reporters. He also attempted to laugh off the incident. "We almost knocked Laos off the front pages," he quipped. "I never realized so many fans were interested in a football team that won only one game." He joked that if Udall could get the Redskins Lenny Moore, the star African American running back of the Baltimore Colts, he would certainly use him. Turning serious, Marshall wrote a brief and defiant letter to Udall, claiming that he had broken no laws and had signed a lease on that basis. Implying that he would pursue legal action, he informed Udall that he had turned the matter over to his attorneys.

"Marshall at first scoffed at my initiative," Udall told me. "He had good reason to scoff as his lawyers had gotten an 'air-tight' lease giving him a free hand from the Stadium Armory Board. The problem was that his lawyers overlooked the Park Service and Interior. We had rights—and we [were] not included as parties in the original contract."

At his office, the irrepressible owner sounded off to reporters. First, he wondered why the government would get involved in such a trifling matter. "I am surprised that with the world on the brink of another war, they are worried about whether or not a Negro is going to play for the Redskins." Second, he doubted that "the government had the right to tell the showman how to cast the play." Then he expressed a desire to discuss the issue with the president. "I could handle him with words. I used to be able to handle his old man." (Marshall claimed to have had unspecified business dealing with Joseph Kennedy years ago, when he was the owner of the Boston football team.)

Marshall also raised some pointed questions. Would an African American have to appear in every contest and event scheduled at D.C. Stadium? For instance, would George Washington University's football team be forced to include blacks? What about Southern colleges that played there? Did Udall also plan to integrate the Army, Navy, and Air Force football squads? What about the National Theater, National Symphony Orchestra, or the White House press and photographers corps? Where would the government draw the line?

He also tried to downplay the charge of discrimination against the Redskins. "All the other teams we play have Negroes; does it matter which team has the Negroes?" Marshall claimed that the Redskins lacked blacks because they recruited players from segregated Southern colleges. Recruiting Southern white players was not a matter of prejudice, he declared, but a business decision. As an owner, he did not want to offend his white Southern radio and television audience by playing blacks. Although he had never signed an African American, he had in the past hired athletes who were Cuban and Native American. He was color-blind when it came to selling tickets and hiring blacks for custodial tasks. As for Udall's ultimatum, Marshall said that his 1961 player roster was frozen. Leaving room to maneuver, however, he claimed that he was always open to the possibility of adding talented players.

The next day, Redskins attorneys attempted to soften some of Marshall's statements. The Redskins, they asserted, had no intention of defying the federal government or breaking any laws. The team would cooperate in seeking a workable compromise.

Udall kept up the pressure. At a press conference on March 28, he gave the Redskins a deadline for compliance. To avoid cancellation of the lease and possible criminal prosecution, the owner must comply with the administration's antidiscrimination policy by October 1, the date of the Redskins' first home game. Marshall could best show compliance by hiring a black player. Udall suggested the possibility of a trade. In a final dig at Marshall, he said that with a black player, the Redskins might actually win some games.

African Americans generally heralded Udall's ultimatum to Marshall. Using ethnically insensitive language, a *Washington Afro-*

American editorial hailed the victory over bigotry. Marshall's "war whoop for bigotry is going to eventually be a whisper. His racial discrimination is in for a real scalping." In a letter to the *Afro-American,* Washington civil rights leader E. B. Henderson urged blacks and whites to boycott all Redskins games until the team integrated its roster. If African Americans and "our liberal friends stay away until the Redskins cease to be all-white, Mr. Marshall will eventually become a true American." In a letter published in both the black and mainstream press, Jackie Robinson, the groundbreaking former baseball player and now vice president of the Chock Full of Nuts coffee company, supported Udall. "Your stand on the hiring policy of the Washington Football team is both inspirational and encouraging. . . .," he wrote. "You have made your position quite clear, we applaud you for it." Marshall dismissed Robinson's statement. "Jackie Robinson is in the business of exploiting a race and making a living doing it. I'm not. He doesn't qualify as a critic."

Marshall also sounded off to African American sportswriter Wendell Smith of the *Pittsburgh Courier.* Asked why he had never hired a black player, Marshall thundered,

> "That's like asking me when I stopped beating my wife. . . . Why do you ask such a question?"
>
> "Because," Smith said, "we want to know."
>
> "Well, I've told you," Marshall responded, "because I haven't seen any I thought were good enough. Does that answer your question?"
>
> It did, said Smith, but would it satisfy the Kennedy White House?
>
> "I don't know," Marshall scowled, "and, frankly, I'm not overly concerned. I don't see how anyone can tell me who to hire, or what to hire."

In mid-April, Udall informed reporters that letters to his office were running about twenty to one against his position. One letter writer asked if he planned to integrate the National Symphony. Udall quipped: "I'll take that up when I'm through with football."

Another writer asked if he was going to insist that an American Indian be added to the Redskins team. "I have news for this person," he told reporters. "My Indian Commissioner, John [Orien] Crow, played football—he is a Cherokee—for George Marshall 30 years ago. Apparently Mr. Marshall pioneered earlier in getting Indians into the game, and all we want him to do is just open his mind a little further."

More pressing issues soon overtook the Udall-Marshall showdown. In mid-April 1961, Americans and the world learned of the Bay of Pigs invasion—an abortive CIA-sponsored effort to overthrow Cuban communist leader Fidel Castro. Holding 1,200 Cuban-exile invaders prisoner, Castro offered to release them for heavy farm and construction tractors. While he and Kennedy negotiated the so-called tractors-for-prisoners deal, through third parties because diplomatic relations had been severed earlier, American civil rights activists were dramatically confronting racism in the American South.

Through Freedom Rides, they sought to test a 1960 Supreme Court decision prohibiting segregation in bus terminal restaurants, restrooms, and waiting areas. The first two-week Freedom Ride, in early May, took a racially mixed band of young activists on two buses from Washington, D.C., to New Orleans. Their first violent encounter in Rock Hill, South Carolina, was mild compared to their reception in Anniston, Alabama, where one of the buses was smoke-bombed and white supremacists clubbed the activists as they escaped the fire and fumes. Eventually, the Freedom Riders were rescued and returned safely to the North.

In late May, another small, racially mixed group of students launched a second Freedom Ride from Nashville to New Orleans. Those activists also met violent resistance. In Montgomery, Alabama, they were beaten with clubs. When John Seigenthaler, a white assistant to RFK, tried to help them, he too was pummeled. When another group of Freedom Riders tried to integrate the bus terminal in Jackson, Mississippi, they were jailed for violating state law. Embarrassed by the incidents of domestic violence, especially at a time when he was cramming for a meeting in Vienna with Soviet premier

Nikita Khrushchev, President Kennedy wanted the Freedom Riders to desist. But they refused.

Whites and blacks alike were distressed by the violence and blatant disregard for individual rights. Democratic senator Mike Mansfield of Montana said the violence in Alabama "should cause us to hang our heads in shame." A Maryland woman who described herself as "a simple housewife" who "might not understand all things" asked President Kennedy how he could sleep at night given the mob action in Alabama. "This is supposed to be a free country with justice and liberty for all. . . . If you can't control the situation in your own country, how do you expect to tell other nations how to rule and run theirs? The whole world's eyes are upon you. . . . Please Mr. Kennedy, if not for your sake or mine, but for our children's sake, . . . do something." Eventually, Attorney General Robert Kennedy ordered federal marshals to the South to protect the young activists.

Kenneth Keating, a Republican senator from New York, contrasted the White House's strong action against the Redskins with its lackadaisical approach to the protection of the Freedom Riders in Alabama. "I cannot help but feel that [Alabama] Governor Faubus and his cohorts need a little more attention than George Preston Marshall and company," he declared on the floor of the U.S. Senate. "The Redskins may be tough on a football field, but the administration apparently has decided that they are easy targets in the political arena."

Kennedy's reluctance to combat racial injustice in America aggressively distressed civil rights leaders. His selection of Harris Wofford, a white lawyer, as his top civil rights adviser was scorned in an editorial in the *Washington Afro-American*. It referred to Wofford as "an apostle of delay." If JFK wanted advice on civil rights, it continued, he should contact a prominent black leader like Adam Clayton Powell, Martin Luther King, Jr., Thurgood Marshall, or A. Philip Randolph. "We don't need any Mr. Harris Wofford speaking for us in this area, thank you, and the less he advises, the happier we'll be."

Thomas Stockett, the *Afro-American*'s answer to the *Washington Post*'s renowned cartoonist "Herblock" (Herbert Block), provided drawings criticizing the lack of civil rights gains under Kennedy.

One showed a space capsule entitled "SPACE PROGRESS" soaring skyward, while RACE PROGRESS moved along below in a dilapidated wagon hauled by a bedraggled horse. Another depicted Fidel Castro offering tractors to Mississippi governor Ross Barnett for imprisoned Freedom Riders. The *Afro-American* also pointed out incidents of racial discrimination in the nation's capital. For example, Hecht's, one of the city's finest department stores, would hire blacks only for menial labor, just as the Redskins did. Similarly, the Library of Congress and District of Columbia Public Library employed African Americans only for low-level government service jobs. And in an incident similar to what happened in Anniston, Alabama, two white District police officers savagely beat a black singer because he was in the company of two white women. Martin Luther King Jr. urged President Kennedy to declare a Second Emancipation Day to rid the nation of all segregation laws, saying, "The colored man is no longer willing to put up with meaningless delays and a crippling gradualism. There's a mighty stirring in this land."

There was also stirring abroad. Soviet premier Nikita Khrushchev encouraged "wars of national liberation" in Africa, Asia, and Latin America. He also demanded an end to the Western presence in West Berlin. The Berlin crisis was the president's main concern in the summer of 1961. When Kennedy refused to surrender treaty rights granting Western access and give up the occupation of West Berlin, war seemed a real possibility. "The president," Udall said, "is imprisoned by Berlin." The crisis was eventually resolved when Khrushchev ordered the East German government to build a twenty-eight-mile concrete wall separating East and West Berlin. Kennedy said: "[A] wall is a hell of a lot better than a war."

Meanwhile, the Kennedy administration continued to chip away at the wall of segregation at home, including the District's professional football team. Marshall remained defiant. "The Secretary and I have nothing to do with one another at all," he told Morris Siegel of the *Washington Daily News*. "My lease is with the Armory Board, not with Interior." He also claimed that Udall's action was inspired by politics, not principle. "We're both in the same business," he huffed, "selling tickets."

American neo-Nazis march outside D.C. Stadium to protest the integration of the Redskins. (Neil Leifer)

When Marshall showed little sign of complying with the integration ultimatum, Udall fired off another warning in July threatening to withhold use of the stadium. "This guy's making a big mistake if he thinks our department merely is trying to get some publicity out of this thing. We're quite serious." Marshall considered Udall's statement "rather vague." Disillusioned with federal interference in his business, he told a reporter that "you can't tell what will happen under the guise of liberalism." Still, he would probably comply with the federal directive, even if it meant hiring "Eskimos or Chinese or Mongolians."

Federally directed desegregation efforts reflected the deep social divisions over civil rights in the 1950s and 1960s. Court-ordered school desegregation provoked Southern resistance and violence. Civil rights activists who conducted sit-ins and Freedom Rides to desegregate public accommodations in the South did so knowing that they risked imprisonment and physical harm. The desegregation of the Redskins may not have provoked violence, but it certainly did elicit a white backlash. The American Nazi Party paraded outside D.C. Stadium with swastika-emblazoned signs reading "America Awake" and "Keep Redskins White!" Udall also received angry personal letters. A man from Tennessee believed the United States was headed for dictatorship "when a football owner is forced to put a nigger on his team." Another disgruntled observer told Udall that if race, instead of ability, was used as a criterion for team membership, then the sport and society would be doomed "to mediocrity and eclipse!" And sports editor Frank Hyde of the *St. Louis Post-Journal* advised Udall to "crawl back into the woodwork."

Other Americans closed their eyes to discrimination. After all, they argued, blacks had plenty of opportunity to play for teams other than the Redskins. Some wondered why African Americans would want to play for a team that was so vocally intolerant. Opponents of forced desegregation, meanwhile, feared a snowball effect. Once the administration compelled the Redskins to employ black players, would it then require the team to hire other unrepresented groups? One critic observed that the Redskins had "no Puerto Ricans, no Christian Scientists, no members of the Raritan Club, and no Pythians. Heavens, Mr. Udall, these people are being discriminated against." Marshall himself took this approach. "Why Negroes particularly," he asked. "Why not make us hire a player from any other race?" "In fact," Marshall continued, "why not a woman? . . . Of course, we have had players who played like girls, but never an actual girl player."

Desegregating the Redskins also became a sort of philosophical football, with liberals generally approving of it and conservatives disapproving of such heavy-handed federal action. Liberals supported federal action for reasons of social justice and public image. "You are doing the right thing by laying it on the line with Marshall," one Philadelphian wrote Udall. "His actions make this country look bad in front of all Ambassadors and representatives of the foreign nations stationed in our nation's capital. Am glad to see the Irishman from Scully [*sic*] Square selected a man with Gutts [*sic*] to run things."

Conservatives interpreted the desegregation order as an unwarranted intrusion by big government, one which threatened democracy and free enterprise. An "aggrieved Redskin fan" asked Attorney General Robert Kennedy to halt "the harassment of private businessmen" by the "cowboy in the New Frontier rodeo." "If Mr. Marshall doesn't want Negro players on his team, that's his business," declared a *Tulsa World* editorial. Others preferred to allow the hidden hand of economics to play out. If Marshall continued to field a team of poor quality, fans would stop attending games, and he would be forced to hire blacks. For some conservatives, federal interference in professional sports smacked of communism, and they accused Udall of trying to become a "sports commissar." Another critic believed that in the near future, federal officials would be dictating where Americans would work. And a Cold War–conscious citizen feared that it would somehow make the nation susceptible to a takeover by Premier Nikita Khrushchev: "Once government sticks its icky fingers into free business, there is a hole in the line big enough for Mr. K to smash through and rack up a winning score for his team."

Others accused Udall of holding a double standard. Why *would* he allow the segregated George Washington University football team to play in D.C. Stadium, but not the Redskins? Why didn't he take action to prevent segregated seating at the home games of the Houston Oilers, the only professional team with segregated seating?

Despite the waves of pointed criticism, Udall would not back down. The president supported his position, as did Attorney General Kennedy and other cabinet members. He explained that George Washington University could use the stadium because they used amateur players. And his department had no control over the facility used by the Houston Oilers, but he could put his own house in order. Learning that only 1 in 474 National Park rangers was black, he promptly recruited 50 minority candidates. As a friendly and symbolic gesture, he took Uzziel Baylor, an African American employee (and mother of Elgin Baylor, the famed Los Angeles Laker) to an exhibition basketball game in Maryland.

Perhaps fearful of jeopardizing the gains that they had already achieved, black players kept a low profile during Udall's challenge. Chicago Cardinal running back Ollie Matson admitted to Shirley Povich that black players "try a little harder when we play the Washington team," but no player criticized Marshall directly or protested the segregated seating policy of the Houston Oilers. When the NAACP asked black players on the Oakland Raiders and San Diego Chargers to boycott games against the Oilers, they refused. Similarly, when the NAACP asked seven Baltimore Colts players, including Lenny Moore and Jim Parker, to sit out an exhibition game in Norfolk, Virginia, against a "segregated team [the Redskins] playing a segregated game in a segregated field for a segregated charity," they refused.

In the spring and summer of 1961, members of the NAACP and the Congress of Racial Equality (CORE) picketed Marshall's home, D.C. Stadium, and the Redskins' exhibition games in the West and South. A letter writer in the *Washington Afro-American* claimed that "the climate of thinking in the District has changed in the last decade to the point that Mr. Marshall's Jim Crow policies do not suit the best interests of the nation's capital or our country." Shirley Povich also kept on the pressure. There was little evidence, he asserted, to suggest that fans "would resent a Negro player on the Redskins, particularly if he could score touchdowns, in living color." In another column, he said that Marshall was "getting more publicity than any loser since Robert E. Lee."

Many sports owners also supported the government's position. Bill Veeck, the maverick owner of the Chicago White Sox baseball team, recommended threatening Marshall with the possibility of having an integrated AFL team play in Washington. William Shea and Jack Kent Cooke, members of the Redskins' board of directors, urged Marshall to yield. Edward B. Williams, who would become a stockholder in 1962, recalled Marshall saying "that under no circumstances would he change" his hiring policy. Football owners, who had recently signed a lucrative television contract and dreaded the bad publicity of Marshall's intransigence, asked NFL commissioner Pete Rozelle to mediate the conflict.

Selected as a compromise candidate the year before, Commissioner Rozelle initially refused to intervene, labeling the controversy "strictly a club problem." But Udall informed him that the government would not back down, and Rozelle, who had a background in public relations, could identify with owners who were embarrassed by the bad publicity. Prompted by Udall, Rozelle recalled scheduling an August meeting with Marshall and persuading him to relent in the best interests of the sport. Following that meeting, Marshall announced that his team had "no policy against the hiring of football players because of their race" and would consider selecting some black players in the upcoming December draft. He mentioned running backs Ernie Davis of Syracuse University and Larry Ferguson of the University of Iowa as possible choices.

Marshall's conciliatory statement prompted a concession by Udall. He would permit the Redskins to field an all-white team at D.C. Stadium in 1961 if they agreed to place a black player on their roster the following year. Udall made it clear, however, that he was not backing down on his commitment to civil rights. "The Kennedy administration," he asserted, "is determined that every American should have a full and equal opportunity to utilize his or her talents in the classroom, in industry, on the playing field, and in all areas of national life."

Some civil rights activists suspected that the compromise was a delaying tactic that would give Marshall a chance to wiggle out of his stadium lease. The *Washington Afro-American* blasted Udall in an August 26 editorial, and Thomas Stockett supported that editorial with a cartoon depicting George Marshall butt-kicking Udall into a free fall. Another sketch portrayed a burly, helmeted football player identified as "Washington Red Skins White Only Policy" stomping on a prostrate figure labeled "Fan Protest" and "Pro Football's Reputation for Fairness."

Other critics, embittered by Marshall's quarter-century color ban, believed that drafted black athletes should refuse to play for

Hat in hand, a beleaguered George Marshall arrives in Washington from California in mid-August 1961. (Star Collection, DC Public Library, © Washington Post)

the racist owner. Refusing to play for the Redskins was crazy talk, argued sportswriter Sam Lacy. Civil rights advocates had "dramatized under threat of the clenched fist and the Dixie jail, the importance of sacrifice for the sake of justice." If they were drafted and

Cartoonist Thomas Stockett depicts the determined resistance of the Redskins to racial integration, in the *Baltimore Afro-American,* August 26, 1961. (Courtesy of the Afro-American Newspapers Archives and Research Center)

given a fair monetary offer, black athletes would be morally obligated to sign with the Redskins. There was a social justice principle at stake. "Suppose Jackie Robinson had taken the position that, since it was a known fact that baseball didn't want him or his kind back in 1946, he could do without it. Where would we be?" Lacy asked.

When it appeared that Stewart Udall might shy away from his effort to integrate the Redskins, the *Washington Afro-American* published this Thomas Stockett cartoon on August 19, 1961. (Courtesy of the Afro-American Newspapers Archives and Research Center)

Meanwhile, on the West Coast, civil rights activists decided to proceed with their threatened boycott of the Redskins game for charity against the Los Angeles Rams. The boycott was organized for August 11, 1961. Local chapters of the NAACP and CORE promised to picket. Letter writers to the *Sentinel* vowed to skip the game. "If the Redskins are not sports enough to hire Negro players, the Negro should be sports enough not to attend their games," wrote one man. The *Sentinel* also ran a blistering editorial supporting the boycott. It could not understand how, "in this enlightened age," an owner of a team in a city with a majority black population would "deliberately exclude Negroes from its player ranks. It is inconceivable that a team representing the nation's capital, when that nation is competing for the minds and loyalties of the dark peoples of the world in a struggle for survival, still sees fit to discriminate in its hiring policies on the mere question of color. It is inconceivable that any true sportsman would deny opportunity for competition purely on the basis of race." Marshall, it concluded, was "a cancer in professional football" that should be removed.

Marshall seemingly was unmoved by the boycott. "I can't do anything about it, From what I gather, most people don't think anything we're doing is wrong," he related to the *Washington Post.* The charity helps black children through its contributions to city boys' clubs, he said. "I don't understand people complaining about something that helps them."

Not all prominent blacks supported protests against the Redskins. Former NFL player Buddy Young opposed picketing because the "Redskins are the greatest advertisement we have," he said. When asked why, he said: "Because they prove how futile it is to operate without our great colored athletes. They are always last. The glory is ours. The suffering is theirs."

The boycott was not very successful from an economic viewpoint. Carrying signs reading "No Jim Crow Charity," "We Protest Racism in Football," and "Marshall's Got to Go," picketers dissuaded hundreds of people from attending the game. But Pye exaggerated by claiming that the boycott and pickets reduced attendance by 15,000 to 25,000. The boycott generally was downplayed by the mainstream media, especially the *Los Angeles Times,* which sponsored the event. In reality, the contest drew 60,000 fans, up 3,000 from the previous year. While not hurt economically, Marshall did suffer additional bad publicity, and protestors promised continued action "until that great day when liberty and justice for all men become a reality."

Pye and Brockenbury kept on the pressure. Marshall, wrote Brockenbury, "is practicing un-American, unlawful, un-Constitutional, un-civilized acts when he keeps Negroes off his team." By allowing other teams with African American athletes to beat him, he was committing gridiron suicide, or "gridicide," as Brockenbury termed it.

In 1961, Marshall was beset by withering attacks from the mainstream press, black writers, boycotts, and the threat of more boycotts to come in Washington, California, and Southern cities where the Redskins had scheduled exhibition games. White and black fans alike were clamoring for an end to Marshall's racial embargo to improve the team and its image. Other citizens, especially Washingtonians, were embarrassed by the team's exclusionary hiring policy because it seemed un-American. Pressure was mounting to "do something about the Redskins." Black frustration also was sweeping the nation in the form of Freedom Rides, sit-ins, and other demands for racial equality. By summer's end, Marshall indicated that he would heed the administration's demand to integrate the team if a qualified black athlete was available in the December draft. But his immediate concern was to concentrate on the upcoming season.

For the Redskins, the 1961 football season was a nightmare. Black residents, who had become a majority of the District's population by 1960, were now becoming increasingly demonstrative against racial injustice. They boycotted games and picketed the stadium with signs reading "People Who Can't Play Together, Can't Live Together." JFK favored home rule for the District and appointed an African American to serve as a district commissioner. He, Udall, and other cabinet officials also honored the pickets. President Kennedy refused an invitation to attend the opening game at the new stadium. The new facility was attractive, but ticket prices were the highest in the NFL, and attendance was modest.

The Redskins opened the 1961 season in San Francisco with a 35–3 loss to the 49ers, as blacks outside the stadium picketed against Marshall's racial ban. "The greater blow for equal opportunity, however, was struck on the field where the thoroughly integrated 49ers won as they pleased," wrote the *San Francisco Examiner*'s Prescott Sullivan. The 49ers far surpassed the Redskins in total yardage, 399 to 35. The Redskins, he continued, "were helpless. Awful. The worst. They could have used some fast colored backs. Hell, for that matter, they could have used the picket line!" The Redskins' only win of the season came against the Dallas Cowboys in the last game of the season. They finished the season with a record of 1–12–1.

Fans and writers heaped abuse upon Marshall and his coaches. An editorial in the *Washington Afro-American* stated that "some psychoanalysis might reveal that the 'Skins, because they realize that they are completely different from any other team in major sports, have developed a complex and will never become effective until their owner shakes the shackles of his warped way of thinking and really rebuilds the team on an integrated basis."

"What's Wrong with the Washington Redskins?" ran the title of a long article in *Sport*. There were multiple answers, according to *Sport* and other publications interested in the question. First, Marshall had failed to establish a decent scouting system. Second, the team was inexperienced at the coaching level and on the playing field. Head coach Bill McPeak, Assistant Coach Ted Marchibroda, and quarterback Norm Snead were all rookies. Indeed, half of the thirty-six-man squad had a year or less of playing experience. Marchibroda held some fond memories of the team because it was his first as a coach. "But let me tell you," he said decades later to Ken Denlinger of the *Washington Post*, "that '61 ball club was poor. We just didn't have the material. We had to go with a rookie quarterback [Norm Snead]." They also had a "slow halfback named Sam Horner—and McPeak would say: 'Sam Horner can't turn the corner.'" A loyal fan later told Denlinger that, as the losses mounted in the 1961 season, he would sputter: "Week after week, we suffer with McPeak." Marshall himself attributed the poor season to inexperienced players and coaches. "Our youth movement," he told a Dallas sportswriter, "was about as successful as Kennedy's Peace Corps."

Marshall's refusal to recruit talented black players was the most common and accurate explanation for the team's lack of success. "The Redskins are hopelessly handicapped by Marshall's white skin policy," wrote Dan Parker in the *New York Mirror*. "The Redskins end zone has frequently been integrated by Negro players," wrote

Washington Post columnist Shirley Povich, "but never their lineup." "Integrated football long ago was accepted by the players and the fans," he wrote again in mid-November, before the Redskins won their final game. "Marshall has been the only holdout. He has keyed the Redskin promotion to his Southern radio-TV network to exploit Nordic supremacy, which in the case of the Redskins has been nil for seventeen games in a row. Washington has been able to cheer one victory in two years." Although some fans continued to defend Marshall's right to exclude blacks, others believed that African American players, especially a fleet running back, would improve the team.

The Washington media hyped the possibility of the Redskins obtaining Syracuse running back Ernie Davis. "A quiet husky football player whose home base is some 400 miles from Washington is rapidly becoming a central figure in the area's 1961 football picture," wrote Martie Zad in the *Washington Post*. University of Maryland head coach Tom Nugent sent letters to all sixty-six members of his football team to fire them up for the October 7 home game against Syracuse. "We must be ready for them and put on a good show for our fans and for the thousands who will come out to see Davis, now that he has a chance to become a Redskin. It will be an exciting day as the Nation's most outstanding back performs on our field." Before a full house, the Terrapins upset Davis and the seventh-ranked Syracuse Orangemen 22–21.

With its abysmal record of 1 win, 12 losses, and 1 tie, the Redskins would have a real opportunity to improve themselves by making a competent selection in the annual amateur player draft held in December. At the NFL draft in Chicago, wrote Povich, "Marshall's position will be right out of a George Orwell novel, *1984*. Big Brother Udall will be watching Marshall for any crime against the state, meaning failure to conform with fair employment practices." Udall, he quipped "is the first Secretary of [the] Interior with a draft choice in the National Football League."

Separate player drafts were held for the two leagues, which competed for the same players, driving up the price of signing them. The AFL selections would take place on December 2, with those of the NFL two days later. In both leagues, weaker teams, in terms of the previous year's winning percentage, would make selections before stronger teams, thus giving them first dibs on the more-talented players. The Oakland Raiders had the first choice in the AFL draft, while the Redskins had the first pick among NFL teams. Ernie Davis of Syracuse was acknowledged by most experts as the premier player in the draft, and Marshall had indicated that talent, not race, would guide his team's draft selections. But adding Davis to the team was hardly a done deal. Marshall could draft him and be unwilling or unable to match the salary offered by an AFL team; he could draft Davis and trade him for several other players; or he could go rogue by drafting North Carolina State's quarterback Roman Gabriel or the University of Maryland's pass receiver Gary Collins, thereby defying the government and continuing the tradition of selecting white players from Southern colleges. The draft was complicated further by Marshall's nemesis, Harry Wismer. The mercurial owner of the New York Titans coveted Davis and promised to outbid any competitor for his services. To give AFL owners more time to sign college players away from the rival NFL, he convinced them to hold a secret draft two weeks earlier than the announced dates of December 2 for the AFL and December 4 for the NFL. In that so-called "sneak" draft, the Titans selected Ernie Davis. Unhappily for Wismer, AFL commissioner Joe Foss nullified the "sneak" draft because he had not been notified and because it violated a draft selection arrangement that both leagues had made with the NCAA. Although irate over Foss's ruling, Wismer vowed to draft Davis on December 2 and offer him more money than the Redskins. "We'll pay top prices for what we want."

The Redskins also expressed strong interest in Davis. In November, Marshall sent Assistant Coach Ted Marchibroda to South Bend, Indiana, to speak with Davis after the Syracuse–Notre Dame game. Marchibroda simply informed Davis that the Redskins might draft him. "It wasn't anything more definite than that," he told the press. "I had permission from his coach to chat with him and I was very much impressed. He's a high-type boy, shy and quiet."

Marshall also solicited help with Davis from Adam Clayton Powell, an African American congressman from New York. He approached Powell one November evening at Duke Zeibert's restaurant. Addressing Powell as "Parson" (because he was a minister at the Abyssinian Baptist Church in Harlem), he asked him to visit Davis after a Syracuse game to put in a plug for the Redskins. Powell said: "You know, George, I've been thinking. One nigger won't be enough. You need more than one. Three or four niggers would be better." "Oh, Parson, you mean a matched set," Marshall replied.

In a late November press conference, Marshall and Coach Bill McPeak fielded questions about Davis and the upcoming draft. When McPeak was asked if he would trade the draft rights to Davis, Marshall interrupted, saying: "that question should be addressed to me because I am responsible for this team. But I shall defer to the coach. He may make a deal or he may not. It's up to him. Naturally, as owner, I would insist upon being consulted before any decision is made." Asked specifically if the Redskins would draft a black player, Marshall hedged: "If we take a Negro, it will be because we think he is the best pick. It won't be because a player is a Negro." Marshall's vague and defiant tone brought a response from Udall. The time for showboating and posturing, he informed the press, would soon be over. At the player draft on December 4, Marshall would have to show his cards.

CHAPTER 10

Hail Victory

George Marshall had cause to be upbeat about the upcoming NFL draft. First, he had decided to avoid the showdown with Udall by selecting Ernie Davis with the first overall pick. Second, he had doubts about his ability to sign Davis and hoped to trade him for a proven professional player. Third, he coveted the attention that he and his team would receive about whether they would sign Davis, lose him to the rival AFL, or trade him. And finally, he must have taken satisfaction in the frustration of his bitter enemy, New York Titans owner Harry Wismer.

For Wismer, the AFL draft in Dallas on December 2 could not have gone worse. Expecting the eight AFL teams to make selections as they had in the earlier "sneak" draft, he opted not to attend the meeting, sending general manager Steve Sebo to select Ernie Davis with the fifth overall pick. True to form, the first three teams drafted as they had two weeks earlier. Oakland took quarterback Roman Gabriel, Denver chose tackle Merlin Olsen, and Dallas selected local running back Ron Bull. But instead of picking Louisiana State University running back Wendell Harris, as they had two weeks earlier, the Buffalo Bills selected Ernie Davis. The Titans seemed stunned by the departure from the earlier pattern. Confident of obtaining Davis, they failed to have a backup plan. After making two frantic telephone calls without reaching Wismer, Sebo chose Sandy Stephens, an African American quarterback from the University of Minnesota.

The next day, without explaining his previous day's absence from the draft, Wismer fumed about losing Davis and again blasted AFL commissioner Joe Foss for nullifying the "sneak" draft. Wismer also claimed that Davis verbally had agreed to a three-year contract with the Titans for $100,000, plus a $25,000 signing bonus. "I asked him: 'are you satisfied?' And he said, 'yes, very much so.'" Wismer claimed that the Bills did not have the money to attract Davis. He vowed to make a trade with Buffalo, to negotiate with Davis, and to pay any price to keep him away from the Redskins and the NFL.

At the NFL draft at Chicago's Shoreham Hotel on December 4, the showdown between Marshall and Udall never materialized. While there was little drama, there was plenty of intrigue. As McPeak later explained to the *Washington Evening Star*'s Morris Siegel, "He told me we had to get a black player. . . . I didn't understand the politics behind it. He didn't know whether he wanted to draft a black or trade for one with experience, but he said he thought he could work something out with Paul Brown. I had no idea who he was talking about, but I knew it wouldn't be Jimmy Brown." Publicly, and only half-seriously, Marshall had offered a second round draft pick for Bobby Mitchell. That proposal was so lopsided it was not taken seriously, but privately, it escalated into an offer of a first-round pick for the Cleveland running back.

Uncharacteristically, Marshall chose not to attend the draft session, authorizing his head coach, Bill McPeak, to make the selections. With the first selection, McPeak took Ernie Davis, the first black player ever chosen by the Redskins organization. Perhaps as a conciliatory gesture to the White House, he took another minority player, halfback Joe Hernandez from the University of Arizona, Udall's alma mater. And in the seventh round, he drafted Ron Hatcher, an African American from Michigan State.

Udall made no public comment about the draft, but later, he privately reiterated his intention of denying the use of the stadium and, if necessary, battling Marshall in court. Udall also expressed satisfaction that Marshall selected a black player because he wanted to end his personal boycott of Redskins football games.

Publicly, the Washington mainstream and black press applauded the Redskins for selecting Davis. "When the Redskins drafted Davis there was the clear understanding by Marshall that Secretary of Interior Stewart Udall was looking over his shoulder like a baleful Big Brother," wrote the *Washington Post*'s Shirley Povich. Marshall had a choice, he continued, of accepting black players or being "placekicked out of the new $24 million stadium which Udall rules." Owing to his team's dreadful record of two wins in two years, Marshall also was losing some of his Southern television audience. Povich noted that CBS had booted the Redskins game of December 3 in favor of the Giants-Packers contest.

That same morning, before the start of the draft and with Marshall's prior approval, McPeak had verbally and secretly agreed to trade Davis to the Cleveland Browns for proven veteran Bobby Mitchell and Leroy Jackson, a black halfback that he asked Cleveland to take with one of its two first-round picks. The deal was kept secret pending its completion in writing and because Mitchell had the remainder of the regular season and possibly postseason games to play. In addition, Marshall wanted to milk the publicity surrounding the selection, signability, and possible trade of Davis.

Rumors of the trade leaked out almost immediately. Baltimore Colts owner Carroll Rosenbloom said two days after the draft: "I'll bet all I own the Browns end up with Davis. I think repercussions in Washington will be considerable when the fans learn the Redskins have traded Davis to a team in their own division." Asked if the Redskins could sign Davis, Marshall boasted: "I think it's no problem." Pushed about whether he had traded Davis, Marshall said: "I wouldn't say so." While misleading, Marshall's statements were not outright lies because he really did not have worries about signing Davis, and he had not traded him officially because the legal paperwork had not been completed.

Meanwhile, Marshall basked in the publicity. When Davis went to New York to receive the Heisman Trophy, President Kennedy asked to meet with him at the Waldorf Astoria Hotel. "We were standing in the anteroom talking," Davis said, "when the doors open and here comes the president. He walked up and introduced himself: 'Hi, I'm Jack Kennedy.'" Then JFK congratulated Davis on winning the Heisman Trophy. "It was the greatest thrill of my life—that and receiving the Heisman Trophy. Imagine a President wanting to shake hands with me." When JFK asked him about his future plans, he replied: "I play in the Liberty Bowl at Philadelphia December 16, sir. After that, I haven't made up my mind." Davis added, "The President may have been interested in whether I was coming to Washington. I couldn't tell him. I'll study all the offers and accept what I think is the best deal." He also mentioned his lack of interest in being a racial pioneer. "I am not interested in the racial issue," he stated. "All I want to do is be a success. I don't feel the Redskins would be making a case for me like Jackie Robinson in baseball. I just don't think about those things."

Davis's indifference toward being a racial pioneer concerned some black leaders. A *Washington Afro-American* editorial, "A Confused Ernie Davis," took issue with Davis's desire to be just a regular guy: "American society has not granted any colored person this privilege." If Davis signed with the Redskins, he would soon learn that not just any guy could rent property on Connecticut Avenue, on Wisconsin Avenue, or in Georgetown. "Any colored person who wins acclaim must share the spotlight of racial accomplishment. He becomes a symbol, and if he's got a miniscule of racial pride, he's proud to be one." The acclaimed Jackie Robinson shared that sentiment. Not wanting to take responsibility for advancing the cause of racial equality, he said, had been taken "by many of the professional people on and off the athletic field [and] gives comfort to the bigot." Robinson attributed Davis's anti-pioneer stance to naivete more than indifference.

Ultimately, Ron Hatcher, the eighth-round draft choice from Michigan State, not Davis, became the first African American to sign a contract with the Redskins. Hatcher downplayed its racial significance. "To me this is just a job," he declared, "nothing else. It is a challenge, yes. But a challenge only in the sense that every new step is a challenge." Nearly always a lightning rod, Marshall brought controversy to the signing ceremony by refusing to be photographed with Hatcher. He did not want to "exploit" the situation, he said, and instructed Coach McPeak to pose with Hatcher instead. Besides being a racist, Marshall seemed to have opposed the invitation to be photographed with Hatcher because he did not want to bring more attention to the twenty-five years of Redskins racial bigotry.

President Kennedy congratulates Heisman Trophy recipient Ernie Davis in New York City. (Cecil Stoughton, White House / John F. Kennedy Presidential Library and Museum, Boston)

Marshall's "sudden act of tender concern" over exploitation brought yet another public rebuke from Shirley Povich. Marshall, he asserted, was a promoter who had made a career of exploiting not only football players, but "laundries, auto races, basketball teams, state fairs, radio-TV, and even the Southern Confederacy, none of them shyly." Still, he continued, Marshall should be commended for yielding to White House pressure to sign an African American player. "It could be the beginning of better football for Washington fans and is certainly the beginning of a more dignified football situation here. Whether Davis or Hatcher, or both, make good is not of the utmost importance. More wholesomeness has been attained." Moreover, if the Redskins failed to sign Davis, it would be for financial considerations, not racial ones. "No longer are colored players born ineligible for the Redskins," he wrote. "That is a gain."

Signing Hatcher was considered a significant story by the regional black press, and the *Afro-American* lifted its quarter-century news boycott, sending its acclaimed sports editor, Sam Lacy, to cover it.

Marshall consented to an interview at his office on 9th and H streets, even though the two men had not talked to one another for years. After offering a grin, a handshake, and a chair to Lacy, Marshall said: "It has been a long time—fifteen, twenty, twenty-five years?" Lacy answered twenty, maybe twenty-five years. "I had no reason to see you before today," Lacy said. "You made your policy clear to me the last time we discussed the matter." But circumstances changed, he said, when the Redskins agreed to lift the racial ban. Marshall, he acknowledged, had shown good faith by drafting three players and signing Hatcher. "We intend to go along with you until we have reason to suspect that your organization is not acting in good faith."

Marshall, according to Lacy, attempted to downplay his record of bigotry by alerting him to a story that had not been written about—namely, his many contributions to the economic advancement of blacks. "For years, I was one of the city's largest employers of colored persons. I was the first laundry operator to use all colored route men. How many do you see on laundry trucks today? I was the first to use colored ushers and vendors at Griffith Stadium athletic contests, and at one time, there were nearly 500 colored persons employed by [the Palace Laundry]." It was one thing to hire blacks for menial jobs, countered Lacy, but it was quite another to employ them in professional capacities. Marshall, he said, believed that African Americans were intellectually suited only for menial work. Marshall made no effort to deny that assertion. When Lacy pressed for the reason that he would not be photographed with Hatcher, Marshall again offered the excuse that he did not want to "exploit the boy." "Why take pictures with Hatcher," he said, "when we have scores of rookies who sign Redskin contracts each year. I don't pose with them." He just wanted Hatcher to play football, not play racial pioneer.

On December 15, the *Washington Post* reported the trade of Davis to the Cleveland Browns for their first draft choice, Leroy Jackson, and a player to be named later, rumored to be Bobby Mitchell, the now-veteran running back. Technically, the Browns acquired only the negotiating rights to Davis. If they lost him in a bidding war with the Bills or Titans, the Redskins would still keep their acquired players in the trade.

Several factors prompted Marshall to trade Davis. First, Davis would be pricy and difficult to sign. Although he had not secured the draft rights to Davis, Wismer had set a lofty salary bar of $125,000 for three years, and Marshall was not about to pay any player, white or black, that much money. Second, he doubted that Davis wanted to play for the Redskins, given his rumored statements about not wanting to be a racial pioneer. Third, he could personally attest to Mitchell's versatility and breakaway speed, having watched him, in a recent October game against the Redskins, score three touchdowns on a 52-yard pass, a 64-yard punt return, and a 31-yard run. And in a 1959 game at Griffith Stadium, he witnessed Mitchell rack up 232 yards on fourteen carries. "The Redskins," noted Shirley Povich, "have scouted him mainly from the rear." Under intense pressure from an increasingly hostile fan base, Marshall wanted a proven black player who could help the team immediately. He divulged that he had initially offered Davis to Baltimore for Lenny Moore, but the Colts had turned him down. "When the deal is fully announced," said Marshall, "I think the fans will agree it should mean immediate victories for the Redskins. Maybe in the long run, it won't turn out so hot. I don't belittle the great ability of Davis and think he'll be great in the NFL. We think we've solved immediate problems confronting us."

Owing to choppy, wintry home-field playing conditions, the Cleveland Browns sought a swift and powerful runner to pair with Jim Brown in the backfield. Mitchell was speedy but slight, featuring shiftiness and balance more than power. Mitchell glided; Brown pounded. Moreover, Mitchell had a military commitment with the Reserves at Fort Meade, Maryland, that made him available only on the weekend. "I was leaving military duty every weekend and starting for the Browns," Mitchell later recalled. "I'd get there Saturday morning, find out what the game plan was, and play the game the next day." Art Modell, who had acquired the Browns in 1961, coveted Davis. "It would have been the greatest backfield in the history of the NFL," he later told Steve Jensen of the *Elmira Star-Gazette*. "We would have surpassed the Paul Hornung–Jim Taylor backfield of the old Green Bay Packers. We would have been better than that." Jim Brown was less enthusiastic about the trade. "I thought Bobby Mitchell was the perfect complement to my style. He returned punts, kickoffs, he had outside speed. He was a touchdown guy. Ernie was the same as me. But all that aside," he continued, "I knew Ernie would be a great, great pro. I was excited to have him playing on the team with me." Soon after starring against Miami in the Liberty Bowl, Davis signed a $200,000, no-cut contract with the Browns. Tragically, in 1962, he was diagnosed with acute leukemia and never played professionally. He died in mid-May 1963.

Mitchell joined the Redskins after the trade became official in 1962. That spring, the team added another experienced African American athlete when it acquired guard John Nisby from the Pittsburgh Steelers. The Redskins had "done a complete turnaround in their hiring policy," beamed Sam Lacy. In all, the roster might include five black players. Moreover, trading a white player—Ray Lemek—for a black one—Nisby—"served to further bolster the belief that Washington's pro football scene will be desegregated this fall."

In all, five African American athletes had a chance to make the Redskins' 1962 roster. Joe Hernandez, however, waited to sign until 1964 and played sparingly for only that one year. Ron Hatcher, the first black to sign with the Redskins, played three games in 1962 before being released. Like Mitchell, Leroy Jackson was a college track star with blazing speed. But unlike Mitchell, he lacked running and pass-catching ability. He played two years but saw limited action. His hands were so bad, said Redskins minority owner Ed Williams, he "fumbled" his bus ticket on the way out of town. Mitchell and Nisby, however, made major contributions. Nisby was selected to three Pro Bowls; Mitchell, four. Mitchell was also elected to the Pro Football Hall of Fame.

Nisby and Mitchell roomed together, but they possessed contrasting personalities. Nisby was assertive, outgoing, and outspoken. Mitchell was reticent, restrained, and reflective. "You talk about two contrasting individuals—me and John Nisby," Mitchell related to the magazine *Black Sports* in 1978. "John was the real free spirit, back then, and he didn't give a darn about anything. A heck of a ballplayer. And Bobby Mitchell, the conservative, quiet, gentleman-type guy. It was really something. The real difference between me and Nisby, of course, was, if something went down, black or white, you heard about it. If it went down on Bobby Mitchell, he clamped down and didn't say anything. But our personalities complemented each other."

Aware of the Redskins' discriminatory policy, both Mitchell and Nisby approached their new team with some apprehension. "I honestly feel good about coming to the Redskins," Mitchell told reporters at the time. Later, he described the move as "traumatic" because he had to endure "verbal abuse" and "a great deal of racial discrimination from the fans and the Washington community."

At his first training camp at Occidental College in California, Mitchell expressed shock, not over matters of race, but over the lack of talent he saw on the field. "I kept waiting for somebody to walk out there who *looked* like they could play football," he recalled. "And I said to Bill McPeak, '*This* is the team?' and he said, 'Oh, yeah, this is the team.' It was a real shock for me because I had come from a team with real personnel. It just scared hell out of me." He encountered more shocks when he arrived in Washington.

An Arkansas native, Mitchell considered Washington, D.C., to be "the North." But shortly after returning from training camp in California, he learned that Washington was not free from Jim Crow. "I began to go places and people kinda got uptight," he remembered. "All of a sudden I thought 'Holy Hell.' Because I hadn't experienced that." There were restaurants that were off-limits. On one occasion, he and Assistant Coach Ted Marchibroda left Redskins headquarters "to a place across the street where the coaches used to eat all the time. He invited me in. We walk up to the door, and all of a sudden, the guy doesn't know him. I was so embarrassed for Ted, because I caught on pretty quick. So I said: 'There's another place where I've been wanting to eat.' I didn't even know the name of the damn place. I just pointed to the first joint I saw." Mitchell, as Ken Denlinger relates in the *Washington Post*'s publication *Redskins: A History of Washington's Team,* also remembered being spit on while dining at Duke Zeibert's restaurant.

Despite a hostile racial climate, Mitchell faced enormous pressure to perform at a high level. "It was a real traumatic thing to come from a winning football team, great surroundings, where your coach and management looked after you, to come here, where you were being called 'nigger' every day, and every time you run down the field, some guy's throwing something at you—it was really a terrible situation. And we're talking about the 60s. To have all that on your shoulders and try to perform," he continued, "you had both white and black who couldn't stand for you to make a mistake. I didn't have the luxury of dropping the ball; I didn't have the luxury of not gaining yardage and having a bad day—it just wasn't allowed."

Mitchell minimized his role as a racial pioneer. "I'd been through being a first before," he stated. "At Illinois, I was selected to integrate a dorm. And with a white student, not an athlete." He also downplayed comparisons with Jackie Robinson. He believed that his Hall of Fame career would have been even more stellar had he been able to handle the racial pressure as well as Robinson. "I wasn't quite as tough as Jackie," he told the magazine *Black Sports*. The racial slurs "affected me greatly—and I haven't forgotten them."

Less sensitive, John Nisby found "little difference playing with the Redskins and playing with the Steelers." The stamina, focus, and discipline required to play the game well, he said, enabled him to block out outside distractions, including racial slurs.

Second-year Redskins quarterback Norm Snead recalled to me that virtually all of the Redskins players considered the color barrier "ridiculous." Mitchell and Nisby, he remembered, were talented players and "great human beings" who were "received enthusiastically and with open arms." Nisby recalled that on one occasion, a group of players went to a Virginia nightclub. When the black players were refused admittance, their white teammates left with them.

Mitchell was more guarded about his reception by teammates. "Some of the whites didn't want me there, and the blacks got mad if I'd drop the ball. To the blacks, I had to be perfect. But Norm Snead was great. He just wanted to throw the ball to a guy who would go get it." But some teammates were not welcoming. "They were used to playing mediocre football and still being in the paper," he related. "All of a sudden, I'm raising a little hell on the field, so I was getting in the paper. It was a little tough on 'em. And they got the rumors, too, that maybe I'm making more money than some of 'em." Indeed, Mitchell almost instantly became the highest-paid Redskins player.

Mitchell and Nisby held different views of Marshall. Still in the Reserves at Fort Meade, Mitchell first met with Marshall on a summer weekend. Marshall said: "Bobby, I'm glad to see you. I'm going to take you out of the shadow of Jimmy Brown. Put you out front." When it came time to negotiate a contract, Mitchell asked Washington attorney Turk Thompson to accompany him. When they entered Marshall's office, he asked Thompson why he was there. "I'm with Bobby . . . to help him out." "No, you're not," Marshall bellowed. "Get out of here." Having dispensed with legal counsel, Marshall said to Mitchell: "Bob, I have three things I want to say to you. First, you must remember you're in a political town and I want you to stay out of politics. Secondly, I just want you to be a good guy. And third, I don't want you to ask for too much money."

Almost immediately, Mitchell failed to heed two of Marshall's three directives. In late April 1962, he and another Fort Meade reservist, Dick Schaffrath of the Philadelphia Eagles, agreed to hold an autograph session at the Presidential Arms in Washington with the proceeds from the fifty-cent admission fee going to support the Democratic National Committee. Mitchell also wanted a raise in salary. "That was a little tough for [George] Preston Marshall to take," he recalled, because Marshall believed that the quarterback should be the highest-paid team member. But Marshall eventually relented.

To Mitchell, Marshall was "a nice man" who "never came across to me as a bigot or showed any behavior in that manner," he related in an interview with me. When he made those remarks, however, he was still employed by the Redskins and was hesitant to criticize the organization's founder. He was less guarded about other people in the organization who did not treat him as well as the owner. Overall, fans, some teammates, and many former players were not welcoming. "My problem with them," he told *Black Sports,* "was that I knew that I was performing quite well and I knew that I was the best thing that had happened to them in some time. And yet, I was not received in that manner away from the field. Of course, I had the usual problems that any black guy has being the star of the team. There were certain players who just couldn't accept that. . . . But I dealt pretty well with that because I could play pretty well on Sundays. But I just wasn't accepted in the manner I felt I should've been by the people. And particularly the ex-Redskins. They just didn't quite open their arms to me."

Mitchell also downplayed the team's history of racism. He attributed Marshall's lily-white hiring record to personality and business. Marshall, he insisted, was genetically stubborn and resisted advice to integrate the team. He was also a savvy business executive who fed on the prejudice of his mainly white Southern audience. "We had trains coming here from down South," he told *Black Sports*. "'Dixie' was the National anthem and you had to stand up there and sing it or he'd give you the devil. But that's how he made his money. He was a businessman and he was doing the same as IBM and everyone else: He was capturing his market. It was tough when we had to go down to some of those Southern towns to play exhibition games, but [George] Preston Marshall and the Redskins were always in the black, never in the red, because the Southern people kept him in good stead."

Nisby was less charitable toward Marshall. "I never appreciated the man at all, because of the stand he took on blacks prior to my arrival here. My relationship with the front office wasn't really that great." He also had difficulty accepting Bill McPeak as head coach because he had outperformed him and had taken his job at guard with the Steelers. His dismissive attitude toward McPeak and his demand for a salary increase after the 1963 season brought his release and an end to his football career.

In late April 1962, Mitchell signed a contract with the Redskins for a reported $20,000, the highest in team history. His signing, remarked African American columnist Cal Jacox of the *Norfolk New Journal and Guide*, "should erase all doubts as to the future of the club's new hiring policy." At the photo-free signing, Marshall hurled some words of defiance at the Kennedy White House. Udall's big-stick ultimatum had no influence on his decision to hire black players, he claimed. "Our lawyers and for that matter some of the secretary's own legal talent told him he could not keep us out of the stadium," he bellowed. "We wanted Mitchell because he was the best available offensive back in the league and for no other reason." If he was responding to a White House ultimatum, he continued, he would have added only one token black player, not several, to the roster.

With the addition of Mitchell and Nisby, the Redskins approached the 1962 season with cautious optimism. So did their fans. Some African Americans, still resentful over Marshall's longtime racial ban, continued to boycott games. Others came out to games for the first time or ended their boycott. If Marshall could have a change of heart, said one fan, so could he. *Los Angeles Sentinel* columnist L. I. Brockenbury probably expressed the sentiment of most black fans when he stated in a June 1962 column that the Redskins now deserved the support of black fans.

Marshall himself expressed optimism over what he called the team's "new look." The Redskins, he said poolside from a Beverly Hills resort, had added "sting" to their offense with Mitchell, Jackson, Nisby, and fullback Bill Barnes, who was acquired by a trade with the Eagles. "Fans around the league certainly are familiar with Mitchell's ability. He and young Jackson give us a commodity we've lacked—a breakaway threat. And this should make Snead even more valuable to us," he said. Marshall was so promotion-minded, said Melvin Durslag of the *Los Angeles Herald Examiner,* that he probably would claim that the integration of professional football was his idea.

At guard, Nisby helped to anchor the offensive line, while Mitchell was converted to flanker to capitalize on his agility and speed. Both players distinguished themselves. In the first game at Dallas, which ended in a tie, Mitchell ran back a kickoff for a ninety-two-yard touchdown and scored on two passes from Snead. In the second game at Cleveland, he caught a fifty-yard pass in the final minutes to upset the Browns, 17–16.

The Redskins' first home game was against the St. Louis Cardinals. Udall accepted Marshall's invitation to be a special guest. Once again, Snead and Mitchell, the city's "greatest battery since Walter Johnson and Gabby Street," brought the team victory. Mitchell caught touchdown passes of forty and twenty-three yards. After Mitchell's first score, Udall recalled the remarks of a foghorn-voiced black man seated near him: "Thank God for Mr. Udall."

"It could only happen in Washington, of course," wrote UPI Washington correspondent Lyle Wilson, "that a politician, merely by a commitment to civil rights, could turn a losing football team into a winner."

After the first six games, Redskins fans were nearly euphoric, the team having amassed a league-leading record of 4 wins, 0 losses, and 2 ties. "The Redskins Find a New Kick—Winning," ran a mid-October article in *Sports Illustrated.* "They think they can lick any team in football," remarked Coach McPeak, "and some of this is due to Bobby Mitchell because the kids know he can break up a ball game at any time from any spot on the field." New York Giants coach Allie Sherman called him "the greatest open field runner in the league." And a reporter for the African Negro Press news service described him as "running through opposing lines like [Mississippi] Gov. Ross Barnett was after him." "We don't know how long it will last, but *OUR* integrated Washington Redskins are now in first place in the National Football League. And we join hundreds of thousands of fans in the District of Columbia in shouting joyfully 'Go, you Redskins!'" editorialized the *Washington Afro-American.*

Marshall, too, was pleased with the "new look" Redskins. In early November, prior to a home game against the Cowboys, Marshall consented to an interview with Frank Boggs of the *Dallas Times Herald.* Asked if he anticipated a merger of the two professional football leagues in the foreseeable future, he said: "There's no reason for one. The other league has nothing to offer." When the topic turned to the Redskins, he attributed the team's early success to the acquisition of Mitchell and the maturation of first-year players like Norm Snead.

> Q.—How have the Redskin fans reacted to your breaking the color line?
>
> A.—They haven't paid any attention to it. Only thing that ever interested them is can they play football. That's the most important thing.
>
> Q.—Once, you were picketed because of not playing Negroes. . . . Did that picketing ever bother you?
>
> A.—No.

Bobby Mitchell is tackled after running a double-reverse for a short gain in an October 8, 1962, game against the L.A. Rams at D.C. Stadium. (Star Collection, DC Public Library, © Washington Post)

Q.—Were you forced by Stuart [*sic*] Udall (secretary of [the]interior) into breaking the color line, or did . . .

A.—No, No, No! He had nothing to do with it.

Q.—Just how valuable has Mitchell been to your club?

A.—Well, I think one of the biggest things you can put down is the fact that he has made 11 touchdowns in seven games, so just figure it out for yourself. That's a tremendous answer.

Cartoonist Thomas Stockett portrays a grateful George Marshall giving thanks for Bobby Mitchell in the *Washington Afro-American,* September 29, 1962. (Courtesy of the Afro-American Newspapers Archives and Research Center)

Mitchell was elated to be a pass receiver with the Redskins: "I think catching a pass is the greatest experience in football." With the arrival of cold weather, he complained, Cleveland coach Paul Brown had given him few opportunities at running back. "Late in the season, when the ground became a little hard, he'd come up to me before a game and tell me, 'It's not your kind of day.' Of course, he put me in there for running back kickoffs and running back punts and running with short flare passes. But when it came to carrying from scrimmage, it was all Jimmy Brown. I wondered if the footing was all right for me to run with kicks and passes, why couldn't I carry the ball from scrimmage too?"

The Redskins could not sustain their strong start, ending the season with five consecutive losses. Still, they attained their best record in years, with 5 victories, 7 losses, and 2 ties. Mitchell led the league with seventy-two receptions and also tallied eleven touchdowns to earn selection to the Pro Bowl. For the third consecutive year, Nisby also was selected to play in the Pro Bowl. Nisby was given a modest raise to $13,000 for the coming year. Rewarded with a $5,000 increase to $25,000 yearly, Mitchell celebrated by buying a gun-barrel-gray Corvette Stingray.

Other events besides the five consecutive football losses brought Washingtonians back to reality. Sam Lacy reminded them that "nothing could be more cruel" than watching Ernie Davis aimlessly wandering the corridors of the National Institutes of Health in Bethesda, Maryland, wondering if he would ever play football again. In mid-October, there was a daunting confrontation between President Kennedy and Premier Khrushchev over the placement of Russian missiles in Cuba. That same month, there was also a civil rights standoff between JFK and Governor Ross Barnett over the admission of James Meredith, the first black to attend the University of Mississippi. Redskins defensive tackle Ed Khayat was called to duty in the Mississippi National Guard to help quell riots over Meredith's admission. Closer to home, more than 50,000 fans attended a Thanksgiving Day championship football game at D.C. Stadium between St. John's (mainly white) and Eastern (mainly black) high schools. At the game's conclusion, won by St. John's 20–7, a melee—or race riot, as some reports described it—erupted between black and white fans and players. Forty people were injured and fourteen arrested.

Although racial injustice persisted, the successful integration of the Washington Redskins won praise for the Kennedy administration. Black sportswriter L. I. Brockenbury of the *Los Angeles Sentinel* called the desegregation of the team "earth-shaking," and Sam Lacy termed it "a revolution in Washington." *Ebony* listed the desegregation of the Redskins as one of the many civil rights achievements of 1961. Indeed, more progress toward racial equality was made that year, the magazine declared, than in any other year in the 1950s. Sportswriters dubbed Udall "coach of the year" and the "most valuable player" in the NFL. Other writers, losing their perspective, called the integration of the Redskins an achievement comparable to James Meredith's successful efforts to enroll at the University of Mississippi. "The integration success story of the Kennedy administration," wrote *Boston Globe* Washington correspondent Wilfrid Rodgers, "didn't take place in Mississippi but here in the back yard of the nation's capital."

As Jackie Robinson and other black leaders were quick to point out, John Kennedy was not fully committed to civil rights. He moved cautiously and occasionally reneged on campaign promises for fear of alienating white Southern members of Congress. Foreign policy also took precedence over civil rights. Yet unlike the Eisenhower administration, the Kennedy White House took positive steps to combat racial injustice. One of those modest steps was the successful showdown with the bigoted owner of a professional football team in the nation's capital.

Ironically, the forced integration of the Redskins did not seem to produce a just result. The transaction that brought Bobby Mitchell to the Redskins turned out to be completely one-sided. The Cleveland Browns, one of the first teams to reintegrate the sport, received a Heisman Trophy winner who never played professionally due to circumstances beyond his control. The Redskins, owned by a racist owner who had steadfastly resisted integration, obtained a future Hall of Famer. But George Marshall would not have long to enjoy his good fortune.

CHAPTER 11

Running Out the Clock

In December 1962, Washington Pigskin Club president Lawrence Oxley sent Marshall a light-hearted letter lifting the "Curse" that his organization had placed on the team for its ban against black players. The removal of the Redskins Curse, however, did not bring immediate success. Marshall had made some organizational changes, adding the acclaimed trial lawyer Edward Bennett Williams as a team director and stockholder in March 1962 and moving the team training camp from California to Dickinson College in Carlisle, Pennsylvania, the next year. He also continued to draft African American players, selecting defensive back Lonnie Sanders from Michigan State in the second round in 1963. But overall, the 1963 team regressed, winning only three of fourteen games. Snead had an off year, completing only thirteen touchdown passes, down nine from the previous year. He also was intercepted twenty-seven times. Mitchell continued to dazzle, however, snagging sixty-nine passes for 1,436 yards, seven touchdowns, and another selection to the Pro Bowl.

Besides the lack of on-field success, the year was marked by the massive March on Washington on August 28, when some 250,000 people gathered at the Lincoln Memorial to show their support for the goal of racial equality. On that day, Martin Luther King Jr. eloquently expressed the hope of all blacks for racial justice in his "I Have a Dream" speech. Mitchell's wife, Gwen, participated in that demonstration, as did Redskins quarterback Norm Snead. When

National Guardsmen encircled Snead as he signed autographs for adoring fans, Jack Walsh of the *Washington Post* remarked: "That's the most protection Snead has had all year." Reserved and not much of a joiner (he had yet to join the NAACP), Bobby Mitchell did not participate in the march. He believed that he contributed to the cause on the field. "Look at the strides we have made in sports. Tremendous!" he told a reporter for *Sport*. "I don't have to apologize to anybody. Everytime I run down that field, I am doing something tremendous for the Negro race." Having a racial bigot as a boss and paymaster also may have prompted Mitchell's lack of activism. Eventually, he overcame his reserve and became a champion of opportunities for blacks, especially in sports as head coaches and front-office executives.

The year also was marred by the devastating and shocking assassination of President Kennedy in November. As the nation mourned, NFL commissioner Pete Rozelle callously decided to proceed with Sunday games. One of the Redskins' three wins came in Philadelphia only two days after President Kennedy's death. It was a somber victory.

George Marshall also experienced life-altering health issues in 1963. The previous year, he had entered the hospital for a hernia operation and made a full recovery; yet all was not well. Marshall's physician diagnosed him with arteriosclerosis (hardening of the brain arteries). As was his custom, he went to Miami Beach, where he spent much of the winter at the posh Kenilworth Hotel owned by Redskins stockholder Leo DeOrsey. There, Marshall appeared to be physically and mentally feisty as usual, holding court on a variety of issues. He informed Floridians that he preferred California oranges. He told Orange Bowl officials that their pageant and game had become boring and needed punching up. He advised Miamians that they did not have a big enough population to support a pro football franchise and that their sports pages contained too much information on horse racing. He supported Commissioner Rozelle's investigation of gambling in pro football and said fellow owners, like Art Rooney, should serve as better role models by forgoing the racetrack. His demands of hotel employees demonstrated his characteristic pettiness. In the hotel dining room, he requested a chocolate ice cream cone. The waiter informed him that ice cream was served in dishes, not cones. "You'll bring me a cone," Marshall blared. "I saw a kid come out of the kitchen with a cone the other day, so I know you've got 'em back there." He got the cone.

While in Miami, Marshall learned that he and sixteen other men had been selected as charter members of the Pro Football Hall of Fame. Located in Canton, Ohio, under the direction of former Redskins general manager Dick McCann, the hall would hold its inaugural induction ceremony in mid-July 1963. Besides Marshall, inductees included deceased Giants owner Tim Mara, ex-commissioners Joe Carr and Bert Bell, and George Halas and Curly Lambeau. Besides front-office types, the list included former players like Jim Thorpe, Red Grange, Bronko Nagurski, Ernie Nevers, Don Hutson, and Sammy Baugh. Asked for his reaction to his selection to the hall, Marshall said: "It makes you feel old. . . . Well let's face it I am old. I hope they don't try to stuff me and put me in a showcase."

Over the next few months, he began to fail physically and mentally. He departed from routine by extending his stay in Florida, missing the opening day of the Washington Senators baseball season for the first time ever. When his associates saw him, they were stunned that this titan had morphed into a frail old man. He couldn't remember names. Still, he managed to maintain his rigid routine of arising at ten, having breakfast prepared by his cook, and working the rest of the day at Redskins headquarters. But he knew he was not well.

In mid-July 1963, just as the Redskins were about to begin training at their new camp in Carlisle, Pennsylvania, he entered Georgetown Hospital for rest and tests. There the diagnosis of arteriosclerosis was confirmed. He also suffered from diabetes, a stomach aneurysm, emphysema, and a weakened heart. While in the hospital, he suffered a mild stroke that further affected his ability to speak, walk, and make judgments. As George Clifford of the *Washington Daily News* put it: "Perhaps nothing worse could happen to a man of Marshall's talents. His life and success were predicated upon his ability to transmit his never-ending stream of ideas. The difficulty in communications had to be particularly frustrating for him."

Marshall had to forgo the Hall of Fame induction ceremony, a decision that must have pained him because he so relished being the center of attention. Longtime Redskins associate Milton King represented Marshall at Canton.

In town in mid-August for a Bears-Redskins exhibition game, George Halas and Commissioner Pete Rozelle visited Marshall in the hospital. Marshall, nearly sixty-seven, and Halas, a year older, had been rivals for more than thirty years. Marshall's friend Morris Siegel of the *Washington Evening Star* was present and reported on the meeting. Shaken and near tears at the frail appearance of his onetime roaring rival, Halas tried to be upbeat. "Hello, Dynamite," he greeted. "Good to see you again."

"Sit down, Georgie," Marshall whispered. "You brought the commish, eh? You never change, Georgie. Still trying to get the edge." Halas turned to Rozelle and recounted the many rule changes Marshall had initiated, including opening the game to more passing. "We got those rule changes through by a three-to-two vote. Remember, George?" Rozelle asked who voted against them. "You'd never guess," Marshall said. "Two damn good passers, Benny Friedman and Curly Lambeau."

When Siegel asked what team Friedman coached, Marshall promptly and correctly identified the Brooklyn Dodgers. Halas tried to tease additional conversation, but Marshall remained mainly unresponsive. Halas did coax a smile when he said the gate for that evening's game might total $200,000. And as he left, Marshall thanked him for the flowers he had sent. "Nice of you," he said. "The girl doesn't forget the man who doesn't forget. See you at the game tonight." Marshall attended the game in a wheelchair, but he stayed for only a half before leaving.

Halas, joined by Pittsburgh Steelers owner Art Rooney, last visited Marshall in 1968 at his Georgetown home. Marshall lay speechless and nearly comatose, so Halas and Rooney had to do all the talking. "It was very hard and very awkward," Rooney told Roy McHugh of the *Pittsburgh Press.* Then Halas asked Marshall's nurse if there was any alcohol in the house. She produced a quart of whiskey, and Halas poured himself a water glass full and downed it. Halas, recalled Rooney, "got loose, real loose, talking to Marshall about a lot of things that happened in the past," and soon Marshall was smiling and crying. Rooney told him that he would need his wheelchair to get Halas home and Marshall smiled again. "I was real proud of Halas that day," Rooney said.

With Marshall addled mentally, board members Milton King, Leo DeOrsey and Edward Williams, all attorneys, petitioned the court to take control of the team temporarily. NFL rules prohibiting ownership in other professional sports leagues forbade the other stockholder, Jack Kent Cooke, from helping to run the Redskins. Cooke, who lived in California, was busy establishing the Los Angeles Lakers professional basketball and Los Angeles Kings professional ice hockey franchises.

Sam Lacy insensitively claimed that Marshall's mental deterioration derived from being forced to hire black players. But Coach Mike Nixon had noticed signs of dementia in Marshall as early as 1960. "There was no scouting system," he complained to the *Washington Post*'s Bob Addie. "We literally drafted players out of those magazine previews. Marshall wouldn't let me send my coaches out in the spring to scout other teams for trade material. But Marshall was on the decline physically at the time and I didn't know it. That accounted for a lot of his idiosyncrasies."

With Marshall sidelined at his Georgetown home with round-the-clock nursing care, DeOrsey became the face and acting president of the franchise. He was a fifty-eight-year-old tax attorney who held 13 percent of the Redskins' stock, valued at $10 million. Marshall retained 52 percent; Cooke held 25 percent; and Williams and King held 5 percent each. "Mr. Marshall is our head man. All I'm doing is substituting for him until he gets back," he told the press. All football decisions would be handled by Coach McPeak. With a history of heart problems, DeOrsey was asked by reporters who would be in charge if he became incapacitated. "We haven't gotten around to naming an assistant to the assistant," he replied. "I imagine it would be quite a scramble."

The team scrambled on the field and in the courts for the remainder of Marshall's life. In 1964, McPeak traded Norm Snead to the Philadelphia Eagles for quarterback Sonny Jurgensen. He also acquired the respected linebacker Sam Huff from the New York Giants and drafted the explosive African American running back Charley Taylor, whom he eventually converted to receiver.

In late July 1964, DeOrsey and Marshall traveled to Carlisle, Pennsylvania, to watch the team work out. DeOrsey told the team that Marshall was "'the Big Chief' and always will be." The two men were visiting, he said, "to see, and be seen, rather than heard." Marshall, accompanied by a chauffeur and two nurses, arrived in an air-conditioned limousine and watched practice from a wheelchair. Vince Promuto, one of the team's captains, assured him that the team was starting to gel and prospects looked promising for a winning season. Marshall responded: "It's too early to tell." Marshall was right. Jurgensen's pass-throwing brilliance, Huff's defensive prowess, and the explosiveness of Mitchell and Taylor were not enough for a winning season. The team had a high-powered offense but won six games and lost eight, a record they duplicated the following year.

One of those wins, in late October 1964, came against the Bears. Once again, Halas visited Marshall on the sideline before the game. "Good to see you. So really good, Chief," Halas said. Marshall's response was only tears. "You've been great for our game," Halas said. "It's like old times." Marshall's only reaction was more tears.

With DeOrsey's death in April 1965, Williams took control of the team. As acting president, he replaced Coach McPeak with famed quarterback Otto Graham, who had been coaching at the Coast Guard Academy. Graham guided the team to a 7–7 record in 1966 (the NFL extended the regular season to fourteen games beginning in 1961), but won only five games in each of the next two years and was replaced by Vince Lombardi, the legendary coach of the Green Bay Packers, who agreed to head the team for fifty shares of stock. Although he had lost Bobby Mitchell to retirement, Lombardi led the Redskins to a record of 7–5–2, their first winning season since 1955. Unfortunately, after that season, Lombardi was diagnosed with colon cancer, and he died in September 1970. His stock was bought back by the Redskins. Bill Austin succeeded Lombardi as coach in 1970, but he lasted only a year.

The team's scramble in the courts was more tenacious than some of their battles on the field. With multiple motions and affidavits, two wills, imprisonment for contempt of court, and charges of fraud, lying, and ethics violations, the legal tangle went on for eight years. "George Marshall Still Center of Controversy" ran the headline of a 1968 Walter Pincus story in the *Washington Post.*

With Marshall's health in decline, the administration of the team became an issue. In December 1963, DeOrsey, King, and Williams had petitioned the court to act as Marshall's conservators because he was incompetent to protect his own interests or the interests of the Redskins. The petitioners argued that Marshall's children from his first marriage—George Jr. and Catherine—were estranged from him, lived outside the area, and had little familiarity with the affairs of the Redskins. George Jr. operated a boat delivery business in Fort Lauderdale, Florida, and Catherine lived in New York City with her husband and children. On December 12, District Judge Alexander Holtzoff recognized DeOrsey, King, and Williams as Marshall's temporary conservators. The next day, he appointed Washington attorney John J. Carmody to serve as guardian of Marshall's interests pending the outcome of a hearing to determine the permanent appointment of conservators.

In January 1964, Marshall's children legally challenged the right of DeOrsey, King, and Williams to act as their father's conservators. The children argued that they should be the conservators, not the minority stockholders who had a conflict of interest. Two of them—DeOrsey and Williams—still owed payment to Marshall for their stock purchases. In 1962, Marshall allowed them to buy Redskins stock for a modest down payment with the balance spread over several years, probably to reduce his tax burden. He sold Williams 38 shares for $58,463 and DeOrsey 130 shares for $200,000. With the 38 shares purchased from Marshall and another 12 shares acquired from King, Williams controlled 5 percent of the Redskins,

DeOrsey 13 percent, and King 5 percent. It would be self-serving, the children asserted, for three minority stockholders to control Marshall's majority interest. They accused the temporary conservators of ripping off Marshall's estate by granting themselves exorbitant salaries, paying King's legal firm hefty fees for representation in court against their claims, fudging the profit margin, and refusing to sell the team to outsiders to keep control. They also claimed that the temporary conservators prevented Marshall from seeing them.

The temporary conservators refuted the charges. They were friends and longtime associates of Marshall, they asserted, with no intention of fleecing Marshall or his estate. King, for example, was Marshall's personal attorney, and he had been vice president and treasurer of the team since 1937. Moreover, Marshall himself had suggested the stock purchase arrangement, and as early as 1962, he had asked DeOrsey to serve as his stand-in on team matters. There had been no serious offer to buy the team from outside sources. They also pooh-poohed the charge of separating Marshall from the children. The estrangement had occurred years earlier. Marshall did not want the children to serve as conservators, they maintained, nor did he want contact with them. Marshall's court-appointed guardian, John Carmody, told the court that he had spoken with Marshall in the hospital on two occasions, and the owner, who appeared to be clear-headed, said that he wanted the three minority stockholders to run the team. In mid-August 1964, the court ordered DeOrsey, King, and Williams to serve as permanent conservators. The children promptly appealed that decision.

Meanwhile, DeOrsey's death the next year further complicated matters. George Marshall Jr. sought to replace DeOrsey as conservator, but King and Williams objected, and the court supported their position. Williams became acting president of the Redskins, with King continuing as vice president and treasurer. DeOrsey's 130 shares of stock went to his widow, and she eventually sold them for $1.3 million to King and Williams, who retired them.

While pursuing their appeal of the court's ruling on the conservatorship, the Marshall children learned of their father's will. In 1958, while still lucid, Marshall executed a will leaving each of his children $10,000 yearly for their lifetimes. The bulk of his estate, however, would go to establish a charity—the Redskins Foundation—to benefit underprivileged children in Washington, D.C., Maryland, and Virginia. Marshall stipulated that the Redskins Foundation "shall never use, contribute, or apply its money or property *for any purpose which supports or employs the principle of racial integration in any form*" (italics added). Oddly enough, he also stipulated that his money should not be given to any group practicing religious discrimination. In other words, Marshall considered it perfectly permissible to practice racial, but not religious, discrimination.

The children, both in their forties, were determined to change the will because they had been shortchanged. In early July, the children, accompanied by two lawyers, entered Marshall's home and read to him a document purporting to be a new "will" dividing his entire estate equally between the son and daughter. "I hereby emphasize that I want my property, including my Redskin stock, to go to my own flesh and blood and not to any other person or group," the "will" read. Marshall also allegedly stated that he understood the new arrangement and consented to have his name signed to the document by his son in the presence of two lawyers.

King and Williams were incredulous. Virtually vegetative at this point, Marshall could not possibly have understood the proceedings, they maintained. Medical specialists agreed.

King and Williams demanded possession of the July 2 "will." When a judge ordered George Jr., to deliver it, he refused, claiming that Williams would destroy it. He also appealed the judge's decision to surrender it. When he persisted in his refusal to produce the will, the judge cited him for contempt and sent him to jail. At a presentence press conference, George Jr. railed against Williams, saying that he was "engaged in a conspiracy to obtain the Redskins." He also charged him with holding his father in isolation. "When I came to see my father in June," he declared, "Mr. Williams had the door locked. I had to break in." After three weeks in jail, George Jr. agreed to turn over the will. He was released in February 1967.

The Marshall children were not sympathetic characters. Fond of wearing sharkskin suits, George Jr. conveyed the image of a money-grubbing predator conniving with his equally greedy sister to change their father's will as he lay senseless. "Redskin Fight Gets Disgusting," Morris Siegel titled his column in the *Washington Evening Star.* "Common courtesy requires a certain amount of respect, not ghoulish legal scavenger hunts aimed at determining what will happen to his interests when he is in fact no longer here." While cold, calculating, and manipulative, the children were on target when they charged the conservators with having a conflict of interest.

The court did not see it that way, however. In January 1968, the U.S. Court of Appeals, in a unanimous 3–0 decision, ruled in favor of King and Williams. The conservators, said the Court of Appeals, "were uniquely qualified to run the Redskins," and the Marshall children "have not presented, either in District Court or in this court, any examples of wrongdoing by the conservators." The Appeals Court also directed the children to surrender the suspect "will." "Conservators have a statutory right to possession of the personal property of the ward," it ruled. The legitimacy of that 1966 "will" would be determined later by another judicial panel.

After a stormy career, Marshall died quietly in his sleep at the age of seventy-two on August 9, 1969. An innovator and promoter with a sharp mind and knack for remembering names, dates, and incidents, he spent the last seven years of his life virtually mindless. "His bright, inventive mind had not an idea in years," wrote the *New York Times'* Arthur Daley. "Yet he once had thrown off ideas like sparks from a generator." His death was noted in major newspapers from across the country. A *Cleveland Press* writer said that if Marshall had planned his funeral, he would have insisted upon baton twirlers and a band loudly playing "Hail to the Redskins."

Instead, a sedate memorial service was held at the Washington Cathedral, where former president Dwight D. Eisenhower lay a few months earlier. Six former Redskins players—John Allen, Jim Castiglia, Al Demao, Henry Krause, Wayne Millner, and Joe Tereshinski—carried the casket, draped in burgundy and gold. Head coach Vince Lombardi, who himself would die the following year, represented the Washington Redskins, whose players, including Bobby Mitchell, attended a separate service at their training facility in Carlisle, Pennsylvania.

The Washington service was attended by Marshall's children, a few friends such as Morris Siegel; some ex-players, including Cliff Battles and Riley Smith; former coaches Dutch Bergman, Joe Kuharich, and Bill McPeak; stockholders Edward Bennett Williams and Milton King; and several fellow owners, including George Halas (Bears), Art and Dan Rooney (Steelers), Charles and William Bidwell (Cardinals), and Art Modell (Browns). Art Rooney contended that Marshall "did more for the progress of professional football than any other man." NFL commissioner Pete Rozelle delivered a humdrum eulogy that remembered Marshall as an innovator who popularized the professional game. "All of us who participate in some form of the game, and millions who enjoy viewing it," he said, "are beneficiaries of what his dynamic personality helped shape over more than three decades." He also praised Marshall for helping to keep the game free of corruption. "He had a fierce commitment to keep the sport clean and above reproach," Rozelle stated. Marshall's death had come in the midst of a legal squabble over his will, and the *Washington Post*'s Bob Addie observed, perhaps with only slight exaggeration, that at a social gathering at the Shoreham Hotel after the service, the lawyers outnumbered the mourners.

On August 14, Marshall was buried, appropriately enough considering the team's name and history, at the Indian Mound Cemetery in Romney, West Virginia.

After his death, Marshall's personal assets and 520 shares of Redskins stock, estimated to be worth $5–6 million, remained in legal limbo for three more years. Eventually, in January 1972, the conservators and the Marshall children reached a court-approved settlement. The 1966 "will" was deemed invalid. George Marshall Jr. and his sister, Catherine, were each awarded $750,000 tax-free. The three minority stockholders—Cooke, King, and Williams—took controlling interest in the Redskins by buying 260 of Marshall's 520 shares for $3 million and then canceling them. Together, the three men held 350 shares—Cooke, 250; King, 50; and Williams, 50—with the Redskins Foundation retaining 260 shares. (In 1974, the Redskins Foundation sold its shares to the three men for about $6 million, and those shares were cancelled.) The court also invalidated the anti-integration proviso relating to the Redskins Foundation.

• • •

The Washington Redskins are Marshall's legacy. At a home game against the St. Louis Cardinals in early November 1967, Redskins alumni honored Marshall with a "Day," placing his bronze likeness in front of the public stadium that he had helped establish.

He also helped establish the popularity of professional football. He brought the sport into the television age, establishing a network to carry his team's games and convincing other owners to televise all away contests to stimulate fan support. His suggestion to divide the league into divisions, with a season-ending championship game, was a master stroke. The first championship game between the Bears and Giants in 1933 netted $23,500, with players on the winning team each earning $210. Thirty years later, the championship game, again between the Bears and Giants, took in $125,000 in ticket sales, plus nearly $1 million in television revenue, with the winning players each receiving more than $30,000. By the twenty-first century, the major networks paid the NFL more than $20 billion to broadcast games, including the Super Bowl with its spectacular halftime musical extravaganza. The 2011 Super Bowl between the Green Bay Packers and the Pittsburgh Steelers attracted more than 111 million U.S. viewers, making it the most watched program in the history of U.S. television. The winning Packers players each received $83,000, with the Steelers players each receiving half that amount.

Marshall took most of the credit for the establishment of D.C. Stadium. Although the stadium would be publicly financed, it probably would not have gotten approved without Marshall's thirty-year commitment to rent it for Redskins home games. One reason that he caved in to the government's integration demands was because he did not want to be denied the use of a stadium that he considered his offspring. D.C. Stadium, he boasted to Curly Grieve of the *San Francisco Examiner* in September 1961, "is the apex of my whole sports career. It is the biggest milestone of my life. It is a tremendous thing to get that most beautiful stadium in the world for Washington." Like a proud father, he considered his offspring far lovelier than others. "Not a single bench in the park—even arm chairs in the bleachers. Not a post to obstruct the view. Sixty percent of the seats under cover. Parking for 12,000. It will be the last word. I've never felt so exhilarated about anything."

Marshall, like many other white supremacists, steadfastly resisted an idea—racial integration—whose time was overdue. Owing to the protests of Protestant, Catholic, and Jewish religious leaders in the District, that offensive and mean-spirited provision was removed, and the Redskins Foundation has helped thousands of needy children. Ironically, Marshall provided young black men with the clothing off his back, both indirectly and literally. Catherine Marshall asked Cliff Battles to retrieve her father's expansive and expensive wardrobe shortly after his death. Battles, in turn, arranged for an official with the Congressional Country Club to obtain the suits, tuxedos, and sportswear for distribution. The clothes went mainly to black caddies, who wore portions of them while shouldering golf bags at one of the nation's most exclusive courses.

Not surprisingly, black leaders were reluctant to pay tribute to Marshall. Sam Lacy was astounded to find that many white observers found positive things to say about him. "As for myself," he wrote in the *Baltimore Afro-American,* "I find it difficult to overlook the fact that if it had been left to George Preston Marshall, there never would have been any colored players in professional football. He persisted until the very end in holding the line on lily-whiteism." Indeed, through his will, Marshall persisted in his bigotry even after death. And Cal Jacox wrote in the *Norfolk New Journal and Guide,* "All those flowery tributes paid to the late George Preston Marshall . . . will never erase a general impression in the minds of Negro fans that when it came to racial bias, the man bitterly and stubbornly opposed integration and was a staunch advocate of lily-whiteism in professional sports."

In many ways, Marshall's life resembled that of another legendary sports titan: baseball's Ty Cobb. True, the older Cobb was an athlete and Marshall was not, and Marshall's team had won a national title and Cobb's had not. But both men were Southern-born racists with combative and toxic personalities. Both attempted to intimidate the opposition with braggadocio and bullying. Both were dreadful husbands and fathers. Both were estranged from their families, and both were intense competitors and self-promoters. Each had a flair for making money, Cobb in the stock market and Marshall with a laundry and football business. Each was elected as a charter member into the Halls of Fame of their respective sports. And both died with few friends. When Marshall was inducted as a charter member into the Washington, D.C., Hall of Stars during halftime of a Cowboys-Redskins game in November 1979, there was no family member there to accept a gold ring in his honor. Jack Kent Cooke accepted on behalf of the Redskins. In their wills, both Cobb and Marshall created foundations to help needy youngsters. Cobb's foundation, however, did not promote segregation. In short, both men made monumental contributions to their respective sports, but they were also monumental embarrassments. Fortunately, both sports recovered from the flawed characters and mean-spirited actions of these two giants.

Epilogue

George Marshall's final years coincided with one of the most turbulent times in twentieth-century America. Protests against the unpopular, and seemingly interminable, Vietnam War jolted college campuses and disrupted the Democratic presidential nomination contest. In April 1968, the assassination of Martin Luther King Jr. ignited looting, burning, and rioting in dozens of American cities, including Washington, D.C.

Black sections of the city, some only blocks from the White House, erupted in violence. The owner of the Florida Avenue Grill, near Howard University and Griffith Stadium, stood guard over his property for hours with a shotgun. In his autobiography *The Good Life,* Ben Bradlee, the executive editor of the *Washington Post,* wrote that "smoke spiraled into the warm spring air, and sirens pierced the night. Sirens and the sound of breaking glass, as the looting began. . . . This was an honest-to-God race riot, born of anger and frustration, dedicated to a demand for attention." Twelve people died, nearly 1,100 were injured, more than 6,000 were arrested, and 1,200 buildings were torched, with an estimated loss of $27 million. For ten days, the capital of the free world was placed under curfew and guarded by 12,000 federal troops, about the same number of soldiers President Lincoln had ordered to defend the city when he launched the first Bull Run offensive against the Confederacy.

Violence shattered American cities again in June following the assassination of Senator Robert F. Kennedy in Los Angeles. To honor the fallen presidential contender, Washington officials renamed the Redskins home arena RFK Stadium. A battered and bewildered electorate turned to law-and-order Republican candidates Richard Nixon and Spiro Agnew, hoping to end an ugly war and restore domestic tranquility. Nixon's narrow election ended eight years of Democratic control of the White House. Having served as Interior Secretary under presidents Kennedy and Johnson, Stewart Udall left government service, never to return. He spent the rest of his life writing, making speeches, and trumpeting a variety of environmental causes. He died in March 2010 at the age of ninety. A grateful Bobby Mitchell "found him to be a tough, straight-ahead type of person," a characterization that George Marshall probably would have shared.

Bobby Mitchell also ended his eleven-year career after the 1968 season. Like many other Redskins players, Mitchell did not have high regard for Otto Graham, who had become head coach in 1966. Graham switched him to running back for the 1967 season, mainly because Charley Taylor had become the primary receiver, but that experiment was not very successful. He played sparingly in 1968, totaling only fourteen receptions for 130 yards. It was the only time since his rookie season in 1958 that he failed to average more than 10 yards per catch, well below his 15.3 yard-per-catch average. Vince Lombardi, who replaced Graham in 1969, encouraged Mitchell to return for another season as flanker, but the physical grind of training camp and pulled hamstring muscles convinced him to retire. Lombardi then persuaded him to pursue front-office positions, and he accepted a job with the Redskins as an assistant director of scouting and remained with the team in a variety of executive roles for more than thirty years, retiring in 2003.

Perhaps because of his friendship with and admiration for Robert and Ethel Kennedy, Mitchell became more outspoken on matters of civil rights. In 1967, he came to the defense of heavyweight boxing champion Muhammad Ali, a recent convert to Islam who refused induction into the armed services for religious reasons. A year later, he became a director of the National Negro Industrial and Economic

Union. Headed by Jim Brown and partially funded by a $500,000 grant from the Ford Foundation, that organization provided advice and support to blacks seeking to establish businesses.

Mitchell also championed education. In 1971, in an interview with the Department of Labor magazine *Manpower,* he urged blacks to attend college to prepare for careers other than athletics because of the long odds of playing any sport professionally. Some colleges, he said, including his alma mater, the University of Illinois, discouraged athletes (especially blacks) from taking difficult courses like medicine, engineering, and dentistry because they were academically challenging and time-consuming, and, in particular, took time away from the practice field. Mitchell recalled that when he tried to enroll in dental school at Illinois, the athletic department intervened, saying: "You can't go in there. We can't control what will happen to you, and we don't know if you can make it." Mitchell said he always resented that interference "because I might have been a heck of a dentist. It should have been my decision. Yes, they were worried about brains, too. But being black wasn't the whole thing. They did it to whites, too."

Because of embedded societal racism, the playing field was rarely level for blacks. Black and white athletes played, trained, practiced, and traveled together, but off the field, they rarely socialized. Mitchell went home to Washington, D.C., while his white teammates lived in racially exclusive suburbs in Maryland and Virginia. In college, Mitchell learned from teammate Ray Nitschke that Illinois coach Ray Eliot distributed more under-the-table alumni money to white players than black players. Although Mitchell himself was always well paid, blacks in professional football generally got less money than whites. They also received far fewer offers to do television advertisements than whites. Even though Jim Brown was perhaps pro football's greatest player, he appeared in few commercials.

When Mitchell's son, Robert Jr., expressed an interest in athletics, Mitchell discouraged it. And when Robert Jr. graduated from Stanford and NFL scouts invited him to tryout camp, Mitchell again dissuaded him. "There was this thing in my head about the lack of opportunity," he stated. "Who knows? Maybe he would have been the next great runner-receiver in the NFL. Maybe not. The point is, I did not push him to find out. I'll live with that guilt for the rest of my life." After graduating from Stanford University, Robert Jr. obtained a law degree from Georgetown and became a Washington attorney.

Mitchell's goal was to become the NFL's first black coach or general manager. "I would like to run a football team someday," he declared in 1971. "This is my third year in management, and I'm in no hurry. Management has to learn that I'm capable, and they have to make up their minds whether they want a black coach, which of course is the seat of the problem." The "seat of the problem" was the prevailing racial stereotype among professional sports executives that African Americans lacked the "necessities"—the intellectual gifts—for leadership positions on the field or front office. With only a few exceptions, African American professional football players were excluded from so-called "thinking" positions—center, linebacker, and especially quarterback. Fritz Pollard in the 1920s and Joe Lillard in the early 1930s excelled at the quarterback position, but from 1946 to 1968, only three African Americans played quarterback, and two of those made only cameo appearances. The aptly named Willie Thrower of Michigan State was drafted by the Bears, and he tossed three passes in 1953. That same year, George Taliaferro made a few starts at the position under center for the Baltimore Colts. And in 1955, Charlie Brackins threw two passes for the Green Bay Packers. Another thirteen years would elapse before Marlin Briscoe of the Denver Broncos played the position—and the following year, he was converted to a receiver.

Scouting and coaching were also positions restricted mainly to whites. In the late 1950s, only Buddy Young, Emlen Tunnell, and Lowell Perry served as professional football scouts. Perry became the first African American assistant coach, signing with the Steelers in 1957. Other than Fritz Pollard in the 1920s, no African American served as a head coach until the late 1980s. Several newspapers in 1978 reported that Mitchell, who had risen to become director of scouting, was about to be named general manager. Instead, principal owner Edward Williams selected Bobby Beathard, a white executive who had previously worked for several other NFL teams, including the Atlanta Falcons and the Miami Dolphins. In 1989, Jack Kent Cooke, who had become sole owner of the Redskins four years earlier, named Charley Casserly general manager, even though Mitchell had served as the assistant general manager since 1981.

After being bypassed twice for the general manager job, Mitchell expressed regret over his decision to go into administrative work. Perhaps if he had gone into coaching, he told the Hall of Fame luncheon audience in Canton in March 1989, he might have become the first black head coach. At a time of frustration and hurt, he slammed NFL owners for hypocrisy. They gave only "lip service" to the professed goal of providing coaching and front-office opportunities for qualified blacks. "All I've ever seen is the put-down," he said.

For the upcoming league meeting, owners invited only essential personnel. Mitchell interpreted that condition to mean that no blacks would attend the meeting. NFL owners also plotted to prevent blacks from obtaining the experience to become head coaches. "The owners say blacks are not qualified. Right. They can say that because they are not training them to the extent that they become qualified," he maintained. Customarily, one had to serve as an offensive or defensive coordinator before being appointed a head coach. "There are 30, 40 assistant coaches in the league," he continued, "but they're not actually assistant coaches. Instead, they are assistants to the assistants." He noted two exceptions: Tony Dungy, defensive coordinator of the Steelers, and Dennis Green, the receivers' coach of the San Francisco 49ers, both of whom would later become head coaches. As it turned out, that year, Al Davis appointed offensive line coach Art Shell to lead the Oakland Raiders, the first black head coach since the 1920s.

In 2003, the NFL adopted the "Rooney Rule," obliging teams to interview minority candidates for head coaching positions. Named for Steelers owner Dan Rooney, son of Art Rooney, the rule has been well received, but its effectiveness is debatable.

Mitchell was also disappointed over his delayed selection to the Pro Football Hall of Fame. He was eligible for the hall five years after his retirement in 1969 but again and again, he was not voted in.

At the time of his retirement, he ranked fifth in total touchdowns, second only to Raymond Berry in career receptions, and second only to Jim Brown in combined total net yards (15,459 to 14,078). Receiver Lance Alworth of the San Diego Chargers and Dallas Cowboys was elected in 1978 in his first year of eligibility, even though he had only twenty-one more receptions than Mitchell (542 to 521) but scored six fewer touchdowns and amassed nearly 4,000 fewer combined total net yards.

In the book *Redskin Country,* Mitchell remembered people telling him that his selection to the Hall of Fame was only a matter of time. But as time went by, he began to wonder. "It's sorta like a guy coming out of college his senior year and everybody tellin' him he'll be the No. 1 pick. And the phone don't ring. First round, second round, third round." He began to think if only he had caught a few more passes and gained some additional yards rushing, he would be selected. He then visited the hall and was impressed by his statistics in several different offensive categories. "I'm leading in some of them. I'm all over the place, but not in it. That blew my mind." Ironically, Washington sportswriter Morris Siegel, who had condoned Marshall's racial ban through his silence, became a champion of Mitchell's selection to the Hall of Fame. The hall's selectors, he wrote in 1980, "ought to be impeached" if they did not promptly include Mitchell. Eventually, in 1983, Mitchell joined the Hall with Sid Gillman, Bobby Bell, Paul Warfield, and his Washington teammate quarterback Sonny Jurgensen.

Mitchell retired from the Redskins in January 2003 without having achieved his goal of becoming the NFL's first black general manager. "The only reason I stayed in all these years," he once said, "was the hope that somebody would eventually say: 'Hey, Bobby Mitchell's good enough to do that.'" The Redskins never did. But Mitchell was comforted somewhat when he learned that the Baltimore Ravens in 2002 had named Ozzie Newsome the NFL's first African American general manager.

Mitchell experienced one additional slight from the Redskins, although it may have been unintentional. He was deeply hurt in 2002 when the Redskins, under new coach Steve Spurrier, distributed his

No. 49 jersey to tight end Leonard Stephens. That decision brought a public outcry. No other player since Mitchell had worn that uniform, and it should be officially retired, Mitchell's supporters claimed. Although wounded, Mitchell remained silent. "But my family and my friends and I, we grieved about it all year. . . . People kept saying to me, 'Why don't you say something?' But I kept thinking about [Stephens]." Eventually, Coach Spurrier declared that the uniform number had been distributed through an oversight. "No one will be wearing Bobby's number during any season." Still, the only uniform the Redskins have retired officially is Sammy Baugh's number, 33.

As a player and administrator, Mitchell experienced the worst and best of times with the Redskins. During the 1960s, he and other black players stimulated fan interest, but the team did not have a winning season until 1969, the year after Mitchell retired. But fans continued to attend games, if only to vent their frustration. A reporter once asked running back Pervis Atkins if the boos bothered him. He replied: "No, I'm a beer drinker, and booze doesn't bother me."

The Redskins resurgence began with Coach Vince Lombardi in 1969 and continued under Coach George Allen, who had recently been fired by the Los Angeles Rams. Given a multiyear contract and full authority over personnel issues, Allen built a winning team by trading draft picks for quality veterans. The Redskins enjoyed winning seasons every year from 1971 through 1977, went to the Super Bowl in 1972 (where they lost, 14–7, to the Miami Dolphins during their perfect season), and reached the playoffs five times. Despite a sparkling .691 winning percentage, Allen was not rehired following a contract dispute with owner Edward Bennett Williams. The team took a step back under Jack Pardee, whose three-year record stood at 24–24 when he was replaced by Joe Gibbs.

Gibbs became the most successful Redskins coach in history, amassing a regular and playoff-game record of 140–65–0 from 1981 through 1992. Under his direction, the team won four NFC Eastern Division titles and appeared in four Super Bowls, winning championships in the 1982, 1987, and 1991 seasons. "You can get a smile on anybody's face in this organization, and really in this area, if you only ask about the '80s," declared Bobby Mitchell. "Fans were excited. We were the talk of the league. Even teams that didn't like us couldn't help but say good things about us."

Ironically, the team that had excluded African Americans for three decades won the January 1988 championship game behind Doug Williams, the first black quarterback to win a Super Bowl. His scintillating performance, in a 42–10 victory over the Denver Broncos, put to rest the ridiculous racial notion that blacks lacked the intellectual "necessities" required for field leadership; and it provided closure for many African Americans who had continued to resent the team for its racial ban. "A lot of people know that the Redskins were the last team to integrate, and a lot of people told me that I put them in a bad position," Williams stated. "You'd be surprised how many people said they had to cheer for the Redskins because I was playing." Bobby Mitchell expressed a similar sentiment. "I had friends of mine in this town who knew I played for the Redskins and loved me, but hated the Redskins because of the [racial] legacy. After Doug Williams, they loved the Redskins. It made a complete transition. After Doug, some people said, 'Now, we're okay.'"

Without dismissing their past and the many contributions of George Marshall, the team displayed racial sensitivity by hiring blacks as scouts, administrators, and members of the band and cheerleading squads, as well as eliminating the racially charged language from their fight song in the mid-1960s. In his book *Quarterblack,* Williams stated that the "Redskins have a top-caliber franchise in every regard."

On the field, the Redskins never again shunned the widely available pool of talented black athletes. As the team's first black player, Mitchell bore the brunt of racial abuse and won over most bigoted fans with scintillating play. His trailblazing effort made the path easier for later African American Redskins players, such as running backs Larry Brown, Mike Thomas, Timmy Smith, and George Rogers and wide receivers Charley Taylor, Roy Jefferson, Art Monk, and Gary Clark. Similarly, Doug Williams exploded the myth that black quarterbacks lacked the intellectual wherewithal for field generalship, thus throwing the position open to future stars like Daunte Culpepper, Steve McNair, and Donovan McNabb, acquired by the Redskins from the Eagles in 2010.

From the beginning in 1937, the Redskins won favor with Washington-area fans. Marshall drafted future star Sammy Baugh, fielded a competitive team, won two national championships in 1937 and 1942, and attracted customers, including women, with entertaining halftime shows. When professional football reintegrated after World War II, Marshall refused to play along, and his team suffered, experiencing only three winning seasons from 1946 through 1968. The team's lack of competitiveness and a boycott by many black fans brought a modest decline in attendance, but not enough to move Marshall. "I never had a losing season at the gate," he boasted.

The addition of Bobby Mitchell and other black athletes did not bring immediate success, but it did improve the team's competitiveness, raise expectations, and salve a community's wounded conscience about its blemished heritage. In the mid-1960s, the Redskins continued to lose, but white and black fans stormed the turnstiles anyway. In October 1965, *Sports Illustrated* reported that the Redskins had become a social phenomenon. Not only did middle-class blacks and whites attend games, but so did the area's power brokers, who wanted "to be seen seeing the Redskins." On one Sunday, for example, eight of the nine Supreme Court justices attended the game. Other loyal fans included media figures Ben Bradlee, Art Buchwald, Robert Novak, and David Brinkley, and members of Congress. "We could get a quorum of the House anytime we ring a bell," declared Redskins official Ray Slattery.

The metropolitan region became giddy in 1971 after the team won its first five games under new coach George Allen. After losing its first game of the season against the Chiefs in Kansas City, twenty thousand fans greeted the team when it arrived at Dulles Airport. Two days later, Washington mayor Walter Washington asked to address the team at Redskins Park, the new practice facility in Maryland. "We're going through a tough time in our city right now," he told players. "We're out of money. I can't pay people. The city is divided along economic and racial lines. We have a drug problem. We are facing a workers' strike. But you know what? You guys are making my job easier. Every Monday morning, instead of talking about all the problems in the city, people are talking about the Redskins." "There was tremendous support for us, at a time when the community was going through some pretty tough times," Redskins cornerback Pat Fischer recalled to Thom Loverro in *Hail Victory*. "What we were doing gave people something in common to rally around."

African American writer Sterling Tucker expressed similar sentiments in the *Washington Sunday Star*. "THE WASHINGTON REDSKINS ARE HOTTEST THING TO HIT WASHINGTON SINCE THE RIOTS OF 1968!!!!" If extraterrestrials visited RFK Stadium, he wrote in October 1971, they would witness "the elite and the ignorant, the accomplished and the deprived, the young and old, the rich and poor, the black and white—anxious and cheering their team to victory as though it were a life-and-death matter." Following three decades of lily-whiteism and the riots of the late 1960s, he continued, the Redskins "are undoubtedly the principal ownership group helping to heal some wounds, instill some pride, restore some faith, and provide a source of new motivation."

Richard Nixon was one of the team's most ardent fans. In the 1950s, as vice president, he occasionally watched games with Marshall from the owner's box. Listening to Marshall's "priceless comments," he recalled, was more entertaining than a "double-feature movie." Later, as president, he befriended George Allen, who had coached at his alma mater, Whittier College. Conservative, no-nonsense, and paranoid, Allen was once referred to as "Richard Nixon with a whistle." Nixon sent him congratulatory notes and reportedly, during the 1971 playoff game, Allen used a play recommended by the president—an end-around by Roy Jefferson that lost thirteen yards.

Fans and the Washington media went into a frenzy when the Redskins went to the Super Bowl in 1972. The *Washington Post,* observed acclaimed journalist Frank Deford in a 1979 *Sports Illustrated* article, sent far more reporters to cover that event than had covered the first moonwalk some years earlier. "Both the *Post* and its rival daily, the *Star,*" he wrote, "have excellent sports sections, but they go berserk as soon as the 'Skins suit up. Radio and TV are worse, they ignore every other sports experience, except possibly the exactas at Laurel."

As the fan frenzy continued through the 1980s and 1990s, the

Redskins outgrew the 53,000-seat RFK stadium. In 1997, owner Jack Kent Cooke oversaw the completion of a new $250-million stadium in Landover, Maryland. Jack Kent Cooke Stadium (renamed FedEx Field in 1999, when new owner Dan Snyder hawked the naming rights), is a five-level, concrete oval slab seating ninety thousand people. "It has all the charm of an office park or suburban mall," said one longtime fan. Another complained that the new facility attracted too many of the "cell-phone-yapping crowd." Still another griped that the seats were so far away, it was like watching the game "from a space shuttle." In terms of overall value—ticket prices, parking, traffic, tailgating, and atmosphere—*Sports Illustrated* in 2007 ranked FedEx Field twenty-eighth out of the thirty-two NFL stadiums. Nonetheless, the stadium is consistently sold out except for its hideously priced luxury-level boxes. And according to *Forbes,* the franchise in 2010 was the fourth most valuable in global professional sports, trailing only the British soccer franchise Manchester United, the Dallas Cowboys, and the New York Yankees.

Several factors combine to help explain the Redskins' mystique. First, other sports in the area lacked the devoted following of the professional football team. District colleges abandoned their football programs, and fans were just not drawn to professional basketball and hockey. The Washington Senators twice abandoned the city, and the District was without professional baseball for thirty-four years prior to the arrival of the Nationals in 2005. True, the professional debut of Washington Nationals pitcher Stephen Strasburg rivaled the hype and interest of a Redskins game, as John Feinstein pointed out in a June 2010 issue of *Sporting News Magazine.* But that event was a one-time-only occasion.

Nor did the Redskins suffer much competition from high culture. Washingtonians, especially its political elite, were not enamored of ballet, opera, or symphonies. "High culture is about as popular in official Washington as stock-car racing in the Ivy League," wrote R.W. Apple Jr. in the *New York Times.*

Psychologically and socially, the Redskins also provided a common bond for the metropolitan community. That bond was strengthened after the White House integrated the team in 1962. It was further steeled by the team's on-field successes of the 1970s and 1980s. The Redskins also served as a distraction following the riots of 1968 and the Watergate political crisis of the early 1970s. Democratic senator Edward Kennedy and Republican secretary of state Henry Kissinger put aside partisan politics on Sundays at RFK Stadium. Richard Nixon explained that Washington was "a city without identity. Everybody comes from somewhere else." People who move to the city, many for political reasons, he continued, "need an identity with the city. And the Redskins provide that. The Redskins are the only thing in Washington that the people think of as 'ours.' Nobody in Washington gives a tinker's dam about the Kennedy Center or the Washington Symphony." In December 1974, *New York Times* writer Christopher Lydon expressed a similar sentiment in an article titled "Redskins: Washington's Common Bond":

> In a city of transients—a city long denied self-government, one that has little college football to speak of and, between the departure of baseball's Senators and the arrival of basketball's Bullets, had no other team—the Redskins are a hometown rallying point, a common denominator for a peculiar body of fans.

George Marshall deserves much of the credit for making Washington, D.C., a Redskins town. He provided the press with a steady stream of colorful interviews, pronouncements, and antics that brought publicity to the team. He also promoted the games as family entertainment by establishing a marching band, halftime extravaganzas, and a catchy team fight song. The acclaimed sportswriter Frank Deford said that the words of "Hail to the Redskins" were as familiar to him growing up in Baltimore in the 1940s and early 1950s as "Ring-Around-a-Rosie" and "Hark, the Herald Angels Sing." Adding entertainment, Marshall informed the *Saturday Evening Post* in 1938, "seemed to help in giving the customers the idea that they belonged to the team and the team to them."

Marshall also promoted his home games as energy-charged social events akin to Derby Day at Churchill Downs. Sunday afternoons were a time when the fashionably dressed Washington elite gathered to see and be seen. When reviewing planned seating for the new D.C. Stadium, he insisted upon high-backed, wide seats to accommodate women in fur coats. He also urged his players to take off-season jobs in the area and to socialize in classy saloons like Duke's. In 1947, only a decade after moving to Washington, Marshall sold all season tickets. "We have become the first city in the National Football League ever to sell out our season tickets," he boasted to *Washington Post* sportswriter Bob Addie. "When people die, they leave the tickets to relatives and friends in their wills. We have a waiting list of more than 10,000 people looking for season tickets and the list increases every year."

In the end, Marshall must be portrayed mostly as a tragic figure. He spent his final years unable to communicate and unable to enjoy his one passion: the Washington Redskins. His obsession with the team and making money cost him two marriages and his relationship with his two children. His bigoted racial views hurt his team competitively and marred his reputation historically. One of the sport's pioneers, he would be considered an iconic figure if not for his racism. He integrated the team only when the Kennedy administration forced him to do so. Little did Marshall realize that adding black players would energize the team and lift the burden of Jim Crow from his proud organization. Like the Boston Red Sox, the last Major League Baseball team to integrate, the post–Marshall Redskins have overcome their sullied past, championed racial diversity, and enjoyed a cultlike hold on their racially diverse and ever-expanding fan base. Hail White House blitz. Hail victory.

Acknowledgments

An author who takes twenty-five years to write a book not only has a problem with procrastination, he also accumulates massive intellectual debts that are impossible to repay. I am indebted to Allison Trzop, an associate editor with Beacon Press, who recommended expanding an essay of mine into a book, helped prepare and repair the proposal, became its in-house champion, and, once the contract was signed, gently prodded me not to take another twenty-five years to complete the manuscript. When Allison departed Beacon Press to enter Harvard Law School, she left me with a superb editorial coach: Joanna Green. I am grateful to Joanna for her deft editing, keen suggestions, good humor, gentle prodding, and enthusiasm for the project. Her feedback and suggestions, along with those of the production and publicity teams, made for sharper prose and fewer mistakes of style and grammar. I alone am responsible for the book's errors and shortcomings.

Few professionals are more gracious and helpful than librarians. Jim Douglas, head of library services at Nichols College, has assisted me with interlibrary loan requests and introduced me to *ProQuest,* a marvelous Internet service providing access to historic newspapers. I offer heartfelt thanks to Jim and other librarians (too numerous to mention individually), who guided me at the University of Arizona, Binghamton University, the Boston Public Library, Howard University, the Martin Luther King Public Library in Washington, D.C., and the Pro Football Hall of Fame. Photo archivists Faye Haskins at the Martin Luther King Public Library and John Gartrell at the *Baltimore Afro-American* helped track down images for the manuscript. School archivist Lori Ito Hardenbergh provided valuable information on George Marshall's years at Washington's Sidwell Friends School.

I am fortunate to teach at a small college where departmental turf wars are virtually nonexistent and colleagues are warm-hearted and supportive. This cozy atmosphere is attributable, in large measure, to Alan Reinhardt, our sage and solicitous academic dean (now provost). Alan has been a longtime friend and an ardent supporter of this project from the beginning. Colleagues Andrea Becker, Maureen Butler, and Kathy Piniarski cheerfully offered administrative assistance. And Susan Veshi also came through in the clutch. I thank my officemate Art Duhaime for his good advice and good nature. I also am grateful for longtime friends Don Leonard and Den Sexton for good times and good cheer. Being honored with the college's Robert Stansky Distinguished Professorship has facilitated my work by reducing my teaching load and providing a generous stipend for travel and research. I am grateful to History Department colleagues Ed Warren and Paul Lambert for taking on some of my teaching and administrative duties.

The late Secretary of the Interior Stewart Udall took the time to correspond and talk with me about the Redskins and offered warm words of encouragement. When I was an upstart historian just starting to write on this topic, Bobby Mitchell graciously encouraged and corresponded with me; but he declined subsequent requests to be interviewed for this book. Author Phil Hoose, scholars Donald Spivey and David Wiggins, and ESPN journalist Howard Bryant offered encouragement and wise counsel.

I am indebted to the editors of the *Journal of Sport History* for permission to use portions of previously published articles: "Civil Rights on the Gridiron: The Kennedy Administration and the Washington Redskins" (Summer 1997): 189–208; and "Outside the Pale: The Exclusion of Blacks from the National Football League, 1934–1946" (Winter 1988): 255–81.

My family has been a blessing. My four children, their spouses, my in-laws, and my sister all have supported my work in numerous ways. My eight grandchildren, budding All-Stars every one, have been sources of joy, exhaustion, and comic relief, as have my students—including the non–All Stars. My greatest obligation is to my wife, Sandra, for her common sense, uncommon sacrifices, ready laughter, and unstinting love and support. She has read the entire manuscript and saved it from numerous flaws. To her I dedicate this book.

Notes on Sources

This book began as an inquiry into the environmental policies of the Kennedy administration and morphed into a book about the racial integration of the Washington Redskins. While doing research at the Stewart Udall Papers at the University of Arizona, I came across a folder on the Washington Redskins. Why, I wondered, would a cabinet member involved mainly with national parks and natural resources have a sizable file on a football team? The answer appeared as "Civil Rights on the Gridiron: The Kennedy Administration and the Desegregation of the Washington Redskins," published in 1987 by the *Journal of Sport History*. I had planned to expand that essay into a book but became sidetracked with other projects. Fortunately, in 2002, ESPN.com editor Eric Neel reignited my interest in the topic by including "Civil Rights on the Gridiron" in a series entitled *Page 2 Goes to Washington*. There, the essay caught the attention of Allison Trzop, an editor with Beacon Press, and she suggested expanding it into a book.

There is an old saying that journalism is the first draft of history. That observation certainly applies to my study of the integration of the Washington Redskins. I have relied heavily on Boston, New York, and Washington, D.C., mainstream dailies and upon African American weekly newspapers, especially the *Baltimore Afro-American* and *Washington Afro-American*. Along the way I have been informed, influenced, and entertained by legendary columnists such as Bill Cunningham of the *Boston Post,* Arthur Daley of the *New York Times,* Sam Lacy of the *Baltimore Afro-American,* and Shirley Povich and Bob Addie of the *Washington Post.*

For the launch and operation of George Marshall's NFL Boston franchise from 1932 through 1936 I scoured the *Boston Evening American, Boston Evening Transcript, Boston Globe, Boston Herald,* and *Boston Post.* For Marshall's involvement with the Washington Redskins from 1937 through 1964, I examined the *New York Times, Washington Evening News, Washington Star, Washington Post,* and *Washington Times-Herald.* There is also a sizable newspaper clippings file on microfiche relating to Marshall at the Pro Football Hall of Fame. Leigh Montville provided valuable information, especially recollections from former Boston Redskins player Riley Smith, in a 1981 *Boston Globe* article, "Funny, But They Were the Boston Redskins." Jim McCabe also covered the topic in his *Globe* piece "Football Footnote: They Played Five Years in Boston."

For the efforts of African Americans to break down racial barriers in professional football and in other areas of American life I have been guided by several black newsweeklies, including the *Baltimore Afro-American, Boston Guardian, Chicago Defender, Pittsburgh Courier,* and *Washington Afro-American.* Those newspapers, especially in the years after World War II, also provided information on Marshall and the Redskins' ban against black players, as did the *New York Amsterdam News, Atlanta Daily World, Cleveland Call and Post, Los Angeles Sentinel, Norfolk New Journal and Guide,* and *Philadelphia Tribune.* I also have benefited from Andy Piascik's *Gridiron Gauntlet: The Story of the Men Who Integrated Pro Football*; Alan H. Levy's *Tackling Jim Crow: Racial Segregation in Professional Football*; Charles Ross's *Outside the Lines: African Americans and the Integration of the National Football League*; and Alexander Wolff's *Sports Illustrated* article, "The NFL's Jackie Robinson."

I have had the good fortune to interview, chat, and correspond with the late Stewart Udall on both the Redskins and environmental matters. His papers at the University of Arizona contain "Reports to the President" and a file of correspondence, a press conference transcript, and newspaper clippings on the integration of the Redskins.

The John F. Kennedy Library in Boston holds a lengthy Stewart Udall oral history.

There are dozens of good books on the Kennedy presidency. Among the best are James Giglio, *The Presidency of John F. Kennedy*, and Herbert S. Parmet, *JFK: The Presidency of John F. Kennedy*. For Kennedy and civil rights, I have consulted Carl M. Brauer, *John F. Kennedy and the Second Reconstruction*, and Nick Bryant, *Bystander: John F. Kennedy and the Struggle for Black Equality*. For civil rights in general, I have examined Raymond Arsenault, *Freedom Riders: 1961 and the Struggle for Racial Justice*; John Hope Franklin's autobiography, *Mirror to America*; Harvard Sitkoff, *The Struggle for Black Equality*; and Jules Tygiel, *Baseball's Great Experiment: Jackie Robinson and His Legacy*.

For the political, racial, and social scene in Washington, D.C., I have depended upon David Brinkley, *Washington Goes to War*; Katharine Graham, *Katharine Graham's Washington*; Constance Green, *The Secret City: A History of Race Relations in the Nation's Capital*; and Brad Snyder, *Beyond the Shadow of the Senators: The Untold Story of the Homestead Grays and the Integration of Baseball*.

Redskins followers and football fans in general are fortunate to have available several excellent histories of the Washington franchise, including Ken Denlinger and Paul Attner, *Redskin Country: From Baugh to the Super Bowl*; Thom Loverro, *Hail Victory: An Oral History of the Washington Redskins*; *Redskins: A History of Washington's Team*, from the staff of the *Post*; and Richard Whittingham, *Hail Redskins: A Celebration of the Greatest Players, Teams, and Coaches*. Steve Sabol, president of NFL Films, has produced a fine film on the subject, *NFL History of the Washington Redskins* (Warner Brothers, 2008).

A number of quality books deal with the history of the NFL and its players and coaches. My work benefited from Myron Cope, *The Game That Was: The Early Days of Pro Football*; Bob Curran, *Pro Football's Rag Days*; Arthur Daley, *Pro Football's Hall of Fame*; and Richard Whittingham, *What a Game They Played*. Former players Jim Brown, Roosevelt Grier, John Mackey, Lenny Moore, Woody Strode, and Doug Williams all have written books about their NFL playing days, and Paul Brown has written about his coaching career with the Cleveland Browns in *PB: The Paul Brown Story*.

The colorful George Preston Marshall attracted considerable attention from the Boston, Los Angeles, New York, and Washington press. His wife, Corinne Griffith, wrote about him in *My Life with the Redskins* and in *Antiques I Have Known*. Marshall himself wrote about football in "Pro Football is Better Football" and "Speaking Out: Baseball Isn't Our National Sport," both *Saturday Evening Post*. The most revelatory articles on Marshall are Robert Boyle's *Sports Illustrated* piece "All Alone by the Telephone"; Ed Linn's article in *Sport*, "Big Noise in Washington"; and Thomas Sugrue's "Soapsuds and Showmanship" in *American Magazine*.

For legal wrangling over Marshall's will and estate I have relied on accounts in the *Washington Evening Star* and *Washington Post*, and on two books about Redskins minority owner Edward B. Williams, Robert Pack, *Edward Bennett Williams for the Defense*, and Evan Thomas, *The Man To See*.

For biographical material on Shirley Povich, I have depended upon his memoir *All These Mornings* and on the tribute edited by his three children and colleague George Solomon, *Shirley Povich: All Those Mornings At the Post*.

Sam Lacy, Povich's contemporary at the *Baltimore Afro-American*, wrote an excellent memoir with Moses J. Newson entitled *Fighting for Fairness: The Life Story of Hall of Fame Sportswriter Sam Lacy*. I have also benefited from reading tributes to the late Lacy in the *Baltimore Afro-American*, *New York Times*, and *Washington Post*, and from an interview with one of his colleagues, Talibah Chikwendu, now executive editor of the *Washington Afro-American*.

I found the most thorough and reliable interviews with Bobby Mitchell to be the online piece "Catching Up with Bobby Mitchell" and Paul Fine's "Historically Speaking" from *Black Sports*. The Pro Football Hall of Fame also holds a large file of newspaper clippings on Mitchell. In June 1985, Mr. Mitchell corresponded with me about integrating the Redskins. However, he declined my requests to be interviewed for this book.

For the saga of Ernie Davis, I examined several online articles from the *Elmira* (New York) *Free Press* and from Robert Gallagher's *Ernie Davis*.

Despite being a Native American head coach of the Boston Redskins and a character, William "Lone Star" Dietz received scant attention in the Boston press. Fortunately there is a credible biography by Tom Benjey, *Keep A-Goin': The Life of Lone Star Dietz*. Another compelling character, Redskins' broadcaster and minority stockholder Harry Wismer, received widespread coverage in the New York and Washington press. I also found valuable a short portrait of him in Ted Patterson's *The Golden Voices of Football* and in Robert Boyle's "Horatio Harry." Wismer's memoir, *The Public Calls It Sport,* is interesting but somewhat unreliable. For information on Washington, D.C., civil rights activist E. B. Henderson, I consulted his personal papers at Howard University, pored over his numerous letters to the editor of the *Washington Post,* and read the family tribute to him, *Molder of Men: Portrait of a 'Grand Old Man'—Edwin Bancroft Henderson*.

Besides Bobby Mitchell, other NFL personalities, most now deceased, took the time and effort to talk or correspond with me about the ugly topic of racism, including Paul Brown, Otto Graham, Charles O'Rourke, Art Rooney, Pete Rozelle, and Norm Snead. My work also has been shaped by talks with former *Los Angeles Sentinel* sports editor Brad Pye, and longtime, diehard Redskins fan David Kelly.

Notes

Works frequently cited have been identified by the following abbreviations:

BAA	*Baltimore Afro-American*
BG	*Boston Globe*
BP	*Boston Post*
CD	*Chicago Defender*
GPM	George Preston Marshall
JFKL	John F. Kennedy Library
LAS	*Los Angeles Sentinel*
NYT	*New York Times*
PC	*Pittsburgh Courier*
PFHOF	Pro Football Hall of Fame
SEP	*Saturday Evening Post*
SI	*Sports Illustrated*
UP	Stewart Udall Papers
WAA	*Washington Afro-American*
WP	*Washington Post*
WS	*Washington Star* (also for *Washington Daily Star* and *Washington Evening Star*)

Unless otherwise indicated, the citations of articles by the following writers refer solely to their regularly appearing newspaper columns:

L. I. Brockenbury ("Tying the Score," *Los Angeles Sentinel*); Arthur

Daley and John Kieran ("Sports of the Times," *New York Times*); Sam Lacy ("A to Z," *Baltimore Afro-American*); Shirley Povich ("This Morning," *Washington Post*); Brad Pye Jr. ("Prying Pye," *Los Angeles Sentinel*); Morris Siegel (*Washington Star*)

PROLOGUE

Information for the prologue and for later chapters derives from correspondence and conversations with the late Secretary of the Interior Stewart L. Udall. *"Paleskins"*: Udall, interview with the author, August 21, 1986, Phoenix, AZ. *"considered it outrageous"*: Udall, letter to the author, May 28, 1985. *"We'll start signing Negroes"*: GPM quoted in *Newsweek*, October 15, 1962, 99. *"is the showdown on this"*: Udall quoted in *WP*, December 1, 1961.

CHAPTER 1: BOSTON BEGINNINGS

"Marshall the Magnificent": Kieran, *NYT*, November 28, 1934. *"The sportswriters have had a lot of fun"*: GPM, "Pro Football is Better Football," *SEP*, November 19, 1938, 21. *"Both the buyer"*: ibid. *"I'm guilty"*: ibid. *"The only real regret"*: GPM to Thomas W. Sidwell, January 23, 1934, Sidwell School Archives, courtesy school archivist Loren Hardenbergh. Some writers have incorrectly claimed that Marshall attended Randolph Macon College. He spent a year at Randolph Macon Academy, not Randolph Macon College. *"This space was cleaned"* and *"Long Live Linen"*: Sullivan, *Pro Football's All-Time Greats*, 75–76. *"Whether having a shampoo"*: Jack Walsh, "Redskin Boss Enjoyed Being the Center of Attention," *WP*, May 10, 1969. *"Marshall is not always offensive"*: Ed Linn, "Big Noise in Washington," *Sport* (November 1957), 27. *"SOCIETY"* and *"Who, exactly"*: Sugrue, "Soapsuds and Showmanship," 133–34. *"financial drunk"*: *BP*, July 16, 1932. *"I am a strong believer"*: Linn, "Big Noise," 87–88. *"got the NFL franchise absolutely free"*: Harold Weismann, *New York Mirror*, October 1, 1961, GPM File, PFHOF. *"General D. Pression"*: Beatty, *Rascal King*, 333. *Queen Mary* and the soiree, Bill Cunningham, *BP*, October 4, 1936. *"sign Battles for the Redskins"*: GPM, "Pro Football," 57. *"colloquy"* and *"put Purdue football on the map"*: Austen Lake, undated newspaper clipping, *Boston Evening American*, Washington Redskins Files, PFHOF. *"Lone Star! Lone Star!"*: Benjey, *Keep A-Goin'*, 144. *"is not only one of"*: ibid., 159. *"He felt deeply"*: ibid., 147. *"In the thirties"*: Whittingham, *Hail Redskins*, 12. *"clogged their pores"*: Curran, *Pro Football's Rag Days*, 127–28. "Fact

is": Jordan Harrison Price, "My Grandfather Named the Redskins," *WP*, September 27, 1987. *"Whatever other ethnic faults"*: Addie, *Sportswriter*, 38. *"Dietz was a man"*: Benjey, *Keep A-Goin'*, 278–79. *"Lone Star used to take"*: Curran, *Pro Football's Rag Days*, 128. *"was chortling"*: *BG*, October 23, 1933. *"a genius"*: Benjey, *Keep A-Goin'*, 283. *"Dammit, Dietz"*: There are multiple versions of this perhaps fabricated story; I have relied on Shirley Povich, "George Marshall: No Boredom or Blacks Allowed," in *Redskins*, 21. *"Marshall law has been established"*: Kieran, *NYT*, November 25, 1934. "Marshall Group": *BG*, August 7, 1935. *"I'm a nut"*: *BG*, August 8, 1935. *"We're going to pep up"*: ibid. "Man of big ideas": *BG*, August 7, 1935. *"Just when the announcer"*: *BG*, October 30, 1935. *"hopped onto"*: ibid. *"I went from there"* and subsequent Smith quotes: Leigh Montville, "Funny, But They Were the Boston Redskins, *BG*, October 25, 1981. *"George spends half his life"*: Griffith, *Antiques I Have Known*, 4. *"Then Mint Juleps"*: ibid., 7. *"Well, Welles, I got married"*: Griffith, *My Life with the Redskins*, 8. *"Bursting into Space"*: *BP*, October 8, 1936. *"Scalpings"*: *BP*, October 22, 1934. *"If they had a little more baseball"*: *BP*, October 7, 1936. *"Pro Football Is Booming"*: *BP*, October 4, 1936. *"right in Fenway"*: unidentified newspaper clipping, August 25, 1936, GPM File, PFHOF. *"I don't mind"*: *BP*, October 4, 1936. *"abdication week"*: Cunningham, *BP*, December 11, 1936. *"Redskins May Quit"*: *BG*, December 3, 1936. *"Boston Fumbles"*: *Boston Evening Transcript*, December 7, 1936. *"Pro Football Goes Sissy"*: *Boston Evening American*, December 3, 1936. *"It wasn't so many years"*: ibid. *Their "final salute to"*: *BG*, December 4, 1936. *"we certainly don't owe"*: *BG*, December 8, 1936. *"clean my fingers"*: ibid. *"was raining cows"*: ibid. *"I'm licked"*: *BP*, December 7, 1936. *"But fans in paying quantities"*: ibid. *"agreed that our existence"*: GPM, "Pro Football," 52. *"sporting heritage"*: *New York Herald Tribune*, December 7, 1936. *"He thought he was responsible"*: *NYT*, November 25, 1934. *"there was undoubtedly"*: *BP*, December 8, 1936. *"I just happen to like"*: *BP*, December 11, 1936. *"an insanity"*: ibid. *"You see"*: Griffith, *My Life*, 19. *"atrocious looking"*: Stanley Woodward, *New York Herald Tribune*, December 13, 1934. *"the national capital"*: *BP*, December 8, 1936.

CHAPTER 2: OUT OF BOUNDS

Much of this chapter was previously published in Smith, "Outside the Pale," 255–81. *"was prejudiced as hell"*: Ross, *Outside the Lines*, 45. *"He's a liar"*: ibid. *"It was my understanding"*: Barnett, "Ray Kemp Blazed Important Trail," 3, 8. *"Lillard is not only"*: Bill Grimes, *CD,* October 22, 1932. *"Football players, like anyone else"*: Al Monroe, *CD,* December 3, 1932. *"the lone link"*: ibid. *"easily the best halfback"*: *CD,* January 6, 1934. *the "color of his skin"*: "Too Good for His Own Good," *CD,* September 8, 1934. *"He was a fine fellow"*: *CD,* November 23, 1935. *"For myself"*: Art Rooney, letter to the author, January 15, 1988. *"I can say"*: Cope, *The Game That Was,* 7. *"You just didn't do it"*: Rathet and Smith, *Their Deeds and Dogged Faith,* 220. *"only hypocrites"*: *PC,* January 7, 1939. *"before any of our people"*: *PC,* September 23, 1939. *"In each case"*: *Boston Guardian,* September 9, 1939. *"and the players on the other teams"*: Barnett, "Ray Kemp," 3, 8. *"In ordinary conversation"*: Linn, "Big Noise in Washington," 90. *"In those days"*: Rooney, letter to the author. *"for the good of the sport"*: *CD,* September 22, 1934. *"absolutely the best"*: *CD,* October 20, 1934. *"Simmons is All-America"*: ibid. *"Singh's Slings Sink Cornell"*: *PC,* October 22, 1938. *"Sweet Revenge"*: *PC,* October 29, 1938. *"one of the most amazing exhibitions"*: Henderson, *The Negro in Sports,* 126. *"virtually insurmountable"*: *PC,* November 27, 1937. *"Neither Holland nor Sidat-Singh"*: *PC,* December 3, 1938. *"cyclone-gaited hellion"*: *PC,* September 9, 1939. *"just about the best sprinter"*: Smith, "Outside the Pale," 266. *"In those days"*: Robinson as told to Duckett, *I Never Had It Made,* 22–24. *"the greatest football player"*: Rathet and Smith, *Their Deeds and Dogged Faith,* 210. *"one of the best players"*: Wendell Smith, *PC,* October 29, 1938. *"King Kenny" led*: *PC,* September 23, 1939. *"greater than Red Grange"*: *PC,* November 11, 1939. *"best all-around football player"*: Smith, *PC,* December 10, 1939. *"I have never been so moved"*: *PC,* December 23, 1939. *"You can look"*: Smith, *PC,* November 18, 1939. *"is kept off"*: Harry Culvert, *PC,* December 2, 1939. *"unadulterated hokum"*: *PC,* December 16, 1939. *"open letter"*: Sam Balter broadcast transcript, *PC,* January 13, 1940. *"He played on the same field"*: Brower, "Has Professional Football Closed the Door?" 376. *"had a deep hurt"*: Wolff, "The NFL's Jackie Robinson," 65. *the "sons of Ham"*: Randy Dixon, *PC,* September 3, 1938. *"We've just finished"*: William Nunn, *PC,* October 1, 1938. *"Grin and Bear it"*: Fay Young, *CD,* September 3, 1938. *"sport's bitter pill"*: *Boston Guardian,* November 30, 1940.

CHAPTER 3: THE REDSKINS MARCH

the Redskins "are a team": Povich, *WP,* December 12, 1936. *"that the conservation"*: Sitkoff, *A New Deal for Blacks,* 117. *their "queen"*: Brinkley,

Washington Goes to War, 76. *"If a Washingtonian"*: editorial, *PC*, November 9, 1946. *"This is in direct contrast"*: *Amsterdam* (New York) *News*, May 6, 1939. *"Concert That Awakened America"*: Arsenault, *The Sound of Freedom*. *"When I found out"*: Loverro, *Hail Victory*, 17. *"Finally, I told George"*: Bob Addie, *WP*, August 16, 1969. *"They're here for keeps"*: *WS*, December 17, 1936. *"He looked"*: *WP*, December 20, 1959. *"I liked him"*: Denlinger and Attner, *Redskin Country*, 18. *"I always try to present"*: *WP*, August 10, 1969. *"Hail to the Redskins"*: lyrics quoted in Griffith, *My Life with the Redskins*, 39. *"bare-legged dancing girls"*: *WP*, September 15, 1940. *"Offhand, I would say"*: *WS*, September 16, 1937. *"I never saw"*: *WS*, December 5, 1937. *"At the head"*: Griffith, *My Life*, 61. *"Washing Done" Redskins*: Kieran, *NYT*, December 5, 1937. *"For once in his life"*: ibid. *"There are the two greatest backs"*: *WS*, December 6, 1937. *"It exceeds"*: *WS*, December 6, 1937. *"any more than they could"*: Allison Danzig, *NYT*, December 14, 1937. *"He's the best"*: *WS*, December 14, 1937. *"the hottest thing"*: Danzig, *NYT*, December 14, 1937. *"You dirty"* and continued dialogue: Griffith, *My Life*, 74–75. *"Marshall is the third most interesting sight"*: Sugrue, "Soapsuds and Showmanship," 33. *"It's not merely the contrast"*: *WS*, December 14, 1937. *"With a special train full of Negroes"*: Dan Burley, *Amsterdam News*, September 26, 1947. *"I'm appealing"*: *NYT*, March 1, 1938. *"Why shouldn't I argue with them"*: Kieran, *NYT*, December 5, 1937. *"It was just like"*: *Detroit News*, December 4, 1939, GPM File, PFHOF. *"If that Halloran"*: *NYT*, December 4, 1939. *"could have gone either way"*: ibid. *"the Mastodons of the Midwest"*: Daley, *NYT*, December 8, 1940. *"The Bears are a team"*: Loverro, *Hail Victory*, 22. *"Washington has a confidence"*: Daley, *NYT*, December 8, 1940. *"We're getting ready to play the championship game"*: in *Redskins*, 30. *"showman supreme"*: Daley, *NYT*, December 8, 1940. *"Take the bums"*: *WS*, December 9, 1940. *"That's George Marshall shooting himself"*: Boyle, "All Alone by the Telephone," *SI*, October 16, 1961, 43. *"That's the most humiliating thing"*: *WP*, December 9, 1940. *"73–7"*: in *Redskins*, 31. *"They quit!"*: *WS*, December 9, 1940. *"stunned into dumb silence"*: ibid. *"[N]ine months"*: *WS*, December 9, 1940. *"makes strong men shudder"*: Daley, *NYT*, December 13, 1942. *"The only thing the Bears won"*: Daley, *NYT*, December 14, 1942. *"He had a brilliant football mind"*: *Redskins*, 32. The *"old Gray Mare"*: Daley, *NYT*, December 3, 1944. *"plenty of assistance"*: *NYT*, March 19, 1944. *"man-in-motion play"*: Povich, *WP*, January 11, 1945. *"This is no gentlemen's game"*: Loverro, *Hail Victory*, 29.

CHAPTER 4: LEVELING THE FIELD

"you could have heard": Wolff, "The NFL's Jackie Robinson," 68. *"revealed the national schizophrenia"*: *WP*, March 11, 1949. *"We are not exaggerating"*: Sitkoff, *A New Deal for Blacks*, 324. *"Prove to us"*: ibid. *"They assigned me"*: Strode and Young, *Goal Dust*, 125. *"Everybody got"*: ibid., 126. *"to mongrelize the nation"*: Brinkley, *Washington Goes to War*, 248. *"a sociological laboratory"*: Kennedy, *Freedom from Fear*, 771. *"after our armies"*: editorial, *BAA*, February 3, 1945. *"I always attempted"*: Cope, *The Game That Was*, 250. *"one of the greatest tackles"*: Broadcaster Bill Stern, *PC*, December 2, 1944. *"Not since the days"*: Wendell Smith, *PC*, October 7, 1944. *"the fastest thing in cleats"*: *PC*, October 21, 1944. *"the best running back"*: Frank, "Buddy Totes the Ball," 109. *"unquestionably played"*: ibid., 107. *"only national sport that bars"*: *CD*, October 28, 1933. *"our new league"*: *PC*, February 17, 1945. *"Every red-blooded"*: *Cleveland Call and Post*, November 17, 1945. *the most "Nazified"*: *PC*, January 12, 1946. *"Rams Sign"*: *LAS*, March 28, 1946. *"is not only the greatest"*: ibid. *"Both athletes"*: Wendell Smith, *PC*, August 3, 1946. *"If I have to integrate heaven"*: Strode, *Goal Dust*, 155. *"is just what the name"*: *PC*, August 24, 1946. *"inconceivable to me"*: Brown, *PB: The Paul Brown Story*, 130. *"It's too bad"*: Otto Graham, letter to the author, February 11, 1988. *"If Willis"*: Brown, *PB: The Paul Brown Story*, 244. *"automatically becomes"*: *PC*, January 4, 1947. *"It's a helluva feeling"*: *Amsterdam News*, May 17, 1947. *an "effective slap"*: Wendell Smith, *PC*, December 14, 1946. *"The limitations"*: Lem Graves, *PC*, May 3, 1947. *Pollard "was pessimistic"*: *Amsterdam News*, December 20, 1947. *"Negro stars"*: *Amsterdam News*, September 3, 1949. *"New Thought"*: *Amsterdam News*, December 20, 1947.

CHAPTER 5: THE WASHINGTON WHITESKINS

"Slingin' Sam": Whittingham, *Hail Redskins*, 60. *Marshall not only owned*: Coe, *WP*, December 3, 1959. *"I've never found"*: Linn, "Big Noise in Washington," 90. *"How anyone"*: Bill Henry in unidentified, undated newspaper clipping, GPM File, PFHOF. *"She used to be"*: *WP*, February 13, 1953. *"Please don't blame"*: *WP*, April 30, 1958. *"They used to say"*: Denlinger and Attner, *Redskin Country*, 60. *"At the player draft"*: Brown, *PB: The Paul Brown Story*, 193–94. *"Marshall was a showman"*: Denlinger and Attner, *Redskin Country*, 60. *"It was weird"*: ibid., 37. *"There were only"*: Staff of *Washington Post*, *Redskins*, 55. *"was a very important reason"*:

ibid., 56. *"I wish the people"*: Povich, *WP*, January 10, 1949. *Residents of Cleveland*: *Cleveland Call and Post*, September 13, 1952. *"change people's hearts"*: and *"we'd all be speaking"*: Sitkoff, *The Struggle for Black Equality*, 24, 36. *"Although signs"*: *Cleveland Call and Post*, January 14, 1956. *"an unreconstructed"*: *Cleveland Call and Post*, November 22, 1958. *"I hear you're"*: Boyle, "All Alone By the Telephone," 43. *"I always"*: Loverro, *Hail Victory*, 32. *"There's nothing difficult"*: Daley, *NYT*, November 13, 1949. *"I'm plugged into"*: Edwin "Bud" Shrake, unidentified, undated newspaper clipping, GPM File, PFHOF. *"Partially" Marshall responded*: obituary, *NYT*, August 10, 1969. *"When Marshall saw"*: Staff of *Washington Post*, *Redskins*, 47. *"One thing we're sure of"*: Roscoe McGowen, *NYT*, December 3, 1947. *"has all the permanency"*: Povich, *WP*, January 21, 1946. *"I never wanted"*: *WP*, August 25, 1949. *"Do you know"*: Loverro, *Hail Victory*, 45. *"Naturally, a sudden"*: *WP*, August 24, 1954. *"I have no statement"*: *WP*, August 23, 1954. *"I didn't want"*: Melvin Durslag, *Los Angeles Examiner*, July 6, 1961, GPM File, PFHOF. *"I should have"* and *"an old friend"*: Linn, "Big Noise," 29. *"the most vibrant figure"*: Daley, *NYT*, August 27, 1952. *"My father"*: Loverro, *Hail Victory*, 35. *"He was obnoxious"*: Brown, *PB*, 193. *his definition of "nominal fee"*: *NYT*, December 10, 1949. *"In this business"*: *NYT*, December 17, 1948. *"a 'ridiculous' demand"*: *WP*, January 23, 1959. *"The best thing"*: *NYT*, November 26, 1958. *"the rankest sort of discrimination"*: *WP*, February 8, 1951. *"idiots and screwballs"*: *WP*, May 25, 1954. *"lousy town"* and *"I haven't worn"*: Addie, *WP*, September 10, 1955. *"It could be said"*: Whittingham, *Hail Redskins*, 269. *"Don't worry. They're coming"*: Sullivan, *Pro-Footballs All-Time Greats*, 78. *"but I never had"*: GPM, "Speaking Out," 10. *"enduring romance"*: Addie, *WP*, September 28, 1957. *"but the team"*: Bus Ham, *WP*, November 9, 1957. *"This was the first time"*: Addie, *WP*, January 22, 1957. *"The only reason"*: *WP*, January 8, 1950. *"With this stadium"*: *WP*, April 23, 1958.

CHAPTER 6: THE OWNER, THE JOURNALIST, AND THE HUSTLER

"I don't mind": Francis Stann, *WS*, August 10, 1969. *"He's irascible"*: Addie, *WP*, August 24, 1954. *"Shirley," he said*: Povich et al., *All Those Mornings*, xxiii. *"retired from retirement"*: ibid., 371. *"carnival freaks"*: ibid., 190–92. *"The million-to-one shot"*: ibid., 131. *"responsible for about a third"*: ibid., 132. *"It was the first"*: Graham, *Katharine Graham's Washington*, 243.

"There he was": Povich et al., *All Those Mornings,* 248–49. *"Dinnertime was taken up"*: ibid., 373–74. *"There's a couple of million dollars' worth"*: Povich, April 7, 1939, *WP,* reprinted in *All Those Mornings,* 63–67. *"That was the beginning of press seat integration"*: ibid., 72. *"When he took you apart"*: ibid., ix. *"Marshall was easy to dislike"*: Povich, *All These Mornings,* 86. *"Povich's running battles"*: Bob Considine, *WP,* February 24, 1957. *"Why on earth do you"*: Povich, *WP,* May 3, 1938. *"I have never done any chiseling"*: Povich, *WP,* November 2, 1938. *"In all my experience"*: ibid. *"You run your Goddam Redskins"*: Povich, *All These Mornings,* 88. *"chumps of"*: Povich, *WP,* December 5, 1938. *"I never meant to end a sentence"*: Povich, *WP,* December 6, 1938. *"By what right"*: Povich, *WP,* September 27, 1942. *"strictly malarkey"*: ibid. *"We add that the financial success"*: ibid. *"I guess I won't be needing"*: Povich, *WP,* October 30, 1943. *"I used to wake up"*: Povich, *All These Mornings,* 96. *"Coach Emeritus"*: *WP,* November 4, 1946. *"Co-Coach"*: *WP,* October 10, 1952. *"eminent football authority"*: *WP,* October 29, 1954. *"beloved figure"*: *WP,* November 10, 1947. *"Eleven and a half men"*: Povich, *All These Mornings,* 88. *"Chief of Communications"*: *WP,* November 15, 1948. *"AT&T formation"*: *WP,* December 6, 1946. *"This was one operation"*: Povich, *All These Mornings,* 90. *"You could see"* and subsequent quotes on Marshall's television show: Povich, *WP,* February 13, 1953. *"How come"*: Povich, *WP,* October 15, 1957. *"are losers"*: Povich, *All These Mornings,* 208. *"Let him rap me"*: Linn, "Big Noise in Washington," 28. *"I always have been a hustler"*: Wismer, *The Public Calls It Sport,* 2. *"Marshall, along with Halas"*: ibid., 29. *"He just sat down, ordered a highball"*: Barber, *The Broadcasters,* 46. *"It's not my decision"*: ibid., 47. *"What would you say, Red"*: ibid., 47–48. *"Washington was the seat of power"*: Wismer, *The Public Calls It Sport,* 27. *"In a 20-year period"*: Patterson, *Golden Voices of Football,* 118. *"I was one of the first"*: Wismer, *The Public Calls It Sport,* 129. *"The Redskins are the worst team in pro football"*: Povich, *WP,* October 24, 1954. *"to see them win more games"*: Povich, *WP,* November 28, 1954. *"Our receipts are not as high"*: *WP,* November 6, 1956. *"He was wrong"*: Wismer, *The Public Calls It Sport,* 60. *"Mr. Wismer on this"*: *WP,* January 28, 1957. *"To be critical of"*: Wismer, *The Public Calls It Sport,* 60. *"ludicrous"*: ibid. *"went on a national network"*: Linn, "Big Noise," 27. *"I had the choice"*: ibid. *"Harry Wismer's New York Titans"*: Jack Walsh, *WP,* February 24, 1960. *"Never on Sunday"*: *WP,* February 20, 1962. *"I was born in West Virginia"*: Boyle, "Horatio Harry." *"is available to you"* and *"I*

have always kept myself unspotted": Qureshi and Grissom, "Secret Letters of the Washington Redskins," 27, my thanks to David Kelley for bringing this to my attention. *"titan of finance"* and *"without him"*: Povich, *WP*, February 8, 1963.

CHAPTER 7: THE BLACK BLITZ

"I wish that I had a lot more time": Bob Addie, *Sportswriter*, 304–5. *"were victims of Jim Crow"*: Tygiel, *Baseball's Great Experiment*, 36. *"were the clearest"*: Michael Wilbon, "Lacy's Towering Legacy," *WP*, May 11, 2003. *"sportswriting equivalent"*: ibid. *"the father of modern-day"*: John Oliver, *USA Today*, May 9, 2003. *"That was my introduction"*: William Rhoden, *NYT*, May 17, 2003. *"one of the greatest sportswriters"*: William Gildea, "Pioneering Sportswriter Lacy," *WP*, May 10, 2003. *"was built to carry a pen"*: Early Byrd, *BAA*, May 23, 2003. *"there goes one"*: Addie, *Sportswriter*, 193–94. *"One thing I never quite"*: Lacy with Newson, *Fighting for Fairness*. In the book, Lacy claimed that Altrock threw a wet towel in his father's face. He later told historian Brad Snyder that Altrock actually spit in his father's face. See Snyder, *Beyond the Shadow of the Senators*, 13, 215–16, and 313n79. *"[S]uch a contention"*: Lacy, *Fighting for Fairness*, 36–37. *"The 21-year-old comet"*: Lacy, *BAA*, February 22, 1947. *"brought a flood of blasphemous"*: Ross, *Outside the Lines*, 126. *"Isn't it about time"*: Lacy, *BAA*, September 8, 1956. *"There was a time"*: Lacy, *BAA*, December 29, 1956. *"It is hard to say"*: Lacy, *BAA*, December 8, 1956. *"simply is not telling the truth"*: Lacy, *BAA*, January 12, 1957. *"Marshall's team is the"*: ibid. *"If I didn't go"*: Lacy, *BAA*, January 28, 1961. *"His frequent use"*: Lacy, *BAA*, February 23, 1957. *"Why would any"* and *"If I were still living"*: Lacy, *BAA*, March 2, 1957. *"Inscrutable, bigoted, rude affronts"* and *"Your problem seems to be"*: Lacy, *BAA*, September 27, 1957. *"Washington Confederates"*: Lacy, *BAA*, October 18, 1958. *"exploitation"*: Lacy, "Million Dollar Exploitation," *BAA*, March 15, 1958. *"Too bad"* and *"The fact that Brown and Parker"*: Lacy, *BAA*, November 29, 1958. *"There is only one difference"*: Lacy, *BAA*, February 7, 1959. *"This column has never advocated suicide"*: Lacy, *BAA*, January 14, 1961. *"I'll never salute"*: E. B. Henderson, "Looking Back on Fifty Years," *BAA*, September 11, 1954. *"More than any other factor"*: E. B. Henderson, "Integrated Sports," letter to the editor, *WP*, November 22, 1955. *"one could not help thinking"*: E. B. Henderson, "Democracy and Football," letter to the editor, *WP*, September 20, 1940.

"Democracy will be at its best": C. Herbert Marshall Jr., letter to the editor, *WP,* September 24, 1940. *"And this in the Capital City"*: *CD,* November 16, 1946. *"It seems to me"*: E. B. Henderson, letter to the editor, *BAA,* January 21, 1961. *"disgraceful anti-racial policies"*: Lacy, *BAA,* January 12, 1957. *"When Dixie is played"*: Art Carter, "Pigskin President Blasts Marshall for 'Dixie' Policy of Pro Redskins," *BAA,* December 26, 1959. *"Marshall, to start with"*: Melvin Durslag, *New York Mirror* clipping, August 15, 1961, GPM File, PFHOF. *"I can't purchase that mule"*: Halley Harding, "A Change of Opinion," *LAS,* June 29, 1950. *"I was afraid of white folks"*: Brad Pye Jr., telephone interview with the author, March 1, 2010. *"Negro hater"*: Brockenbury, *LAS,* July 21, 1960. *"Why in the hell"*: Pye, *LAS,* September 19, 1957. *"I would think"*: Pye, *LAS,* July 17, 1958. *"We hope"* and *"knows that George Preston Marshall"*: Brockenbury, *LAS,* August 7, 1958. *"Will the lilywhite Washington Redskins"*: Pye, *LAS,* July 30, 1959. *"has made it clear"*: Brockenbury, *LAS,* December 3, 1959. *"Because George Preston Marshall"*: Brockenbury, *LAS,* August 20, 1959. *"shake Marshall loose"*: Brockenbury, *LAS,* February 18, 1960. *"There should be no place"*: Pye, *LAS,* August 18, 1960.

CHAPTER 8: THE NEW FRONTIER

"never saw a Negro": Giglio, *Presidency of John F. Kennedy,* 159. *"This means"*: *PC,* June 25, 1960. *"Above all"*: Parmet, *JFK,* 250. *"I devoutly hope"*: ibid., 34. *"We can do better"*: Brauer, *John F. Kennedy and the Second Reconstruction,* 43. *"He said that he was going"*: ibid., 48. *"What I want to see"*: *WAA,* October 22, 1960. *"we confidently believe"*: editorial, *BAA,* November 26, 1960. *"look to the Kennedy era"*: Booker, "What Negroes Can Expect From Kennedy," 33. *"we are expecting"*: *PC,* January 14, 1961. *"do not govern alone"*: Sugrue, *Sweet Land of Liberty,* 266. *"The hard-fighting legislator"*: editorial, *WP,* June 24, 1960. *"Washingtonians have"*: *WP,* December 8, 1960. *"with the feeling"*: Cecil Holland, *Detroit News,* January 18, 1961, Redskins File, UP. *"My relations with President Kennedy"*: Udall, Oral History interview, January 12, 1970, JFKL. *"had concentrated more"*: Udall, "Thoughts About the Kennedy Legacy," draft of manuscript, Box 208, UP. *"I long for a flicker"*: Udall Journal, Conservation Trip, 1963, Box 112, UP. *"There is such a thing"* and *"Why doesn't he invite me"*: ibid. *"That's why I named him"*: Adler, *The Kennedy Wit,* 58. *"Don't worry, Stewart"*: Udall, interview with the author, August 21, 1986. *"into sharp focus"*:

Smith, "John Kennedy, Stewart Udall, and New Frontier Conservation," 343. *"a city of"*: Adler, *The Kennedy Wit,* 58. *"If you want a friend"*: Graham, *Katharine Graham's Washington,* 233. *"more interested in politics"*: ibid., 47. *"Opportunities were just dismal"*: ibid., 705. *"If you're not in my joint"*: Garry Clifford, "Even the Matzo Balls Have Punch at Duke Zeibert's, Where the D.C. Elite Meet to Eat," *People,* March 24, 1980, www.people.com/people/archive/article/0,, 20076094, 00.html. *"made it a priority"*: Deford, "It's Tough to Be the Hometown Team in No One's Hometown." *"Never At Anytime"*: Smith, "Civil Rights on the Gridiron," 194. *"Marshall is an anachronism"*: ibid., 195. *"spotting their rivals"*: ibid. *"faces the blackest future"*: Daley, *Pro Football's Hall of Fame,* 221. *"The Redskins had"*: *WP,* December 29, 1960. *"People came from all over"*: "Catching Up With Bobby Mitchell." *"At that time"*: ibid. *"I don't ever remember"*: Denlinger and Attner, *Redskin Country,* 70. *"So it was a situation"*: "Catching Up With Bobby Mitchell." . *"I was a young"*: ibid. *"J. C. was"*: ibid. *"I am very proud"*: ibid. *"athletic ability"*: Brown with Clary, *PB,* 252. *"and I did quite well"*: "Catching Up With Bobby Mitchell." . *"the most dangerous"*: in Lebovitz, "Bobby Mitchell's Uphill Battle," 37. *"Having played two sports"*: John P. Cleary, "Glory Days," *Elmira* (New York) *Star Gazette,* special ed., December 8, 2001, http://www.stargazettesports.com/ErnieDavis/ernie2.html. *"one of the greatest"*: Mackey with Loverro, *Blazing Trails,* 37. *"He had that spontaneous"*: "Ernie Davis," www.answers.com/topic/ernie-davis. *"a bloodless, unemotional spectacle"*: Marshall, "Speaking Out," 14. *"strictly a freak show"* and subsequent quotes: ibid.

CHAPTER 9: SHOWDOWN

This chapter has benefited from correspondence and interviews with the late Stewart Udall. Portions of the chapter have appeared previously in Smith, "Civil Rights on the Gridiron," and "Page 2 Goes to Washington: Civil Rights on the Gridiron." *"the forward pass"*: Giglio, *Presidency of John F. Kennedy,* 161. *"instinctively felt"*: Udall letter to the author, May 28, 1985. *"George Marshall of the Washington Redskins"*: Udall, Report to the President, February 28, 1961, Box 88, UP. *"a throwback to"*: *PC,* January 7, 1961. *"any public facility"*: Udall to GPM, March 24, 1961, Box 90, UP. *"It is certainly"* and *"I think"*: Udall, press conference, March 24, 1961, Box 90, UP. *"He knew that when"*: ibid. *"REDSKINS TOLD"*: *CD,* April 1–6, 1961. *"Washington Redskins Told"*: *PC,* April 1, 1961.*"I don't know what"*:

Washington Daily News, March 25, 1961, Box 88, UP. *"I never realized"*: *Washington Daily News,* April 4, 1961, Box 88, UP. *"Marshall at first"*: Udall, letter to the author, May 28, 1985. *"I am surprised that"*: *Washington Daily News,* March 25, 1961, Box 88, UP. *"All the other teams"*: ibid. *"war whoop for bigotry"*: editorial, *WAA,* April 8, 1961. *"our liberal friends"*: *WP,* May 6, 1961. *"Your stand on the hiring policy"*: Jackie Robinson, *WP,* April 12, 1961. *"Jackie Robinson is in the business"*: *WP,* April 12, 1961. *"That's like asking me"*: *PC,* April 22, 1961. *"I'll take that up"* and *"I have news"*: *WP,* April 15, 1961. *"should cause us"*: *WAA,* May 27, 1961. *"a simple housewife"*: letter in *WAA,* June 3, 1961. *"I cannot help but feel"*: Lacy, *BAA,* May 13, 1961. *"an apostle of delay"* and *"We don't need"*: editorial, *WAA,* April 15, 1961. *"The colored man"*: Martin Luther King Jr., *WAA,* June 10, 1961. *"The president," Udall said, "is imprisoned"*: Schlesinger, *A Thousand Days,* 328. *"[A] wall is a hell"*: Norton et al., *A People and a Nation,* 866. *"The Secretary and I"*: *Washington Daily News,* May 9, 1961. *"This guy's making a big mistake"*: *WP,* July 13, 1961. *"rather vague"* and *"you can't tell"*: *New York Herald Tribune,* July 14, 1961. *"when a football owner"*: Curtis Williams, letter to Udall, April 10, 1961, Box 90, UP. *"to mediocrity"*: Henry Cathles, letter to Udall, May 4, 1961, Box 90, UP. *"no Puerto Ricans"*: Smith, "Civil Rights on the Gridiron," 201. *"You are doing"*: ibid. *"aggrieved"* and *"if Mr. Marshall"*: ibid. *"Once government"*: ibid. *"try a little harder"* and *"segregated team"*: ibid., 202. *"the climate of thinking"*: *WAA,* August 26, 1961. *"would resent"*: Povich, *WP,* April 27, 1961. *"getting more publicity"*: Povich, *WP,* September 10, 1961. *"that under no circumstances"*: Smith, "Civil Rights," 202. *"strictly a club problem"*: Pete Rozelle, letter to the author, June 19, 1985. *"no policy against the hiring"*: GPM to Pete Rozelle, August 9, 1961, Box 90, UP. *"The Kennedy administration"*: *NYT,* August 15, 1961. *"dramatized under threat"*: Smith, "Civil Rights," 203. *"If the Redskins"*: letter to the editor, *LAS,* July 27, 1961. *"in this enlightened age"*: editorial, *LAS,* August 3, 1961. *"I can't do anything"*: *WP,* August 3, 1961. *"Redskins are the greatest"*: *San Francisco Examiner,* September 15, 1961, GPM File, PFHOF. *"No Jim Crow"*: *LAS,* August 10, 1961. *"until that great day"*: Brad Pye, *LAS,* August 17, 1961. *"Is practicing"*: Brockenbury, *LAS,* August 17, 1961. *"do something about the Redskins"*: *WP,* November 9, 1961. *"People Who Can't Play"*: Smith, "Civil Rights on the Gridiron," 203. *"The greater blow"*: *San Francisco Examiner,* September 18, 1961, GPM File, PFHOF. *"some psychoanalysis"*: *WAA,* December

2, 1961. *"What's Wrong"*: Stann, *Sport,* 45–47, 80–82. *"But let me tell you"*: *WP,* October 31, 1998. *"Our youth movement"*: unidentified newspaper clipping, GPM File, PFHOF. *"The Redskins are hopelessly"*: *New York Mirror,* November 5, 1961, GPM File, PFHOF. *"The Redskins end zone"*: Smith, "Civil Rights on the Gridiron," 204. *"Integrated football long ago"*: Povich, *WP,* November 17, 1961. *"A quiet"* and *"We must be ready"*: *WP,* September 3, 1961. *"Marshall's position"* and *"is the first"*: Povich, *WP,* November 17, 1961.

CHAPTER 10: HAIL VICTORY

"I asked him": *WP,* December 3, 1961. *"He told me we had to get a black player"*: Morris Siegel, "Yesterday's Heroes," *Football Digest,* April 1981, 81. *"When the Redskins drafted Davis"*: Povich, *WP,* December 15, 1961. *"I'll bet all I own"*: ibid. *"I think it's no problem"*: Walsh, *WP,* December 6, 1961. *"We were standing in the anteroom talking"*: Gallagher, *Ernie Davis,* 99–100. *"I play in the Liberty Bowl"*: *WP,* December 7, 1961. *"American society has not granted"*: *WAA,* editorial, December 16, 1961. *"by many of the professional people"*: Jackie Robinson, letter to the editor, *WAA,* December 12, 1961. *"To me this is just a job"*: *WAA,* December 16, 1961. *"sudden act of tender concern"*: and other quotes in the paragraph are from Povich, *WP,* December 11, 1961. *"It has been a long time"*: and other quotes in the paragraph are from Lacy, *BAA,* December 16, 1961. *"For years, I was one of the city's"*: ibid. *"have scouted him mainly from the rear"*: Povich, *WP,* December 15, 1961. *"When the deal is fully announced"*: *WP,* December 15, 1961. *"I was leaving military duty"*: Staff of *Washington Post, Redskins,* 56. *"It would have been the greatest backfield"*: Steve Jensen, *Elmira* (New York) *Star Gazette,* special ed., December 8, 2001, http://www.stargazettesports.com/ErnieDavis/ernie2.html. *"I thought Bobby Mitchell was the perfect complement"*: ibid. *"done a complete turn-around"*: Lacy, *BAA,* April 7, 1962. *"fumbled"*: Pack, *Edward Bennett Williams for the Defense,* 75. *"You talk about two contrasting individuals"*: Fine, "Historically Speaking" 57. *"I honestly feel good"*: *WP,* December 15, 1961. *he described the move as "traumatic"*: Bobby Mitchell, letter to the author, June 14, 1985. *"I kept waiting for somebody"*: Fine, "Historically Speaking," 57. *"I began to go places"*: *Redskins,* 57. *"It was a real traumatic thing"*: Fine, "Historically Speaking," 57. *"I'd been through being a first before"*: *Redskins,* 57. *"I wasn't quite as tough as Jackie"*: Fine, "Historically Speaking," 59. *"little

difference": ibid., 57. *"ridiculous"* and *"great human beings"*: Norm Snead, undated letter to the author [June 1985]. *"Some of the whites didn't want me"*: *Redskins*, 58. *"Bobby, I'm glad"*: Howard Tuckney, *NYT*, October 30, 1962. *"Bob, I have three things"*: Fine, "Historically Speaking," 59. *"That was a little tough"*: ibid., 61. *"a nice man"*: Bobby Mitchell, letter to the author, June 14, 1985. *"My problem with them"*: Fine, "Historically Speaking," 61. *"We had trains"*: ibid., 59. *"I never appreciated the man"*: ibid., 60. *"should erase all doubts"*: Cal Jacox, *Norfolk* (Virginia) *New Journal and Guide*, April 28, 1962. *"Our lawyers"*: *Philadelphia Tribune*, May 1, 1962. *"new look"*: Melvin Durslag, *Los Angeles Herald Examiner*, July 12, 1962. *"greatest battery since"*: *PC*, October 6, 1962. *"Thank God for"*: Udall, letter to the author, May 28, 1985. *"It could only happen in Washington"*: *Mesa* (Arizona) *Tribune*, September 27, 1962. *"The Redskins Find a New Kick—Winning"*: Maule, *SI*, 61–63. *"They think they can lick"*: *CD*, October 2, 1962. *"the greatest open field runner"*: *CD*, October 27, 1962. *"running through opposing lines"*: *Atlanta Daily World*, May 1, 1963. *"We don't know how long"*: editorial, *WAA*, September 29, 1962. *"There's no reason for one"*: and the Q&A, Frank Boggs, *Dallas Times Herald*, October 31, 1962. *"I think catching a pass"*: *CD*, November 3, 1962. *"nothing could be more cruel"*: Lacy, *BAA*, September 8, 1962. *"earth-shaking"*: Brockenbury, *LAS*, January 4, 1962. *"a revolution in Washington"*: *BAA*, September 15, 1962. *than in any other year*: "Negro Progress in 1961," 21. *"coach of the year"*: *Cleveland Plain Dealer*, October 13, 1962. *"most valuable player"*: unidentified newspaper clipping, Box 90, UP. *"The integration success story"*: Wilfrid Rodgers, *BG*, undated, Box 90, UP.

CHAPTER 11: RUNNING OUT THE CLOCK

The "Curse": *BAA*, December 15, 1962. *"That's the most protection"*: Addie, *Sportswriter*, 304. *"Look at the strides we have made"*: in Devaney, "Bobby Mitchell: The Power of Confidence," 54. *"You'll bring me"*: Melvin Durslag, "Marshall Has His Say in Miami Sun," *Philadelphia Inquirer*, March 19, 1963, GPM File, PFHOF. *"It makes you feel old"*: Tommy Devine, "Marshall Tops Pro Football Hall-Of-Fame," undated, unidentified newspaper clipping, GPM File, PFHOF. *"Perhaps nothing worse"*: George Clifford, "A Report on Marshall," *Washington Daily News*, September 9, 1963. *"Hello, Dynamite"*: Siegel, "Old Antagonists Hold Reunion," *WS*, August 16, 1963. *"It was very hard"*: Roy McHugh, "The Press Box," *Pittsburgh Press*, August

12, 1969. *"There was no scouting system"*: Addie, *Sportswriter,* 265. *"Mr. Marshall is our head man"*: Jack Walsh, *WP,* September 13, 1963. *"the Big Chief"*: *WP,* July 23, 1964. *"It's too early"*: ibid. *"Good to see you"*: Siegel, *WS,* October 26, 1964. *"George Marshall Still Center of Controversy"*: *WP,* January 28, 1968. Pack provides a detailed and cogent analysis of the legal battle in *Edward Bennett Williams for the Defense,* 73–85. *"shall never use"*: Pack, *Edward Bennett Williams,* 78. *"I hereby emphasize"*: ibid. *"engaged in a conspiracy"*: *WP,* January 13, 1967. *"When I came to see my father"*: ibid. *"Redskin Fight Gets Disgusting"*: Siegel, *WS*, February 18, 1967. *"Common courtesy"*: ibid. *"Were uniquely qualified"*: Pack, *Edward Bennett Williams,* 78. *"Conservators have a statutory"*: David Jewell, "Appeals Court Decides in Favor of Marshall Estate Conservators," *WP,* January 4, 1968. *"His bright, inventive mind"*: Daley, *NYT,* August 26, 1969. *insisted upon baton twirlers and a band,* Bob August, "Football Loses a Stormy Giant," *Cleveland Press,* August 12, 1969. *"did more for the progress"*: Roy McHugh, *Pittsburgh Press,* August 12, 1969, GPM File, PFHOF. *"All of us"*: Bob Addie, *WP,* August 14, 1969. *"is the apex"*: Curly Grieve, *San Francisco Examiner,* September 15, 1961, GPM File, PFHOF. *"As for myself"*: Lacy, *BAA,* August 23, 1969. *"All those flowery tributes"*: Cal Jacox, *Norfolk New Journal and Guide,* August 30, 1969.

EPILOGUE

"smoke spiraled": Bradlee, *A Good Life,* 290–91. For a general treatment of the 1968 Washington race riot, see Ben Gilbert and the staff of the *Washington Post, Ten Blocks from the White House: Anatomy of a Race Riot. "found him to be"*: Bobby Mitchell to the author, June 14, 1985. *"You can't go in there"*: Dave Brady, *WP,* November 28, 1971. *"There was this thing in my head"*: Tom Melody, *Canton Repository,* March 15, 1989, Bobby Mitchell File, PFHOF. *"I would like to run a football team someday"*: Brady, *WP. "necessities"*: Hoose, *Necessities. "lip service"*: Melody, PFHOF. *"It's sorta like"*: Denlinger and Attner, *Redskin Country,* 82. *"ought to be impeached"*: Morris Siegel, *WS,* November 12, 1980. *"The only reason I stayed in all these years"*: *Cleveland Plain Dealer,* February 1, 1983, Mitchell File, PFHOF. *"But my family and my friends and I"*: *St. Petersburg Times,* February 1, 2003, Mitchell File, PFHOF. *"No, I'm a beer drinker"*: *WP,* November 4, 1964. *"You can get a smile on anybody's face"*: Staff of *Washington Post, Redskins,* 115. *"A lot of people know"*: ibid., 166. *"I had friends of*

mine": ibid. *"Redskins have a top-caliber franchise"*: Williams with Hunter, *Quarterblack,* 131. *"priceless comments"*: Povich, *WP,* June 14, 1961. *"but I never had a losing season at the gate"*: GPM, "Speaking Out: Baseball Isn't Our National Sport," 10. *"to be seen seeing"*: Shrake, *SI,* October 4, 1965, 52–54, 61. *"We could get a quorum"*: ibid., 53. *"We're going through a tough time"*: Loverro, *Hail Victory,* 114. *"There was tremendous support for us"*: ibid. *"THE WASHINGTON REDSKINS ARE HOTTEST"*: Sterling Tucker, *WS,* October 24, 1971. *"the elite and the ignorant"*: ibid. *"Richard Nixon with a whistle"*: Deford, "Its' [*sic*] Tough to Be The Hometown Team In No One's Hometown!" . *"Both the* Post *and its rival daily, the* Star*"*: ibid. *"It has all the charm"*: "NFL Fan Value Experience: Washington Redskins," SI.com. On the Strasburg debut, Feinstein, "Audacity of Hype," 80. *"High culture"*: R. W. Apple Jr., *NYT,* July 26, 1998. *"city without identity"*: Deford, "Its' [*sic*] Tough to Be the Hometown Team." *"In a city of transients"*: Christopher Lydon, "Redskins: Washington's Common Bond," *NYT,* December 21, 1974. *"seemed to help in giving the customers"*: GPM, "Pro Football is Better Football," 20. *"We have become the first city"*: Addie, *Sportswriter,* 260–61.

Selected Bibliography

Archives

E. B. Henderson Papers, Howard University, Washington, DC.

George Marshall, newspaper and magazine clippings file, Pro Football Hall of Fame, Canton, OH.

Bobby Mitchell, newspaper and magazine clippings file, Pro Football Hall of Fame, Canton, OH.

Stewart Udall, Oral History, John F. Kennedy Library, Boston, MA.

Stewart Udall Papers, University of Arizona.

U.S. Department of the Interior, Secretarial Subject Files, "Racial Integration of the Washington Redskins." Freedom of Information Act Request, September 30, 1985.

Mainstream Daily Newspapers

Boston Evening American

Boston Evening Transcript

Boston Globe

Boston Herald

Boston Post

Elmira (NY) *Free Press*

New York Herald Tribune

New York Times

Washington Daily News

Washington Evening Star

Washington Post
Washington Times–Herald
Worcester (MA) *Telegram*

African American Weekly or Semiweekly Newspapers

Amsterdam (NY) *News*
Atlanta Daily World
Baltimore Afro-American
Boston Guardian
Chicago Defender
Cleveland Call and Post
Los Angeles Sentinel
Norfolk (VA) *New Journal and Guide*
Philadelphia Tribune
Pittsburgh Courier
Washington Afro-American

Interviews and Correspondence

Paul Brown, telephone interview, February 8, 1988.
Talibah Chikwendu, March 11, 2010.
Otto Graham, telephone interview, February 11, 1988.
David Kelley, telephone interview, October 28, 2009.
Bobby Mitchell, letter, June 14, 1985.
Charles O'Rourke, telephone interview, February 3, 1988.
Brad Pye, telephone interview, March 1, 2010.
Art Rooney, letter, January 15, 1988.
Pete Rozelle, letter, June 19, 1985.
Norm Snead, letter, undated [June 1985].
Stewart Udall, interviews, Phoenix, AZ, August 21, 1986, and Dudley, MA, October 21, 22, 1986.
Stewart Udall, letter, May 28, 1985.

Articles

Only magazine and journal articles (print and online) are referenced here; newspaper articles are referenced in full in the notes.

Barnett, Bob. "Ray Kemp Blazed Important Trail." *Coffin Corner* (December 1983): 3, 8.

Bethel, Kari. "Ernie Davis." *Gale Contemporary Black Biography*, Answers.com, www.answers.com/topic/ernie-davis.

Booker, Simeon. "What Negroes Can Expect from Kennedy." *Ebony* (January 1961): 33++

"Boston Bravery." *Time* (August 19, 1935): 29–30.

Boyle, Robert H. "All Alone By the Telephone." *Sports Illustrated* (October 16, 1961): 37–43.

———. "Horatio Harry." *Sports Illustrated* (October 31, 1960), http://sportsillustrated.cnn.com/vault/article/magazine/MAG1071937/index.htm.

Brooks, Albert N. D. "Democracy through Sports." *Negro History Bulletin* 14 (December 1951): 56ff.

Brower, William. "Has Professional Football Closed the Door?" *Opportunity: A Journal of Negro Life* 18 (December 1940): 375–77.

———. "Negro Players on White Gridirons." *Opportunity* 19 (October 1941): 304–6.

Carmody, John. "The Pro" [on Bobby Mitchell]. *Potomac* (October 12, 1969): 19ff.

"Catching Up with Bobby Mitchell." Fighting Illini.com, Official Home of University of Illinois Athletics. http://www.fightingillini.com/sports/m-footbl/spec-rel/051107aay.html.

Cuneo, Ernest. "Present at the Creation: Professional Football in the Twenties." *American Scholar* 56 (Autumn 1987): 487–501.

Deford, Frank. "It's Tough to Be the Hometown Team in No One's Hometown." *Sports Illustrated* (July 2, 1979), http://sportsillustrated.cnn.com/vault/article/magazine/mag 1095110/5/index.htm.

Devaney, John. "Bobby Mitchell: The Power of Confidence." *Sport* (December 1963): 49–57.

Feinstein, John. "Audacity of Hype: Strasburg Is the Real Deal." *Sporting News Magazine* (June 21, 2010).

Fine, Paul. "Historically Speaking" [on Bobby Mitchell]. *Black Sports* (January 1978): 57–61.

"Football's Most Democratic Team." *Ebony* (December 1955): 104–8.

Franck, Isaac. "Integration in Washington." *Commonweal* 68 (August 15, 1958): 493–96.

Frank, Stanley. "Buddy Totes the Ball." *Collier's* (November 23, 1946): 21–107.

Friedman, Benny. "The Professional Touch." *Collier's* (October 15, 1932): 16–17, 46–47.

Gill, Bob, and Ted Maher. "Not Only the Ball Was Brown: Black Players in Minor League Football, 1933–1946." *Coffin Corner* (Spring 1989): 12–14.

Halas, George. "My Forty Years in Pro Football." *Saturday Evening Post* (November 23, 1957): 34ff., and (November 30, 1957): 34ff.

Henderson, Edwin B. "The Negro Athlete and Race Prejudice." *Opportunity: A Journal of Negro Life* 4 (March 1936), 77–79.

———. "Negro Stars on the Playing Fields of America." *Literary Digest* (March 2, 1935): 32ff.

"Increasing Popularity of Pro Football." *Literary Digest* (December 9, 1933): 24ff.

Jones, P. W. L. "All–Time Negro Football Team." *Crisis* 44 (January 1937): 16–21.

Lawrence, David. "Washington's Worry." *U.S. News & World Report* (April 6, 1959): 120.

Lebovitz, Hal. "Bobby Mitchell's Uphill Battle." *Sport* (June 1961): 37–39, 82–85.

Linn, Ed. "Big Noise in Washington." *Sport* (November 1957): 26–29, 87–90.

Marshall, George. "Pro Football Is Better Football." *Saturday Evening Post* (November 19, 1938): 20–21.

———. "Speaking Out: Baseball Isn't Our National Sport." *Saturday Evening Post* (December 9, 1961): 10, 14.

Maule, Tex. "The Redskins Find a New Kick—Winning." *Sports Illustrated* (October 15, 1962): 61–63.

———. "The Shaky New League." *Sports Illustrated* (January 25, 1960): 49–53.

Nace, Ed. "Negro Grid Stars, Past and Present." *Opportunity: A Journal of Negro Life* 17 (September 1939): 272–74.

"The Nation's Capital: A Troubled City." *U.S. News & World Report* (April 4, 1960): 84–85.

"Negro Athletes and Civil Rights." *Sepia* 13 (June 1964): 35–39.

"Negro Progress in 1961." *Ebony* (January 1962): 25–28.

"NFL Fan Value Experience: Washington Redskins." SI.com, November 7, 2007, sportsillustrated.cnn.com/2007/football/nfl/10/29/fvi.redskins/.

Nocera, Joseph. "The Screwing of the Average Fan: Edward Bennett Williams and the Washington Redskins." *Washington Monthly* (June 1978): 35–41.

Povich, Shirley. "The Washington Redskins." *Sport* (November 1953): 44–47, 95–97.

"Powwow." *Time* (December 12, 1938): 56–57.

"Promoter." *Newsweek* (June 12, 1937): 29.

Qureshi, Samu, and Valerie Grissom. "The Secret Letters of the Washington Redskins." *Washington Post Magazine* (August 2, 2009): 8–13, 25–28.

"Race Problems in the Nation's Capital." *U.S. News & World Report* (September 27, 1957): 34–38.

"Segregation in Washington, D.C." *Negro History Bulletin* 16 (January 1953): 79–86.

Shrake, Edwin. "To Be Seen Seeing the Redskins." *Sports Illustrated* (October 4, 1965): 52–54, 61.

Siegel, Morris. "Yesterday's Heroes." *Football Digest* (April 1981): 81–82.

Smith, Thomas. "Civil Rights on the Gridiron: The Kennedy Administration and the Desegregation of the Washington Redskins." *Journal of Sport History* 14 (Summer 1987): 189–208.

———. "John Kennedy, Stewart Udall, and New Frontier Conservation." *Pacific Historical Review* 64 (August 1995): 329–62.

———. "Outside the Pale: The Exclusion of Blacks from the National Football League, 1934–1946." *Journal of Sport History* 15 (Winter 1988): 255–81.

———. "Page 2 Goes to Washington: Civil Rights on the Gridiron." ESPN.com, March 5, 2002.

Spivey, Donald. "End Jim Crow in Sports: The Protest at New York University, 1940–1941." *Journal of Sport History* 15 (Winter 1988): 282–303.

"Sports as an Integrator." *Saturday Review* (January 21, 1967): 32.

Stann, Francis. "What's Wrong with the Washington Redskins?" *Sport* (August 1961): 45–47, 80–82.

Sugrue, Thomas. "Soapsuds and Showmanship." *American Magazine* 124 (December 1937): 32–33, 131–36.

Telander, Rich. "Shamefully Lily–White." *Sports Illustrated* (February 23, 1987): 80.

"Top Negro Stars in Pro Football." *Sepia* 12 (November 1963): 76.

Trevor, George. "King Football Answers the Great Depression." *Literary Digest* 116 (September 16, 1933): 24ff.

White, Al. "Can Negroes Save Pro Football?" *Our World* 5 (December 1950): 60–65.

Wiggins, David K. "Edwin Bancroft Henderson: Physical Educator, Civil Rights Activist, and Chronicler of African American Athletes." *Research Quarterly for Exercise and Sport* 70 (June 1999): 91–112.

Wilkins, Roy. "Negro Stars on Big Grid Teams." *Crisis* 43 (December 1936): 362–63.

Wolff, Alexander. "The NFL's Jackie Robinson." *Sports Illustrated* (October 12, 2009): 60–71.

Wolff, Alexander, and Richard O'Brien. "Forgotten Pioneer." *Sports Illustrated* (January 16, 1995): 10–11.

Zug, James. "The Color of Our Skin: Quakerism and Integration at Sidwell Friends School." *Quaker History* (Spring 2009): 35–47.

Books

Abrams, Brett L. *Capital Sporting Grounds: A History of Stadium and Ballpark Construction in Washington, D.C.* Jefferson, NC: McFarland & Company, 2009.

Addie, Bob. *Sportswriter.* Lanham, MD: Accent Publishing, 1980.

Adler, Bill, ed. *The Kennedy Wit.* New York: Bantam, 1964.

Arsenault, Raymond. *Freedom Riders: 1961 and the Struggle for Racial Justice.* New York and Oxford, UK: Oxford University Press, 2006.

———. *The Sound of Freedom: Marian Anderson, the Lincoln Memorial, and the Concert That Awakened America.* New York: Bloomsbury Press, 2009.

Ashe, Arthur R. *A Hard Road to Glory: A History of the African American Athlete, 1919–1945.* New York: Warner Books, 1988.

Barber, Red. *The Broadcasters.* New York: Da Capo Press, 1970.

Beatty, Jack. *The Rascal King: The Life and Times of James Michael Curley.* New York: Addison–Wesley Longman, 1992.

Benjey, Tom. *Keep A–Goin': The Life of Lone Star Dietz.* Carlisle, PA: Tuxedo Press, 2006.

Borchert, Robert. *Alley Life in Washington: Family, Community, Religion, and Folklife in the City, 1850–1970.* Urbana: University of Illinois Press, 1980.

Bradlee, Benjamin C. *Conversations with Kennedy.* New York: W. W. Norton, 1975.

———. *A Good Life: Newspapering and Other Adventures.* New York: Touchstone, 1995.

Brauer, Carl. *John F. Kennedy and the Second Reconstruction*. New York: Columbia University Press, 1977.

Brinkley, David. *Washington Goes to War*. New York: Ballantine, 1988.

Brown, Jim, with Myron Cope. *Off My Chest*. New York: Doubleday, Doran, 1964.

Brown, Jim, with Steve Delsohn. *Out of Bounds*. New York: Kensington, 1989.

Brown, Paul, with Jack Clary. *PB: The Paul Brown Story*. New York: Atheneum, 1979.

Bryant, Nick. *Bystander: John F. Kennedy and the Struggle for Black Equality*. New York: Basic Books, 2006.

Carroll, John M. *Fritz Pollard: Pioneer in Racial Advancement*. Urbana: University of Illinois Press, 1998.

Chalk, Oceania. *Pioneers of Black Sport*. New York: Dodd, Mead, and Company, 1975.

Cope, Myron. *The Game That Was: The Early Days of Pro Football*. New York and Cleveland: World Publishing Company, 1970.

Curley, James Michael. *I'd Do It Again: A Record of All My Uproarious Years*. Englewood Cliffs, NJ: Prentice Hall, 1957.

Curran, Bob. *Pro Football's Rag Days*. New York: Bonanza Books, 1969.

Daley, Arthur. *Pro Football's Hall of Fame: The Official Book*. Chicago: Quadrangle Books, 1963.

Daniels, Jonathan. *Frontier on the Potomac*. New York: MacMillan, 1946.

Denlinger, Ken, and Paul Attner. *Redskin Country: From Baugh to the Super Bowl*. New York: Leisure Press, 1983.

Duberman, Martin B. *Paul Robeson: A Biography*. New York: Ballantine, 1989.

Duckett, Alfred. *I Never Had It Made: An Autobiography*. New York: Putnam, 1972.

Franklin, John Hope. *Mirror to America: The Autobiography of John Hope Franklin*. New York: Farrar, Straus and Giroux, 2005.

Gallagher, Robert. *Ernie Davis: The Elmira Express*. Washington and Baltimore: Bartleby Press, 2008.

Giglio, James. *The Presidency of John F. Kennedy*. Lawrence: University of Kansas Press, 1991.

Gilbert, Ben, and the Staff of the *Washington Post*. *Ten Blocks from the*

White House: Anatomy of the Washington Race Riots of 1968. New York: Frederick A. Praeger, 1968.
Graham, Katharine. *Katharine Graham's Washington*. New York: Vintage, 2002.
———. *Personal History*. New York: Knopf, 1997.
Green, Constance M. *The Secret City: A History of Race Relations in the Nation's Capital*. Princeton, NJ: Princeton University Press, 1967.
———. *Washington: Village and Capital, 1800–1878*. Princeton, NJ: Princeton University Press, 1962.
Grier, Roosevelt. *Rosey: An Autobiography*. Tulsa, OK: Harrison House, 1986.
Griffith, Corrine. *Antiques I Have Known*. New York: Frederick Fell, 1961.
———. *My Life with the Redskins*. New York: A. S. Barnes, 1947.
Harris, David. *The League: The Rise and Decline of the NFL*. Toronto and New York: Bantam, 1986.
Henderson, Edwin Bancroft. *The Negro in Sports*. Rev. ed. Washington, DC: Associated Publishers, 1949.
Henderson, James H. M., and Betty F. Henderson. *Molder of Men: Portrait of a "Grand Old Man"–Edwin Bancroft Henderson*. New York: Vantage Press, 1985.
Hoose, Phil. *Necessities: Racial Barriers in American Sports*. New York: Random House, 1989.
Kennedy, David. *Freedom from Fear: The American People in Depression and War, 1929–1945*. New York and Oxford, UK: Oxford University Press, 1999.
Lacy, Sam, with Moses J. Newson. *Fighting for Fairness: The Life Story of Hall of Fame Sportswriter Sam Lacy*. Centreville, MD: Tidewater Press, 1998.
Levy, Alan H. *Tackling Jim Crow: Racial Segregation in Professional Football*. Jefferson, NC: McFarland & Company, 2003.
Litwack, Leon. *Trouble in Mind: Black Southerners in the Age of Jim Crow*. New York: Knopf, 1998.
Loverro, Thom. *Hail Victory: An Oral History of the Washington Redskins*. Hoboken, NJ: John Wiley & Sons, 2006.
———. *Washington Redskins: The Authorized History*. Dallas: Taylor Publishing, 1996.
Mackey, John, with Thom Loverro. *Blazing Trails: Coming of Age in Football's Golden Era*. Chicago: Triumph Books, 2003.

Moore, Lenny, with Jeffrey Jay English. *All Things Being Equal: The Autobiography of Lenny Moore*. Champaign, IL: Sports Publishing, 2006.

Norton, Mary Beth, et al. *A People and a Nation: A History of the United States*. 5th ed. Boston: Houghton Mifflin, 1998.

Pack, Robert. *Edward Bennett Williams for the Defense*. Bethesda, MD: National Press Books, 1988.

Parmet, Herbert. *JFK: The Presidency of John F. Kennedy*. New York: Penguin, 1983.

Patterson, Ted. *The Golden Voices of Football*. New York: Sports Publishing, 2004.

Piascik, Andy. *The Best Show in Football: The 1946–1955 Cleveland Browns*. Lanham, MD: Taylor Trade Publishing, 2007.

———. *Gridiron Gauntlet: The Story of the Men Who Integrated Pro Football, in Their Own Words*. Lanham, MD: Taylor Trade Publishing, 2009.

Povich, Lynn, et al., eds. *All Those Mornings . . . At the Post: The 20th Century in Sports from Famed Washington Post Columnist Shirley Povich*. New York: Public Affairs, 2005.

Povich, Shirley. *All These Mornings*. Englewood Cliffs, NJ: Prentice Hall, 1969.

Rathet, Mike, and Don R. Smith. *Their Deeds and Dogged Faith*. New York: Balsam Press, 1984.

Reeves, Richard. *President Kennedy: Profile of Power*. New York: Simon & Schuster, 1993.

Reeves, Thomas C. *A Question of Character: A Life of John F. Kennedy*. New York: Free Press, 1991.

Rhoden, William. *Forty Million Dollar Slaves: The Rise, Fall, and Redemption of the Black Athlete*. New York: Crown, 2006.

Robinson, Jackie, as told to Alfred Duckett. *I Never Had It Made: An Autobiography*. New York: Putnam, 1972.

Ross, Charles K. *Outside the Lines: African Americans and the Integration of the National Football League*. New York and London: New York University Press, 1999.

Schlesinger, Arthur. *A Thousand Days: John F. Kennedy in the White House*. Boston: Houghton Mifflin, 1965.

Sitkoff, Harvard. *A New Deal for Blacks*. New York and Oxford, UK: Oxford University Press, 1978.

———. *The Struggle for Black Equality.* Twenty-fifth-anniversary ed. New York: Hill and Wang, 2008.

Smith, Robert. *Pro Football: The History of the Game and the Great Players.* Garden City, NY: Doubleday, 1963.

Snyder, Brad. *Beyond the Shadow of the Senators: The Untold Story of the Homestead Grays and the Integration of Baseball.* Chicago: Contemporary Books, 2003.

Staff of the *Washington Post. Redskins: A History of Washington's Team.* New updated ed. Washington, DC: Washington Post Books, 2000.

Strode, Woody, and Sam Young. *Goal Dust: The Warm and Candid Memoirs of a Pioneer Black Athlete and Actor.* Lanham, MD: Madison Books, 1990.

Sugrue, Thomas. *Sweet Land of Liberty: The Forgotten Struggle for Civil Rights in the North.* New York: Random House, 2008.

Sullivan, George. *Pro Football's All–Time Greats: The Immortals in Pro Football's Hall of Fame.* New York: G. P. Putnam's Sons, 1968.

Thomas, Evan. *The Man to See.* New York: Simon and Schuster, 1991.

Tygiel, Jules. *Baseball's Great Experiment: Jackie Robinson and His Legacy.* New York: Vintage Books, 1983.

Whittingham, Richard. *Hail Redskins: A Celebration of the Greatest Players, Teams, and Coaches.* Chicago: Triumph Books, 2004.

———. *What a Game They Played: An Inside Look at the Golden Era of Pro Football.* Lincoln: University of Nebraska Press, 1984.

Williams, Doug, with Bruce Hunter. *Quarterblack: Shattering the NFL Myth.* Chicago: Bonus Books, 1990.

Wismer, Harry. *The Public Calls It Sport.* Englewood Cliffs, NJ: Prentice Hall, 1965.

Index

Page numbers in italics refer to illustrations.